Feminist Methodology

Feminist Methodology

Challenges and Choices

Caroline Ramazanoğlu
with Janet Holland

Los Angeles | London | New Delhi
Singapore | Washington DC

First published 2002

Reprinted 2009

SAGE Publications Ltd
1 Oliver's Yard
55 City Road
London EC1Y 1SP

SAGE Publications Inc.
2455 Teller Road
Thousand Oaks, California 91320

SAGE Publications India Pvt Ltd
B 1/I 1 Mohan Cooperative Industrial Area
Mathura Road
New Delhi 110 044

SAGE Publications Asia-Pacific Pte Ltd
33 Pekin Street #02-01
Far East Square
Singapore 048763

British Library Cataloguing in Publication Data
A catalogue record for this book is available from the British Library

ISBN 978-0-7619-5122-3 (hbk)
I5BN 978-0-7619-5123-0 (pbk)

Library of Congress Control Number available

Typeset by M Rules
Printed and bound in Great Britain by
CPI Antony Rowe, Chippenham, Wiltshire

Contents

1

Introduction

Introduction

There are many possible approaches to feminist methodology. We start from the problems that arise when feminist social researchers set out to tell 'better stories' of gendered social realities than others. We examine the methodological challenges and choices that they face on the way. We do not prescribe what feminist methods must be, or specify how feminist researchers should proceed. Rather, we want to consider how feminist approaches to social research have been shaped by some of the concerns of western philosophy and epistemology, how feminist responses to these concerns have struck out in differing directions through a variety of methodological problems and solutions, and whether, despite this diversity, there is any sense in which feminist methodology is feminist, and the struggles have been worthwhile.

    Methodology is not generally taken to be an exciting area, and those involved in researching gender may well wonder why they should take an interest in methodological problems rather than just getting on with the job. But any researcher who sets out to understand gender relations and grasp their impact on people's lives has to consider: how (or whether) social reality can be understood; why conceptions of sexuality and gender have some meanings rather than others; how people make sense of their experiences; and how power inhabits knowledge production. In seeking knowledge of gender through social research, feminists make decisions about how to produce and justify their knowledge, whether they do so intentionally or not, and we argue that these decisions matter. They affect what can be known and what gets to count as authoritative knowledge. Decisions about methodology are particularly powerful in the politics and practices of knowledge production.

Feminists (like all other social researchers) have to establish and defend their claims to knowledge of social life, because there is no certain or absolute knowledge against which the truth of everything can be measured. If feminist knowledge is to be believed, it has to be made believable, but there is more than one way of making and justifying knowledge claims (and many ways of failing). There are taken-for-granted distinctions in western thought, for example, between the authority of knowledge produced through scientific procedures, and that of knowledge produced in literature, horoscopes or dreams. It is easy to class feminist knowledge as unscientific, biased and lacking in authority. But the problems raised by feminist methodology are not peculiar to feminism: they are also problems for social research more generally.

We do not attempt to review the full range of feminist adventures in methodology or all areas of feminist expertise, since these are now extensive. Instead, three themes run through the book. The first thread of our argument is that debates on feminist methodology are framed by disagreements in western philosophy over how ideas about the social world can possibly be related to people's experiences of social life, and to actual social realities. These preoccupations mean that the feminist approaches to social research currently debated in western universities can be very different from other ways of thinking about producing knowledge. Anne Seller (who has taught philosophy in the UK and the USA) says that taking her feminist ideas and debating tradition to the Mother Theresa Women's University in India confronted her with her own cultural specificity as a philosopher (Seller 1994). She found that her tools for thinking with were characteristically western: 'the more abstract and theoretical our formulations, the more culturally specific they become' (Seller 1994: 243). Feminist approaches to methodology entail choices between different strategies for specifying connections between ideas, experience and reality, or for claiming the impossibility or irrelevance of specifying such connections.

Second, we argue that feminist responses to these debates have led to methodological dispute and diversity within feminism. It is problematic that knowledge of gendered lives (like any other claims to knowledge of social reality) cannot be claimed as simply and generally true (in the sense that this knowledge directly and accurately describes an actual reality). Feminists have to find ways of making their knowledge believable, and for evaluating competing knowledge claims, but there is more than one way of connecting feminist ideas with women's experiences and with particular conceptions of reality.[1]

Third, despite this divergence, feminist research is imbued with particular theoretical, political and ethical concerns that make these varied approaches to social research distinctive. Feminist knowledge is grounded in experiences of gendered social life, but is also dependent on judgements about the justice of social relationships, on theories of power and on the morality of social investigation. Feminist researchers are not necessarily in agreement on the meanings and consequences of experience, justice, power, relationships, differences and morality but, despite this divergence, they can potentially negotiate common moral and political positions.

The intertwining of these three themes illuminates critical contradictions in feminist efforts to produce and justify authoritative knowledge of gendered social life across a range of approaches to social research. It follows that this book is an argument *for* methodology since it is not possible to produce a neutral text *on* methodology, or to resolve feminism's inherent contradictions. It is also an argument for the importance of practical, empirical investigation in producing knowledge of gendered social life.

Three challenges to feminist methodology

Feminists have made a range of claims about the position of women in relation to men, and about male domination of social theory. As a result, recent feminism and its claims to knowledge have confronted three rather different sources of criticism.

First, challenges to feminist knowledge claims have come from dominant approaches to science, reason, progress and truth, and the situation of this thought in relation to women's experience (and to other ways of thinking, colonial and imperial history, and the uneven development of global capitalism). Feminists have been criticized for failing to produce adequately rational, scientific or unbiased knowledge (on the understanding that their critics use methodologies that are adequate in these respects). As academic feminist research developed, feminists came under increasing pressure from the wider academic community to justify their knowledge in terms of, for example, rationality, validity, rules of method, control of subjectivity and political bias. Feminist thought has been treated in many academic institutions as marginal, or as intellectually inferior to existing modes of thought (Arpad 1986; Stanley 1997). When feminists judge gender relations to be unjust and want to change them, they are implying that they have knowledge of what social relations between women and men actually are, and are expected to provide acceptable grounds for claiming that others should take this knowledge seriously. By being openly politically committed, feminists are charged with failing the test of producing generally valid and authoritative knowledge.

Second, challenges come from women's varied experiences of cultural differences, social divisions and power relations. For example, claims that patriarchal power, sexuality or reproduction are key mechanisms in the oppression of women ignore other factors (such as racism, systems of production, nationalism, heterosexism, ablebodiedism, and the complex relations between them) that shape women's lives in differing ways, and complicate relations between women (Brah 1992; Moraga and Anzaldúa 1983). Western feminists have been extensively criticized for relying on an undifferentiated category of 'women', in what Audre Lorde (1983: 99) terms the 'pathetic pretence' that differences between women do not exist.[2] These criticisms signal variations in personal experiences of the complex interrelations of power between women. They target the intellectual and ethical implications of producing knowledge of gender as if 'women' were a unified category of being throughout history and all over the world. They also question whether it is possible to produce knowledge of gender when gendered power relations are only one aspect of people's lives. Issues of difference fracture, politicize and personalize all approaches to understanding gender.

A third challenge has shifted English-language feminism from a long period of engagement with scientific method, liberalism and Marxism (Jaggar 1983; Maynard 1995) to close encounters with aspects of postmodern and poststructuralist thought that question the foundations of feminist knowledge and methodology (Hekman 1992; Nicholson 1990). Feminist knowledge claims are tangled in tensions between knowledge of gender relations that take the existence of women for granted, and theories that take apart the grounds of feminist claims to knowledge, and treat 'women' and 'gender' as products of ideas rather than of embodiment, patriarchy or social construction. Poststructural and postmodern thought abandons any notion of methodology as able to produce knowledge that describes actual reality.

These three sources of challenge have thrown divided feminist researchers further into dispute. Feminists are constantly rewriting feminism and its histories with some common elements, but no general consensus (see, for example, James and Busia 1993; Kumar 1989; Mohammed 1998). We consider that disentangling the resulting methodological confusion is important, both in order to clarify how knowledge of gendered lives is produced, and because different methodological challenges and responses have different epistemological, political and ethical implications. The decisions that feminist researchers make matter.

Since feminists agree on so little, and their many critics tend to oversimplify and unify diverse feminist positions, we take the rest of this chapter to sketch some points of definition that outline our concerns.

What is gender?

Feminism provides theory, language and politics for making sense of gendered lives, but no orderly position on pinning down the contradictions of 'gender'. This term can cover both how specific people experience sexuality and reproduction, masculinity and femininity, and the boundaries and interstices between them, and also variable cultural categories for conceptualizing what is lived and thought. In feminist theory, there has been considerable debate about the nature and interrelationships of sex, reproduction, identity, gender and power. We argue that sexuality, reproduction, subjectivity and gender can be taken to be interrelated – not wholly independent of embodiment, but also socially and politically constituted. Since what gets constituted and interrelated varies, gender cannot be known in general, or prior to investigation.

There are considerable differences, however, between thinking about gender in terms of: (1) what people (and their bodies) are; (2) what people do; (3) what relationships and inequalities they make; (4) what meanings all these are given; (5) what social effects ideas of gender can produce. There are also differences in conceptualizing how gender is interrelated with other ways of identifying and categorizing people, for example in racialized relationships and categories of analysis. Rather than any agreed feminist position, there are deeply felt disputes.

For the purposes of this book, we discuss feminist methodology with reference to social research on gendered lives (rather than, say, 'women', 'sex/gender' or 'sexual difference'). *We take gender to include: sexuality and reproduction; sexual difference, embodiment, the social constitution of male, female, intersexual, other; masculinity and femininity; ideas, discourses, practices, subjectivities and social relationships.* While gender can be analysed from differing perspectives and with differing assumptions, we argue that feminist knowledge of gender should include practical social investigation of gendered lives, experiences, relationships and inequalities. We see the investigation of the similarities and differences across the diversity of gendered lives as a potentially radical and emancipatory project that the term 'gender' can serve.

What is feminism in the twenty-first century?

Feminism covers a diversity of beliefs, practices and politics, and these overlap and interact with other beliefs, practices and politics. For every generalization that one can make about feminism it is possible to find 'feminists' who do not fit, or who do not want to fit. By the end of the nineteenth century, the term 'feminism' in the English-speaking world generally indicated the advocacy of women's rights. In the UK and the USA, by the late nineteenth and early twentieth centuries, women were actively campaigning around education, political representation, working conditions, health, sexuality, motherhood and legal rights, as well as on more specific local issues. But these were not necessarily campaigns for all women (for example, in the UK, there were campaigns to gain access to the professions for middle-class women and access to contraception for working-class, married mothers). These and other campaigns were also marked by various forms of radical feminist consciousness that targeted male power over women's minds, bodies, sexuality or labour, but this was not generally respectable or politically acceptable (Bland 1995). Other countries produced diverse campaigns around both general and specific interests and concerns, often connected with struggles for national independence, civil rights, democracy and modernization.

By the end of the twentieth century, feminism referred both more specifically and more generally to theories of male dominance that took relations between women and men to be political, and feminist struggles to be political activity on behalf of women in general. Feminism, therefore, entails some theory of power relations. Feminist conceptions of gendered power have been a critical factor in developing distinctive feminist theories and practices, but there is no unified theory of power, and feminists have drawn on a variety of ways of thinking about how to conceptualize power, the exercise and effects of power, and what can be done to change specific power relations and practices. As our concern here is with methodology, rather than the range of theory, we have not pursued variations in feminist conceptions of power. What these theories have in common is a concern that different knowledges of gender relations have different political and ethical implications. In these theories, any claim that all women are similarly subordinated, and so can and should act collectively, rubs up against actual experiences of differences between women, and different ways of conceptualizing power (Sanday 1981).

The feminism that developed in the last 30 years or so still attracts criticisms for its supposedly powerful consensus, and its tyranny in imposing hatred of men and denying fun and femininity to women (Gill 1997).[3] In practice, late twentieth-century feminism developed, alongside many other political movements and activities, as an unstable intellectual, political and practical activity grounded in a sense of women having some common political interests across their social divisions, and so having some potential interest in acting together to transform unjust gender relations. Feminist notions of liberation, emancipation and social transformation imply freedom from oppression and freedom to live differently, but this is a slippery area of debate, difference and disagreement, rather than one of agreed concepts, aims or strategies (Ahmed et al. 2000).

Feminist notions of social transformation are rooted in varied experiences of gender subordination, expressed in varied theories of gender and power, and incorporate a range of moral and political judgements on what constitutes injustice. If the subordination of women is taken to be unjust, then it is unjust wherever it occurs, and strategies for tackling particular injustices imply some general notion of justice. This gives feminism a problematic relationship to women-in-general. Feminism depends critically on establishing: first, that a category of women (female persons, clearly differentiated from male persons) exists; second, that women do have some common conditions of gendered existence, despite the social and cultural divisions between them, and despite the interests that women can share with men; and, third, that there are universal criteria of justice/injustice. Feminism in this cloak of well-meaning universalism has been unmasked as a form of western cultural imperialism seeking to incorporate all women into a particular set of western values and categories (Mohanty 1988). Challenges to feminist universalism mark a central contradiction in feminist politics. There is a critical difference between building limited generalizations about women's social existence (based on specific histories, experiences, cultures, localities and relationships) and making universal generalizations about 'women' (based on prior theory).

The characteristics of feminism remain open to dispute since women's movements have developed at different periods, in different languages and cultures, and in differing ways. The diversity of women's struggles around the world constitutes a challenge to claims that feminism is a western invention. All over the world women are occupied in struggles for more humane and just societies through action on 'women's issues', which takes various forms and adopts various cultural expressions. The extent and limits of common experiences, visions of alliances and social divisions are well exemplified in the global women's conferences organized periodically by the United Nations (see, for example, Basu 1995; Brah 1992; Sum 2000). There has never been a shared theory of gender oppression or male dominance; a unified vision of justice and liberation; a common approach to the production of knowledge; agreed knowledge of the extent of women's differences; or a consensus on truths about gender.

Any definition of feminism can, therefore, be contested. But a review of developments in western feminism since the nineteenth century, and of the activities of women's movements around the world that are in critical tension with western feminism, suggests the following key characteristics of the feminism that is the focus of this book.

1 *Feminism is diverse and decentred.* There is no political centre to provide an authoritative definition of common goals and strategies for liberation. So there is no ruling on what does or does not constitute feminist methodology.
2 *Feminism is exclusionary.* Despite its diversity, any definition of feminism excludes 'non-feminism', or 'not-quite-feminism', thus exposing fragmentation among feminists and divisions between women. This leaves as problematic who (if anyone) has the power to define boundaries for whom, and whether, or how, feminists can speak for 'women'.
3 *Feminism implies a unified subject.* Women can only constitute the subject of feminism if they share a gendered social position. Feminism, therefore, requires some concept of a community of women who really exist. This raises the question of whether 'women' (and so 'men') are a real collectivity with political interests in common, rather than a variable social category.
4 *Feminism entails some claim to common interests between women.* Attempts to define feminism and its goals in some neutral way encounter real divisions of political interest, and so differing experiences of power, inequality and injustice between women. Any specific goals of social transformation can be very actively contested. Gender cannot be separated in practice from other social relationships, including those that empower and privilege some women over others. Nevertheless, feminism addresses women across their social differences, on the grounds that common interests can be found wherever gender relations are unjust. If women really have nothing in common, and no gendered inequalities or injustices exist, the rationale of feminism disappears.
5 *Feminism implies a case for emancipation.* Feminism can only be justified where gender relations are unjust/oppressive, and people are able to choose to change them. Feminist claims to knowledge of gendered lives carry dreams of resistance, agency and emancipation across social divisions and the complexities of social existence. But emancipation also raises numerous problems about how change for the better is conceived, by whom, for whom and why.

Are feminists women?

Any notion of 'we' implies either universal humanity (all of us human beings) or requires some specification and justification of the boundaries of the particular category of being in question. (Which of us human beings does this particular 'we' refer to?) Feminists cannot speak for 'we humans', 'we women' or 'we feminists' without specifying the nature and boundaries of the collectivity or category they speak for. The notion that women are a community with a shared social position whose lives can be investigated by women researchers who share this common position has been extensively criticized. In this book, we use 'we' to refer to us, the authors addressing you, the reader, unless we specify otherwise.

As an alternative to assuming that there are always two rigid, natural categories, 'women' and 'men' (which could clearly identify feminists as women speaking on behalf of women), 'women' and 'men' can be seen as socially constituted, and so variable, gender categories. There is no certain knowledge, though, on what aspects of gender identities exist at birth, the consequences of genetic variation, or of variable interaction with environments. It does seem increasingly likely that what is innately gendered, what develops in interaction with specific environments, and what is learned interact in ways that are both variable and not fully understood. Gender categories can operate differently in different periods and cultures in identifying what some people share with those like themselves and do not share with those unlike themselves, with particular reference to sexuality and reproduction. What people with male/female labels share in any given instance cannot be known in advance and so needs investigation.

Confusions about the significance of embodied differences, and their relation to social identities, arise because there can be political struggles around what sense is made of sexual and reproductive difference. There are not in practice two mutually exclusive, wholly natural, gender categories, and official attempts to classify international athletes as definitively male or female have made clear the impracticality of drawing clear boundaries around individual bodies. Instead, there is an area of intersexuality, normative confusion and social regulation, where differing cultures draw, disrupt and regulate their gender boundaries differently (Sawhney 1995).

The UK, for example, has only two gender categories (male/female). Newborn babies whose genitals do not mark them as clearly fitting into either category are assigned a gender that is recorded on their birth certificate and may not legally be changed. Such babies may be deemed to require surgery, or other medical intervention, to 'improve' the fit with their assigned gender. Other ways of conceptualizing gender can allow more than two gender categories or different or more flexible boundary systems (Sawhney 1995). Intersexuals and transsexuals in the UK, as in the USA, may support existing gender boundaries by seeking clear assignment as either man or woman. Alternatively, they may disrupt rigid boundaries by asserting their difference and refusing to 'fit' (Hird 2000).

Once it is established that what it means to be woman/man/neither-woman-nor-man, can be different within different ways of knowing and being, feminist researchers cannot simply take 'women' as the subject of feminism, and cannot assume that the feminist is simply a woman. If a feminist methodology has distinctive rules, a politically sympathetic man should (in theory) be able to use them. If only women can do feminist research, where does this leave intersexual or transsexual researchers? (Problems can arise in practice if a researcher's claim to share feminist politics or have knowledge of women's experience is disputed.) Since understanding power relations is central to feminist research, investigation of gendered lives by feminists includes the study of men and masculinity (Holland et al. 1998; McKee and O'Brien 1983; Sharpe 1994). The more male-oriented field of men's studies is also informed by feminist theory and politics (Ramazanoğlu 1992a).

These problematic characteristics of gender, feminism and feminists both shape and constrain the development of feminist methodology. There is an enormous feminist literature on knowledge, methodology and science, but considerable confusion and contradiction within modern feminism (and in the many criticisms of feminism) about where feminists stand in relation to notions of science, reason, method and truth. In the next section we outline the context and the key characteristics of methodology that have both shaped feminist approaches to social research, and encouraged the diversity of these approaches.

What is methodology in social research?

Methodology in social research is concerned with procedures for making knowledge valid and authoritative. But questions of truth and authority are extensively disputed in western philosophy, and can be thought of in different terms in other ways of thinking. Attempts to clarify the problems and possibilities of feminist methodology range from abstracted debates on science, truth and epistemology to the details of fieldwork practices (Cook and Fonow 1990: 71).

For our purposes, different approaches to methodology in social research are different responses to how, or whether, the knowledge people produce about social life can be connected to any actual reality. Philosophers disagree on the possibilities of connections being made between:

1 *ideas* (theories, concepts, consciousness, knowledge, meanings) through which people imagine or make sense of reality and experience, for example in conceptions of 'family';
2 *experience* (how people live and make sense of the social world, and each other, in their everyday lives), for example in everyday experiences of 'family life', its meanings, relationships and practices;
3 *material and social realities* (things, relationships, powers, institutions, and impersonal forces that really exist and can have effects on people's lives whether people are conscious of them or not), for example relations between sexual partners, or parents and children, that actually exist independently of people's knowledge of them.

Different conceptions of 'family' clearly have different political implications, and there are also ethical issues in how knowledge of the 'family' is produced and used. The methodological choices open to feminist social researchers in connecting ideas, experience and reality provide the main theme of this book.

Connecting ideas, experience and reality

Feminist methodology is one set of approaches to the problems of producing justifiable knowledge of gender relations. Any claim to know social reality, though, is fraught with difficulty. Western philosophers disagree on what claims can be made about connections between knowledge and reality, or whether any claims are possible. Positions vary from claims that knowledge can directly describe or mirror reality, to claims that all that researchers can know is ideas, or the particular shared language through which knowledge claims are expressed.

Modern scientific method is a form of the pursuit of truth, in the sense that scientists do aim to specify connections between ideas (scientific theories), experience (what our senses and experiments tell us) and reality (what actually exists independently of human thought). Alternatively such connections can be deemed problematic or impossible. Although these concerns with making and contesting connections run through western thought, they run in different directions. There are particularly sharp disagreements over: whether social reality can exist independently of people's ideas about it; whether experience can exist independently of the ideas/language that give meaning to experiences; where ideas come from, and whether/how they are powerful. Disputes over how, or whether, connections can ever be made, and social reality ever actually known, provide the methodological context within which feminist approaches to methodology have developed.

While feminist methodology is rooted in conceptions of scientific method as the means of producing authoritative knowledge of social reality, these roots do not grow into clear pathways through debates on methodology. Feminists too are divided over where ideas come from, how people make sense of experience, whether social reality can be connected to ideas and experience, and what evidence is evidence of. Claiming connections (or being unable to specify connections) between ideas, experience and reality can be thought of as a social process of knowledge production. This requires further reflection on who is doing the knowing, the nature of mind, self and subconscious, whether individuals can produce knowledge, or whether they always do so as part of a community, and what it means to be reasonable. For feminists, this process is intrinsically political, and has ethical implications.

Further philosophical disputes about cause and effect, determinism and free will affect conceptions of human agency. Agency implies that people have the ability to choose their goals and act (more or less rationally) to achieve them, as opposed to actions and ideas being determined by one's social position, genes, subconscious, impersonal historical forces, or other factors. Western feminism has recognized that agency is difficult to establish, but has been reluctant to dispense with a notion of individual agency, however philosophically problematic. Most versions of feminism assume that people have some power to make choices and act on them (unless forcibly rendered totally helpless) and so can be held morally responsible for their actions. But this notion of individuality and agency is not common to all cultures, and is never a simple one to defend.

Methodology in social research entails:

1   a social and political process of knowledge production;

2   assumptions about the nature and meanings of ideas, experience and social reality, and how/if these may be connected;
3   critical reflection on what authority can be claimed for the knowledge that results;
4   accountability (or denial of accountability) for the political and ethical implications of knowledge production.

It is these concerns that situate the roots of feminist methodology in modern western thought, despite feminism's engagements with other ways of thinking and other cultures.

Method is not methodology

Although they are often confused, it is useful to make a clear distinction between methodology and method in social research. Used loosely, 'method' indicates a general approach to research, as in 'empirical method', 'scientific method' or 'Marxist method'. More specifically, the notion of method simply refers to techniques and procedures used for exploring social reality and producing evidence (such as ethnography, interviews, observations, focus groups, questionnaires, life histories, documentary analysis, laboratory experiments, analysis of texts, objects or images). Different disciplines tend to specialize in a particular range of techniques, but there is no fixed relationship between particular methods or research techniques used in social research and particular methodologies.

The characteristics of methodology in social research

A methodology in social research comprises rules that specify how social investigation should be approached. Each methodology links a particular *ontology* (for example, a belief that gender is social rather than natural) and a particular *epistemology* (a set of procedures for establishing what counts as knowledge) in providing *rules* that specify how to produce *valid knowledge* of *social reality* (for example, the real nature of particular gender relations).

A key feature of feminist methodology is the implication that the relevant rules can provide criteria for judging between competing knowledge claims. For example, in judging feminist knowledge to be 'better' than patriarchal knowledge, or in deciding between conflicting feminist accounts (despite the problem of not being able to establish once and for all what 'better' means). There are different methodologies because different schools of thought have different rules for producing and justifying knowledge. We sketch the common characteristics of methodology briefly here.

An ontology is a way of specifying the nature of something

Different methodologies depend on different beliefs about what really exists, and so on different notions of the essences of things. Those things that are social (for example, education, families, relationships) are generally conceived in western thought as essentially different from those things that are natural (for example, rocks, trees, reproductive organs). Other cultures have other systems of classification, and other notions of essence and difference. Different ontologies offer different beliefs about social existence. Critical debates in feminism, for example, have developed over the 'true nature' of sex, sexuality and gender (Jackson and Scott 1996). The notion that masculinity and femininity are natural states pinned to male and female bodies has been contested, as has the belief that 'sex' is what is biological while 'gender' is what is social. There are also more complex beliefs about the interrelations of bodily differences and their social forms that indicate how difficult it is to understand the interactions of ideas, bodies and their physical and social environments. *Feminists can have different ontological beliefs (and so different theories) about the nature of reality and the objects of their research.*

An epistemology is a way of specifying how researchers know what they know

Different epistemologies (for example, empiricism, realism) offer different rules on what constitutes legitimate knowledge, and what criteria establish knowledge of social or natural reality as adequate or valid. Differences within and between epistemologies are many and complex, and have diversified over the years. From the perspective of feminism, the development of methodology has been influenced, in particular, by philosophical struggles over how far knowledge (of the natural world or God, or social life) is produced through *reasoning*, through *ideas* in people's minds, or from evidence available to the *senses* (particularly through systematic observation and experiment).

Empiricist epistemologies, for example, offer rules on how to move from the evidence of our senses, and private experiences, to general and certain knowledge of what is really there. There are many versions of empiricism, and it is difficult to embrace them in a brief definition, but empiricists rely on their observations and experiments to make connections between human experience, external reality and ideas about what really exists. Despite disagreements between empiricists, Ted Benton suggests that 'the touchstone of empiricism [is] that there is no knowledge *a priori* ("prior to" or independent of experience) which is at the same time informative about the world, as distinct from our ideas, or the meanings of the terms we use' (Benton 1978: 22).

The common sense of western thought largely takes for granted that knowledge of reality rests on factual evidence that can be observed, and that these facts (if properly interpreted) can indicate what is real, independently of the researcher's values. The inferiority of women was scientifically established in the nineteenth century in this way (by examining brain size and bodily differences, observing behaviour, and so on). Feminists have challenged these 'facts' by arguing that patriarchal or racial prejudices and power relations were present in the initial ideas and in the research method, producing 'bad' theory, and that the evidence of inferiority does not 'fit' reality or accord with experience.

Realist epistemologies assume, in contrast to empiricism, that although reality is not fully available to the senses, it can still be grasped. Theory (of what reality is like) is required in order to imagine what is hidden from the senses and cannot be directly observed. Reality (for example, the reality of 'patriarchy') may or may not be imagined correctly. Realist epistemologies do not require the separation of fact and bias, as theory must come both from the reasoning mind and from the material conditions in which the thinker lives. Karl Marx, for example, claimed to have 'discovered' the logic of capitalism, which could not simply be deduced from evidence or experience. Marxists also 'discovered' that social class is a more fundamental social division than gender. Feminists have countered this conclusion by arguing that a gender-blind theory is inadequate for understanding people's experiences of the realities of gendered social relations.

Since different epistemologies (and their many variations) specify differing relations between knowledge, experience and reality (or deny that researchers can access reality independently of how they think about it), it is not surprising that *feminists can draw on differing epistemologies.*

Validity is a way of establishing what counts as true

In recent western scholarship (in modern and postmodern debates on scientific method, scientific knowledge and truth) feminists have thought about the investigation of social life through debates on what social reality is like and whether/how reality can or cannot be validly known (in the sense that connections between knowledge of reality and actual reality can be specified). Feminists have had to contest what counts as reliable knowledge (in the sense of what can be replicated by other researchers) and valid knowledge (in the sense of representing reality), and how (or whether) such knowledge can be achieved. In order to challenge existing knowledge of women's inferiority, and to have their challenges taken seriously, feminists have either to validate their claims to knowledge of social life/gender through existing scientific methods, or to propose other criteria for justifying their knowledge and how it is produced. *Feminists can draw on different rules for establishing what counts as true, or can regard valid knowledge as impossible (in the sense that connections between knowledge and an independent reality cannot be specified).*

Power makes a difference to who is able to know what

Feminist methodology always entails some theory of power, since the power to produce authoritative knowledge is not equally open to all. Feminists therefore question who has the power to know what, and how power is implicated in the process of producing knowledge. (Can the pregnant woman determine what is going on in her body in the same way as the obstetrician? What is the relation between medical professionals and those whom they treat? Whose knowledge is authoritative/legitimate? Why are the obstetrician, the midwife, the mother and the father differently situated in relation to knowledge of childbirth? Why does the attribution of birthing knowledge and skills vary between cultures?)

Questions about the nature of power and where power lies are critical to the political/ethical implications of producing knowledge in one way (for example, via medical hierarchy, examinations, professional qualifications) rather than another (for example, via personal experience). *Feminists can draw on different theories of power.*

Knowledge is not separable from experience

Knowledge of social life is shaped by theory, culture and ideas, but does not come only *from* theory or language. It is a historical product, produced in particular social, political and intellectual conditions and situations. Feminist approaches to methodology have to tackle the problem of how to take account of experience when researchers are all personally and variably engaged, experienced and situated in social relations. What people do in everyday life, including researching, teaching or learning, is not separable from the rest of their lives. *Feminists can have different experiences and different conceptions of how knowledge is connected to experience and its meanings.*

Ethics expresses moral judgements, for example on rights, obligations, justice

A feminist methodology implies that researcher bear moral responsibility for their politics and practices. Feminist investigations of the social world are concerned not just with truth, but also with how knowledge is produced and authorized. Judgements about power, justice and the transformation of what is unjust have to be balanced against tolerance of contradiction and respect for difference. These aims are deeply problematic since there is no neutral way of producing valid knowledge of gendered lives across differences, or of judging between different accounts of social reality. The ethical and political implications of defining a relationship as violent are very different from defining it as domestic. *Feminists can adopt different ethical and political positions.*

Accountability allocates responsibility for what knowledge is produced, and how

What feminism adapts from its critique of modern western thought is a moral responsibility for feminist knowledge, through some concept of agency. This entails a general ethic of accountability to a community of women. *Feminists can take differing positions on: defining agency; allocating accountability for knowledge production; conceptualizing a community of women.*

The choices open to feminists in relation to these aspects of methodology indicate that feminism requires some level of political unity from those who are philosophically and methodologically as well as socially and politically divided. Feminist methodology is initially hard for students to grasp because different feminists take different positions in claiming that their knowledge is both in some sense 'believable' and also in some sense 'feminist'. This is sometimes dealt with by referring to 'feminist methodologies', rather than 'methodology'. Multiplying methodologies, however, does not clarify in what respects different approaches have something distinctively feminist about them. We use the term 'feminist methodology' (rather than methodologies) throughout this book for simplicity's sake, but in doing so we take methodology to be a plural term covering a broad area of thought, debate and practice.

Is feminist methodology distinctively feminist?

Since feminists can make choices in relation to all the key characteristics of methodology, the idea of any distinctively feminist approach to methodology is problematic (Harding 1987a) The academic area of feminist methodology was initiated primarily as a way of characterizing existing methods of producing knowledge as masculinist, and of challenging existing understandings of gendered social life. In general, feminists were critical of ways of producing supposedly scientific knowledge of social life that claimed to be politically neutral, or gender-neutral, while in practice promoting, reproducing or ignoring men's appropriation of science and reason (Clegg 1975; Stanley and Wise 1993).

Sandra Harding comments: 'For feminists it is moral and political rather than scientific discussion that has served as the paradigm – though a problematic one – of rational discourse' (1986: 12). Since there is more than one moral/political position within feminism, claims for a distinctive feminist methodology have always been debated and contested by feminists. If feminist methodology is not distinctive in terms of women studying women, or in its methods/techniques, or in its epistemologies and ontologies, or in its conceptions of rationality and validity, then any distinctiveness must come from the relations between epistemology and politics in feminist research. The following four points summarize this position:

1 *Feminist methodology is not distinguished by female researchers studying women.* Since feminist consciousness is not derived from a female body, women do not have a special claim to know gender. Those who are materially and socially more-or-less-female do not necessarily fully share political interests or experience a common social/embodied existence.

2 *There is no research technique that is distinctively feminist.* Feminists have developed, and experimented with, qualitative, politically sensitive research styles and fieldwork relationships, because this suits their purpose of making diverse women's voices and experiences heard. But they can also use a range of quantitative and other techniques. The empirical finding that many feminist researchers use particular qualitative techniques does not mean that feminist research logically or necessarily requires such techniques, or that others cannot use them. There is no research method that is consistently or specifically feminist.

3 *There is no ontological or epistemological position that is distinctively feminist.* Feminists have interacted with a range of existing positions. There are particular differences between: (i) those taking realist positions (indicating a

belief in a real world external to and independent of human knowledge of it, which needs human consciousness/social theory in order to imagine what it is like); (ii) those taking empiricist positions (indicating that knowledge of what is real is limited to the evidence of our senses); (iii) those taking relativist positions (rejecting the possibility of scientific method as a means of accessing social reality). While some have argued that feminist methodology is distinctive in how it locates the researcher in the research process (Harding 1993: 69; Stanley 1992: 31), we take the view that this is also characteristic of other radical approaches to social research (for example, in anti-racist or disability studies). It is a requirement of feminist research to reflect critically on the place of the researcher in the process of knowledge production, but this is also a requirement of good practice in social research more generally.

4 *Feminist methodology is distinctive to the extent that it is shaped by feminist theory, politics and ethics and grounded in women's experience.* Logically, feminist methodology cannot be independent of the ontology, epistemology, subjectivity, politics, ethics and social situation of the researcher. No rules of methodology enable researchers to escape their ideas, subjectivity, politics, ethics and social location. Feminist claims to know what people's lives and relations are like are politically charged. They defy patriarchal 'truths' that women are naturally inferior to men; they defy the reasoning and scientific methods that are blind to male dominance. This defiance ranges from wild excitement at unleashing women's full human potential to cautious programmes of equal rights in limited public spheres, but it rests on the moral and political position that authoritative knowledge of the unjust subordination of women can be produced and justified.

What is distinctive is the particular political positioning of theory, epistemology and ethics that enables the feminist researcher to question existing 'truths' and explore relations between knowledge and power. Because of the social diversity of gender relations, and the variable interaction of gender relations with other power relations, feminist knowledge of women's lives cannot be assumed or generalized without qualification and empirical investigation. Regardless of their epistemological and ontological differences, what distinguishes feminist researchers (of whatever gender) is some shared political and ethical commitment that makes them accountable to a community of women with moral and political interests in common (Code 1991; Nelson 1993). Feminist research is politically *for* women; feminist knowledge has some grounding in women's *experiences*, and in how it *feels* to live in unjust gendered relationships.

These appear to be the only grounds on which something distinctively feminist might be claimed for diverse approaches to methodology. Confusion can arise where people fail to distinguish clearly between methodology and method (see above), but much feminist debate on methodology is unresolved or confusing because feminists have been arguing *for* feminist methodology *from* differing political and epistemological positions. While feminist methodology has its roots in modern debates on reason, science, truth and progress, it has both grown from these roots and developed in various directions. In the chapters that follow, we look at key challenges that feminist researchers have faced in producing knowledge of gender, and how these challenges have been tackled.

The structure of the book

Part I situates feminist approaches to methodology in the context of the challenge of scientific method. We note the cultural particularity of the debates and assumptions that have shaped feminist thinking about possible connections between ideas, experience and reality. Chapter 2 locates the roots of feminist approaches to methodology in particular preoccupations with social research as a pursuit of truth, and particular notions of reason, science and progress inherited from the European Enlightenment and from humanism. The notion of man's mastery of nature, particularly the assumption that human beings, as free selves with agency, can use reason progressively to discover the truth about the natural or social worlds, served both to disparage women and to shape feminist approaches to knowledge production. We argue that feminism in the West was substantially influenced by Enlightenment thought, but also developed in conflict with it, giving feminism a powerful but contradictory methodological heritage. It is the methodological problems and contradictions of feminist responses to a lasting Enlightenment and humanist legacy that are addressed in the rest of the book.

Feminist researchers face particular problems in taking on a political and epistemological responsibility to tell accurate stories of gender (since different stories have different effects on people's lives) without being able to establish accuracy with any certainty. In Chapter 3, we look at the struggles over 'truth' and 'objectivity' in late twentieth-century feminist debates on methodology. Since claims that there are universal criteria for establishing which are the better stories of gender have been challenged, feminists have taken a variety of positions in justifying the knowledge of social life that they produce. This chapter suggests four possible stances towards justifying connections between knowledge and reality, and the confusions that arise from failure clearly to distinguish between them. In the first two, objectivity and subjectivity are seen as separable but as providing contrasting paths to truth claims; in the third, subjectivity and objectivity are taken as problematically inseparable in seeking hidden truths; the fourth position, that of relativism, denies that researchers can specify connections between knowledge and reality.

Chapter 4 examines the consequent question of whether telling the truth is at issue at all. Feminists have to weigh any commitment to science, rationality and rules of method against the relativist claim that the 'knowing feminist' (the self who produces feminist knowledge) and her 'truths' are socially constituted and so are contingent on how they are produced. In trying to resolve these problems within modern thought, some feminists have attempted to move beyond debates on objectivity and truth through notions of a feminist standpoint. While standpoint theories are often dismissed as a unified and simplistic position, we consider conceptions of a feminist standpoint to be a critical area of debate on the possibilities of feminist knowledge. Proposals for a feminist or women's standpoint, from which 'better' knowledge of gender relations can be produced, offer differing approaches to making feminist knowledge plausible and authoritative. These debates bring out key problems in claiming connections between ideas, reality and experience, and the limits of modern thinking in this respect.

Part II marks a shift in approaches to knowledge production by considering whether there is any place left for feminist methodology when feminist claims to knowledge are confronted by the poststructuralist and postmodern critiques that we loosely term 'postmodern thought'. In Chapter 5, we look first at the positive opportunities offered by postmodern thought through deconstructions of the very terms of feminist thinking on methodology. From a postmodern perspective, feminism's inheritance of modern and humanist thought can be viewed as defective. This challenge need not be negative. It can offer escape from the constraints of modern thinking on the pursuit of truth, and propose productive ways of thinking about gender, power and knowledge production. The concerns of postmodern thought and of feminist social research, however, remain different. Postmodern freedoms to think about connections between knowledge and power can appear to unravel feminist politics and ethics. We argue that feminism should retain some distinctive elements in its approaches to social investigation, particularly in studying the institutionalization of inequalities of power, issues of materiality, difference and experience, and the interconnection of politics, ethics and epistemology. Feminists have been concerned about the political and ethical implications of abandoning the entire legacy of humanism and scientific method, but this concern has resulted in a contradiction at the heart of feminism, and varying feminist responses to postmodern thought, rather than a single methodological strategy.

In Chapters 6 and 7 we take up the choices facing feminist social researchers in the aftermath of postmodern thought. Chapter 6 starts from the problem that in empirical social research the researcher and the researched always stand in some relationship to each other. Feminists cannot assume any shared situation of 'being women'. Researchers have the problem of conceptualizing and experiencing multiple differences between 'women', but they also seek to represent gendered realities across differences, and to do so within a normative framework for assessing injustices. There are persistent tensions between pressures to fragment feminism, and pressures to focus on the political concerns of feminism and possible alliances between women. Since reality cannot be directly represented in research texts, representation of the researched and interpretation of data are powerful ways of claiming particular connections or a lack of connections between experience, ideas and realities. We consider the problems facing feminist social researchers in dealing with privilege, and look more generally at the politics of representing 'others' across social, political and cultural differences. Feminism has been shaken by women's resistance to being constituted as 'other', and by accusations about women's exercise of power. The moral agency of the feminist remains a vital factor in reflecting critically on power relations in the research process and in seeking strategic alliances between women, but the choices facing the researcher as the producer of feminist knowledge remain politically and epistemologically problematic.

In Chapter 7 we return to three recurrent and interconnected issues that have run through earlier chapters: (1) whether, or how, feminist knowledge can be grounded in women's experiences if experience cannot be taken simply as true; (2) whether, or how, gendered experience is connected to underlying material realities; (3) whether, or how, there are grounds for deeming any knowledge claim 'better' than another. Different views of possible connections between feminist knowledge, people's experiences and material realities remain sharp points of divergence between feminists. Different epistemological and ontological assumptions offer different understandings of the complexity of social life and the nature of power relations. We consider the case that feminist knowledge cannot be grounded in experience, and then use the example of accounts of rape to explain why, despite the problems of making sense of them, feminists are reluctant to abandon experience as a source of knowledge. This reluctance brings researchers up against the case for claiming connections between experience and material social realities. Despite considerable resistance to any notion of validity, we argue that feminists (and their critics) should work out what criteria they actually use in judging between competing accounts of gendered lives, and how these may be defended. The assertion that feminist knowledge claims are evaluated and authorized within feminist epistemic communities requires further investigation.

Part III is a brief consideration of what choices are encountered in doing a small-scale feminist research project. Once the feminist researcher is located in a social process of doing research, abstract debates on methodology have to be brought down to earth, and their implications worked out in practice. In Chapter 8, we take prospective researchers through the stages of a small-scale feminist social research project, in the light of the challenges to feminist knowledge production that we raise in earlier chapters. The point is not to provide correct answers or propose a model procedure, but to deconstruct a version of the research process from research question to presenting the results. We take the novice researcher through key decisions on the production and justification of feminist knowledge.

In Chapter 9, we conclude that although feminists are as much in disagreement as any other social researchers over how connections or disconnections can be conceived between feminist knowledge, women's experience and gendered social realities, knowledge of gender has flourished. Feminists have risen to the challenges of scientific method, postmodern thought and differences between women in productive ways, despite their disagreements. Feminist knowledge has been effective in grasping hidden power relations, in bringing out the diversity of gendered social existence, and in offering well-grounded strategies for how women can envisage justice, exercise choice and make alliances across their differences.

Notes

1. Sandra Harding has pointed out that different feminists have adopted different ways of knowing. She distinguishes between feminist empiricism and taking a feminist standpoint (Harding 1987b, 1991, 1993), and distinguishes both these positions from the production of male-centred (androcentric) knowledge and from poststructuralist feminism.

2. It is not true, however, that white American feminists of the 1960s and 1970s ignored all differences between women. Shulamith Firestone (1970), Kate Millett (1970) and Robin Morgan (1970), for example, all indicate differences of class, race and sexual orientation in the USA. Millett and Firestone specify interrelations between sex, racism and patriarchy that implicate white women in racism. But all three focus on exposing sex/gender as the key political division between women and men. While judging racism

to be immoral, they emphasize that what women have in common is their subordination to male supremacy in patriarchal society. Analyses such as these of women's common interests in sexual politics have been strongly resisted by women whose own experiences of sexism are intermeshed with other forms of subordination (Joseph and Lewis 1981; Mirza 1997a and b; Moraga and Anzaldúa 1983).

    3. For some current examples of criticism see the Feminism on Trial website.

PART I

FEMINISM'S ENLIGHTENMENT LEGACY
AND ITS CONTRADICTIONS

2

Reason, science and progress

Feminism's Enlightenment inheritance

Introduction

When feminist researchers set out to produce knowledge of the social world, their assumptions about what knowledge is, who knows what, and what constitutes adequate social investigation start not from scratch, but from particular ways of thinking about producing knowledge and claiming truth. 'We start, all of us, always, in the middle of ongoing histories of inquiry' (Nelson and Nelson 1994: 500). Feminist social researchers have to establish that knowledge is reasonable, based on evidence and telling some truth, or they must provide some other criteria of authority, or reject established practices of authorization.

In this chapter, we pick out certain assumptions and ways of thinking that became influential during the European Enlightenment, and which gave rise to the nineteenth- and twentieth-century thought on social research within which debates on feminist methodology emerged. We take the term 'Enlightenment' to characterize a significant period of European science, philosophy, politics and society, particularly during the seventeenth and eighteenth centuries. Feminism in the West was substantially shaped by the concerns of the Enlightenment, but also developed in conflict with it. We focus on the consequences for feminism of changes in thought that brought notions of reason, science and progress into dominance.

Feminists have taken critical, though not unified, stances in relation to Enlightenment thought, since it offers a framework of masculinist thinking within which they have struggled to find an authoritative voice. Behind the concerns of feminist methodology lie the major concerns and debates of western philosophy in thinking about how knowledge of the world can be produced and justified. A book on methodology is not a book on philosophy, but methodology is framed by philosophical ideas, problems, traps and disputes. Discussion of methodology entails some reference to technical terms with specific meanings in this context. We do not have space for any fuller introduction to relevant philosophical debates, but we define key terms briefly where necessary and have included a glossary.[1]

Enlightenment thought

Enlightenment thinkers pursued critical questions about the capacities and the rights of rational men to think for themselves. We make no attempt here to do justice to the range, complexity and internal disputes of the European Enlightenment, or to squeeze Enlightenment thought into some unified philosophical position. (There were variations, for example, between British empiricism, French rationalism, German idealism, as well as tensions around the Enlightenment's counter-current of romanticism [Lanser 1997].) We merely pull out some factors in approaches to claiming knowledge of social life that have subsequently both influenced feminist methodology and become a focus for feminist resistance. We approach Enlightenment thought from the current predicament of feminist claims to knowledge, and so from the need to clarify whether feminist knowledge can be authoritative and whether distinctions can be made between better and worse accounts of gendered social life.

We first identify particular ways of thinking about scientific knowledge, and ways of positioning the thinker, that have, directly or indirectly, influenced both feminist thought and feminist claims to authoritative knowledge. This requires clarifying what it is about Enlightenment thinking that has impinged on feminist thought. Second, we consider what modern feminism has challenged in the application of scientific method to social research, as male-centred, emotional and patriarchal. Although feminists have not agreed with each other on exactly what Enlightenment thinkers meant, or on what criticisms are most apposite, they have produced a considerable literature on why feminist researchers need to re-evaluate notions of reason, scientific method, authoritative knowledge and progress.

Reason, science and progress: how Enlightenment thought has shaped feminist approaches to methodology

The Enlightenment thinkers of the seventeenth and eighteenth centuries may seem remote (and often sexist and racist) figures of little direct interest to an international and cross-cultural feminism today. All these thinkers have attracted critics who have, more or less thoroughly, set out to refute their propositions: 'Philosophy may be born in wonder, but it is kept alive by dissatisfaction' (Curley 1978: x). Enlightenment thinkers built on earlier scholarship, but they established particular conceptions of scientific method and epistemology that are still relevant to debates on feminist methodology today. Their approaches to science underpin what came to be commonsense ways of thinking about thinking in the West, and of establishing the truths of the natural and social worlds. The Enlightenment laid the foundations of the modern thought to which postmodern and poststructural thinkers are largely opposed. Since it is not possible here to track all the differing paths that Enlightenment thinkers took, we have been highly selective in picking out issues that influenced the development of feminist methodology.

The rise of reason and science

Enlightenment thinking influenced the development of social research through claims that reason provides the path to freedom and autonomy (Seidler 1986: 222). Enlightenment debates on scientific method, in which discoveries about the nature of the world by individual scholars constitute progress, have profoundly influenced how feminists have thought about producing knowledge. The Enlightenment also provided conceptual tools, scientific goals, and notions of progress and liberty that influenced feminist approaches to conceptualizing and investigating gender relations.

Immanuel Kant commented, in 1784, that the 'motto of enlightenment' is: 'have courage to use your own reason!' (1995a: 1). In Kant's view, enlightenment follows from freedom, leading not just to knowledge, but to progress. Although Jean-Jacques Rousseau queried how far science (as opposed to virtue) had created progress rather than barbarism, he had summarized, in 1751, his sense of enlightenment.

> It is a beautiful noble prospect to view man, as it were, rising again from nothing by his own efforts; dissipating, by the light of his reason, all the thick clouds in which nature had involv'd him; mounting above himself: soaring in thought even to the celestial regions; marching like the sun, with giant strides around the vast universe; and, what is still grander and more wonderful, re-entering into himself to study man, to dive into his nature, his duties, his end. (1995a: 364)

It has been difficult for feminists to position their ways of knowing in relation to this conception of reason, and to decide whether they can or should be 'soaring in thought' so that women can stride around the universe and dive into the nature of wo/man. While this rational pursuit of knowledge of 'man' has framed feminist methodology, feminists have also struggled against this framework. The possibilities and difficulties they encounter come in part from questions pursued by Descartes.

René Descartes's work in the seventeenth century is taken as marking a turning point in the development of a modern attitude towards knowledge of the natural world. Descartes has been termed the father of modern philosophy and, in the period before the emergence of scientific specialisms and professions, he thought that he personally could lay the foundations for all future science (Magee 1987: 80). His questions about how to pursue truth had a powerful impact on thinking about scientific and social research well into the twentieth century, even though his answers were immediately opposed, have been variously interpreted and widely rejected (Bordo 1999). During the Enlightenment, the outlook of educated westerners was completely transformed by the rise of a general commitment to reason. Michel Foucault (1973) shows the historical peculiarity of the new ways of thinking that opened up from the seventeenth century. The new disciplines of the European 'human sciences' emerged into 'new epistemological space'; they took 'man' as their object of knowledge as a result of changes in the arrangement of knowledge (Foucault 1973: xi).

Descartes is taken to have launched philosophy into a modern scientific age through his questions about truth and certainty. His questions are pertinent to feminist social research because he asks: What knowledge can I be certain of? How can I know what is true? What can I know? These questions raise three particular problems. First, they target certainty in the sense of connecting ideas about the world to some underlying reality. Second, thought is not enough; people cannot simply think their way to knowledge of reality that is in some way certifiable. The process of thinking includes imagination and feeling, and even dreaming, since people can think while they are asleep. Descartes needed some way of validating claims to knowledge of truth/reality – how could he know what was true/real and what was dream, trick or illusion? Third, he could not get round this problem by relying on his own experience or the evidence of his senses, since this experience and evidence (however apparently convincing) could be misleading. Given what people can see before their eyes, they might believe that the sun moves around the earth or simply from east to west. But these beliefs have been refuted by astronomers. Science requires some way of being able to determine whether the astronomers are right or, rather, which astronomers, if any, are right. Descartes looked for sure ways of connecting scientific theories both with what people experienced and with some underlying reality.

In Descartes's view, knowing the truth about the natural world requires knowing with the mind/reason, rather than just with the senses or intuition. He did not rule out intuition or the senses as possible means of knowledge, but intuitive or experiential knowledge still needs some form of validation to establish with certainty whether it is true (in the sense of connecting ideas about reality with reality). Descartes concluded that reason is necessary to arrive at decisions on truth, since what truly exists has to be conceptualized through theory as well as observed. 'I understand by the sole power of judgement which resides in my mind, what I thought I saw with my own eyes' (Descartes cited in Russell

1996: 549). Descartes's influence has come from distinguishing between the world *as it really is* (for example, the realities of the solar system) and the world *as the individual investigator sees it* (for example, the sun moving across the sky) (Curley 1978: 10).[2] There have been significant influences on later thought, including feminist debates on epistemology, through what have come to be termed Cartesian doubt and Cartesian dualisms.

Doubt and certainty

Descartes asks, 'is it possible to work out a scientific account of the nature of things which will be perfectly general, intelligible to anyone and absolutely certain?' (Curley 1978: 1). His response assumes that people using their reason can distinguish what is true from what is false. This entails two further assumptions: first, that people have free will, and so are able to exercise choice; second, that the nature of matter is an orderly nature. Since Descartes's aim was to establish the foundations of science, and so of scientific method, he needed to deal with the possibility that he could come to a false conclusion.

Descartes was not only trying to reach the foundations of science, in the sense of discovering fundamental general truths about the nature of the world, but also trying to establish that scientific knowledge was actually possible. To do this he felt that it was essential that the search for truth should start with a search for certainty (Magee 1987: 81). He pursued his quest for certainty to the point where the one thing he could be absolutely sure of was that he was a consciously thinking being, and so he could be certain that he existed – 'I think therefore I am' (Descartes 1995: 184). He still had the problem, though, of how to attain certain knowledge of reality that could not be refuted. (His solution was to derive the certainty of the existence of God from his own consciousness of something more perfect than himself [since he had the capacity to doubt, and was thus less than perfect], and the certainty of a material world from the existence of God.) The general influence on scientific method of this attitude was the development of assumptions about the orderly nature of matter and the possibility that scientific knowledge could grasp this nature.

Cartesian dualisms

In Descartes's view, the essence of mind is not intelligence but consciousness (Kenny 1997: 113). It is this consciousness, or 'mind', that separates men from animals, who are unconscious 'matter'. Having stated that it is necessary to exist in order to think (Descartes 1995: 184), Descartes is taken to have established a dualism between a conscious being (mind) and its objects of knowledge (matter). This drew on earlier dualistic thinking in western and Christian thought, but has had a lasting impact on western thinking about knowledge and science: 'everything in Descartes' system is to be explained in terms of this dualism of mind and matter' (Kenny 1997: 113).

The effect of this separation of mind from matter was to focus scientific investigation on the discovery of an external world (unthinking matter) that really exists, but is not necessarily known about. The means of discovery is through the agency of a knowing self (me, using my mind and guided by reason). My knowledge can then reveal the realities of matter.

Magee points out that this position leads straight to

> a view of the world as split between subjects which are pure thought and objects which are pure extension. This is the famous 'Cartesian dualism', the bifurcation of nature between mind and matter, observer and observed, subject and object. It has become built into the whole of western man's [sic] way of looking at things, including the whole of our science. (1987: 86)

The taken-for-granted dualisms (mind/body; reason/passion; culture/nature; male/female) that have become embedded in European cultures and scientific thinking (albeit with variations) have profoundly influenced the development of feminist resistance to the certainties, and male-centredness, of existing knowledge (for example, in challenging scientific 'discoveries' of women's inferiority to men). Feminists have challenged dualistic or binary thinking by identifying unreason, emotion and injustice in how the separation of mind from body and reason from passion has come to position women. At the same time, the tools for thinking initially available to western feminists were those of scientific methods steeped in these dualistic categories.

An important political consequence of this dualistic thinking was to treat the body as matter to be studied like a machine (a position that, for example, became built into medical textbooks [Martin 1989]). The dominance of reason put the reasoning mind in a position of mastery. The 'knowing subject' – the conscious self who reasons – could master the 'object of its knowledge' – the matter to be known. The natural scientist, the man of culture, could unlock the secrets of nature in order to master her. One consequence of this logic was to conclude that the rational, civilized, cultured man, with his access to certainties, could master the savage, primitive or barbarian, who was subject only to passion or a child-like mind. Rational men also had passions, but these could be mastered by their superior reason. Kant defines 'enlightenment' as part of the process of man coming to maturity, and as 'defining the conditions under which the use of reason is legitimate in order to determine what can be known, what must be done and what may be hoped' (Foucault 1984b: 38).

These foundations of thinking about science have profoundly affected the shape and concerns of feminist methodology (even though the reasoning of individual thinkers has been extensively analysed, questioned and criticized). Since the Enlightenment, rationality and scientific method have come to be greatly valued as keys to unlocking the secrets of both social and natural worlds: the proliferation of knowledge and technology continues. Descartes's path to enlightenment and maturity has been weakened by a range of criticisms and refutations, but the common sense of the West has been slow to dispense with Cartesian dualisms. Scientific reason became very powerful through being defined in opposition to what is outside reason (passion, prejudice, madness, subjectivity, superstition, magic, tradition), even though this opposition has never been simple or uncontested.

Dualistic thinking took a particular political form in making rules for what counts as 'true' (representing actual reality). In the case of astrology, for example, science positions astrologers as unable to access real forces that actually affect human lives, or at least as unable to offer adequate evidence that such forces exist. Scientific explanations give chance, coincidence, self-fulfilling prophecy or delusion, as rational grounds for any apparent 'fit' between astrological cause and human effect. Astrologers claim that astrological knowledge can access real forces that actually affect human life. Astrologers know that astrological knowledge can certainly be true (although there can be inept practitioners), but scientific thought places this certainty outside science. From the perspective of scientific method, feminist research that does not conform to a particular rationality of knowledge production and its rules can be dismissed, alongside astrology, as unable to produce valid and authoritative knowledge.

Feminist scholars argue that the rise of reason and science that swept away competing explanations was not innocent of gender subordination (Grimshaw 1986; Lloyd 1984). In this triumph of dualistic thinking, men are masters of mind, culture and masculinity. It is they who can use reason to master their passions, bodies and objects of knowledge. This positions women as mistresses of passion and emotion, and as closer to nature than are men, in being subject to their bodies. Feminist observations and concepts can be categorized as expressions of feminine passion, or embodiment, rather than as rational, certain or authoritative. Men's naturally superior capacity for rational thought critically distinguishes masculinity from femininity. The rise of modern science entails ways of thinking in which these dualistic categories of thought are both hierarchical and political.

Since Enlightenment thinkers were writing over a considerable period of time, and were always in dispute with others, Enlightenment thought cannot be simplified into one clear view of male superiority opposed to female inferiority. But in much of the common sense of the western thinking that emerged with scientific authority from the Enlightenment, the proper place of women's knowledge is confinement to the realm of the feminine, domestic and maternal, in natural subordination to male mastery (Lloyd 1984: 82). The practical application of Cartesian dualisms to social relations became imbued not only with what were taken to be the natural propensities of male and female, but also with moral implications. As a particular capacity for rational thought came explicitly to characterize dominant forms of European masculinity (Seidler 1994), feminism could only emerge through challenges to the scientific truth that women are less capable of reason than men. It is not surprising that one of the first issues that privileged western women struggled for was access to education and claims to be reasonable.

Unreasonable women

Feminism has brought dramatic changes through challenging men's apparently 'natural' dominance as unreasonable, emotional, political and unjust, and showing 'reason' itself to be socially constituted. Winning political struggles to allow women access to education, and showing how gendered power relations operate in educational institutions and at work, has allowed women to demonstrate their intellectual capacities. This has been part of many wider struggles to question the association of masculinity with culture and mind.

> [A]s Lloyd (1984) shows in her tracing of changing ideas of reason, while ideas may change, their gender inflection may remain. Throughout the history of western philosophy women have been thought inferior or less than fully human, though some philosophers, like Kant and Rousseau, have found them charming and necessary to men's well-being, as long as they keep in their place. [. . .] [F]eminist criticism shows that western philosophy has been consistently masculine in orientation even while it has changed its preoccupations and methods. (Griffiths and Whitford 1988: 6–7)

Some of Kant's and Rousseau's remarks on women's capacities clearly indicate this masculine orientation. Kant exemplifies the excitement of the wave of scientific developments in Europe from the late seventeenth century. He identifies such excitement as properly situated in a male sphere of knowledge where femininity is inappropriate.

> A woman who has a head full of Greek [. . .] or carries on fundamental controversies about mechanics [. . .] might as well even have a beard. [. . .] The fair can leave Descartes his vortices to whirl forever without troubling themselves about them [. . .] and the attraction of their charms loses none of its strength even if they know nothing of what Algarotti has taken the trouble to sketch out for their benefit about the gravitational attraction of matter according to Newton. [. . .] The content of women's great science, rather, is humankind, and among humanity, men. Her philosophy is not to reason, but to sense. (Kant 1995b: 581–2)

As we quote Kant here, the dualism of his assumptions grates on us and, in writing this book, we are clearly challenging his right to construct this notion of a gendered opposition between male 'reason' and female 'sense' (but see Schott 1997).

Kant was also excited by Rousseau's writing. While Rousseau proposed a modern education for men, women's role was to be strictly supportive and subordinate, and this gender distinction was marked by a distinct relation to reason.

> The Most High [. . .] has endowed man with boundless passions, together with a law to guide them, so that man may be alike free and self-controlled; though swayed by these passions man is endowed with reason with which to control them. Woman is also endowed with boundless passions; God has given her modesty to restrain them. (Rousseau 1995b: 570)

Rousseau claims a moral difference between the sexes since it is the business of women (provided for by nature and morality) to be mothers (1995b: 572). He was writing during a period of social and political change in late eighteenth-century France during which women were actively kept out of the new body politic (Gatens 1991: 10). He considered that woman's lack of endowment with reason left her with inferior means of controlling her nature, and so she could be conceived as closer to nature than man. 'Women do wrong to complain of man-made laws; this inequality is not of man's making, or at any rate it is not the result of mere prejudice, but of reason' (Rousseau 1995b: 571). He did not want women to be made miserable by their dependence on men, but thought that their gift of natural cunning enabled them to manage this dependence, and to cultivate docility, modesty and obedience, learning early to submit to the injustices that flow from man's imperfections (Rousseau 1995b: 579). The struggles for women's rights that emerged in varying forms in eighteenth-century Europe demonstrated what women were up against in contesting the rationality of 'man-made inequalities'.[3]

Feminists have tackled the undoubted sexism of such assumptions, but they are divided over how far generalizations about reason and gender were necessarily masculinist, or indeed what the maleness of reason means (Witt 1996: n. 22). Some feminist philosophers have attempted to re-evaluate Enlightenment philosophy, arguing that some Enlightenment thinkers are more sympathetic to women than feminist critics have allowed. Annette Baier (1993), for example, argues that Hume resisted a Cartesian opposition between reason and passion (which the quotations above from Kant and Rousseau exemplify). Hume did think women were different from men, but out of this difference they should produce female judgements to complement and check those of men.

> Some of Hume's more apparently condescending remarks about woman's special role as a 'polisher' and 'refiner' of rougher and more 'boisterous' male energies are distasteful to late-twentieth-century feminists. But we should not fail to appreciate the radically antipatriarchal stand that inspires them and that Hume takes throughout his philosophy. (Baier 1993: 47)

Twenty-first-century feminists, however, might well query any strategy dependent on assumptions of 'complementary but equal', since feminists claim this complementarity as a political relationship. Rational thought since the Enlightenment has commonly defined women in terms of Cartesian dualisms as closer to nature and, therefore, further from reason than men. 'Woman is more closely related to nature than man and in all her essentials she remains ever herself. Culture is with her always something external, a something which does not touch the kernel that is eternally faithful to nature' (Nietzsche cited in Hekman 1992: 111).

Margaret Atherton (1993) contends that Descartes's notion of reason is not gendered, since seventeenth-century women writers used it to argue for better education for women. The problem for feminist researchers now, however, is not whether Cartesian dualisms necessarily associate reason with men, or even whether feminists can detect some alternative feminine capacity for reason that is different. Men's appropriation of reason may not have been inevitable, but various forms succeeded, endured and have profoundly shaped the development of scientific theory and practice. Even in the late twentieth century, those looking for dualistic grounds for disparaging women had a wealth of established thinkers to draw on. In the 1990s, the respected novelist Sir Kingsley Amis could rudely call upon a long tradition of assuming that men are reasonable creatures and women are something different, in stating that 'the word *reasonable* changes meaning with the sex of its user' (1997: 244).

Given that privileged western men did effectively constitute the power of reasoning as male, feminist researchers have to consider whether reason is necessary or reclaimable in some gender-neutral mode. Can or should feminists be reasonable? If feminists can rely on knowledge produced through intuition, passion, subjectivity, experience, for example, do they need rationality in order to produce valid knowledge of gendered social arrangements? This is an issue that we take up in Chapters 3 and 4, but we note here that these questions only arise in the context of preceding, and dominating, dualisms.

Regardless of their own views, feminists have been positioned in relation to reason, science and truth by dominant conceptions of how truth can be known. Feminist claims to knowledge of the social world have depended on assumptions and concerns about science and authoritative knowledge that developed during and since the Enlightenment. They have had to situate themselves in relation to scientific method in order to try to claim an authoritative voice for reasonable women and rational knowledge of gendered social realities.

The idea of scientific method

The triumph of reason legitimated scientific method as the key to understanding and mastering nature. Increasing religious freedom, secularization and the development of individualism in the West facilitated stunning discoveries about the natural world. Technological innovations followed from applying laws of nature and exploring and testing them through experimentation, allowing increasing attention to be paid to the investigation of the natural world. Reason and scientific method became the hallmark of modern education, the means of conferring authority on claims to knowledge, and of deciding between the validity of these claims.

By the late nineteenth century, it was taken for granted that scientific theory, methods and experiment offered the potential for unlocking not only the secrets of nature, but also the secrets of social life. Exactly how social life can be discovered through reason, from ideas, or through the senses, however, has been hotly disputed (Williams and May 1996). Various forms of empiricism, rationalism, realism, idealism, hermeneutics (and the often bitter debates between them), framed struggles over method in the new social sciences.

Feminist methodology has a problematic relationship with notions of scientific method as a means of producing authoritative knowledge. For example, establishing the existence of domestic violence as a social and political problem requires changes in ideology and theory, so that marriage, rights and violence can be reconceptualized. But accounts of experience, statistics or other evidence are also needed as a means of claiming connections between feminist knowledge of domestic violence, actual events and competing meanings. These claims require rules of method that offer criteria for connecting experiences, ideas and reality, and so some claim to authority.

Modern feminist researchers have clearly wanted to establish authoritative knowledge. They have wanted to demonstrate, for example, that women are *not* naturally and morally subordinate to men; that men are *not* naturally creatures of reason; that there is *no* hierarchy of gender given in nature; that societies without gender subordination *are* possible. They have chafed against dualistic conceptions of reason/unreason, and struggled to change the meanings of science. But they have not generally wanted to present feminist knowledge as 'unreason', invalid or not authoritative. Still central to feminist concerns with how best to investigate the social nature of gender relations are problems of how to claim feminist knowledge as worth attending to, without being trapped in the dualistic thinking that opposes 'reason' to 'passion'. Some feminist debate on this issue has retained Cartesian dualisms by posing problems of feminist methodology in terms of struggles between 'objectivity' and 'subjectivity', and we take up these problems in Chapter 3. Generally, though, the development of feminist methodology has meant challenging the dominance of binary thinking in western thought.

Systematic scientific investigation of the natural and social worlds gives particular importance to rules of method, and to the development of expert professions requiring specialist academic training. Feminists have sharply criticized the masculinism of much of this expertise and training. They argue that the institutionalization of expertise also institutionalizes the legitimation of what counts as authoritative knowledge, and the exclusion of certain categories of human subject from the hierarchical institutions that confer such authority (Bleier 1986; Harding 1991; Keller and Longino 1996). But debates on methodology are still located in a specific scientific tradition that feminists in part adopt and in part oppose. Central to this tradition is the scientist or researcher as the human subject of modern humanism.

Modern humanism

While we claim that feminist methodology has roots in modern humanism as well as in the Enlightenment, it is impossible to give a brief, general definition of humanism that is historically accurate and takes proper account of diversity, disagreement and change. Kate Soper comments that, despite this diversity, there is a central humanist belief in the universality of humanity, but that this has led to '"humanist" sparrings for the right to represent the human race, its meaning and destiny' (1990: 231). The aspects of modern humanism that have had a particular impact on feminist approaches to methodology are those concerned with how human beings, as free selves with agency, can use reason progressively to discover the truth about the natural or social worlds, and so provide the potential not only for domination, but also for emancipation.

Michel Foucault (1984b) warns against confusing the Enlightenment with modern humanism in unhistorical attempts to equate them. He sees them as developing in a state of tension, rather than being the same. 'Humanism serves to colour and to justify the conceptions of man to which it is after all obliged to take recourse' (Foucault 1984b: 44). Nevertheless they have become somewhat confused in what has come to be termed 'modern thought' (as constituted in opposition to 'postmodern thought'), and through glossing over the historical complexities and diversity of a long period of reflection, knowledge production and critical debate. In order to clarify the influence of humanism on feminist methodology, we list some relevant characteristics, to which feminists have made varying responses. (It is not the case that all forms of humanism have all these characteristics.)

Characteristics of modern humanism that have influenced feminist approaches to methodology

1   The human subject is capable of rationality. The human subject is the 'I' who can discover the 'truth', and so depends on reason to reach the truth. Rationality is universally valid.
2   The human subject is an individual, rather than a collectivity, an autonomous agent with a self. This notion of self may or may not imply an essential human nature, but it does presuppose a common, universal humanity – although without agreement as to who is properly human or how the boundaries of humanity may be drawn. In order to deny this common humanity to those inferior to the knowing self (for example, slaves, women, workers, colonial subjects, Jews, gypsies, homosexuals), humanity's 'other' can be defined as not fully, or not yet, human – hence, feminine, immature, savage, flawed or deviant (Seidler 2000). This version of humanism therefore simultaneously denies 'difference' (because there is a universal humanity) while allowing the powerful to justify social and political inequalities as natural.
3   The human subject is the agent of his own subjectivity. In a discourse that conflates 'man' with 'humanity', man determines the fate of man. The human subject ('man') can take himself as his own object.
4   Since the human subject, as an autonomous individual with agency, can use reason progressively to discover the truth about the world, he has the potential to emancipate himself, or to be emancipated (from ignorance, oppression, barbarism or immaturity). This power gives the knowing subject (the reasoning man) the power and the right to study humanity, and the scientist, or social scientist, the power and the right to speak for humanity.
5   The human subject is able to contribute to human progress by adding to existing knowledge, through applications of rationality, knowledge, science. In Francis Bacon's terms, man's power is legitimated by his knowledge of what is true. It is in this sense that Bacon claims that knowledge is power (1995: 39).

We have oversimplified these aspects of modern humanism in order to bring out a characteristic attitude in western thought that has shaped feminist approaches to social investigation. But it is an attitude that has also provoked feminists into spirited resistance (Jaggar 1983; Johnson 1994). Modern humanism provides feminism with deeply contradictory goals and paths to knowledge, which have both liberating and dominating potential.

Progress and emancipation

In presenting the ideas of feminist writers in the UK and the USA between the eighteenth and nineteenth centuries, Alice Rossi comments that these authors 'were heirs to the happy Enlightenment conviction that reason would lead the way to a progressively better social order, free of the superstitions that had in the past bogged down mankind. [. . .] These writers believed deeply that reason, if properly cultivated through education, could set men and women free' (1973: 3).

During the twentieth century, these liberal notions of progress and individual notions of agency were increasingly questioned (Young 1985), but the urge towards emancipation has persisted.

Progress and emancipation, in the sense of freedom from male domination and rational transformation of gendered inequalities, has been central to feminism, but also intensely problematic. The emancipation or liberation of women presumes a clear category of women who are subject to some common form of patriarchal oppression from which individual women can be liberated. This assumption of universal humanity and universal rights transcends actual inequalities and differences and so overlooks power relations between women. This has been a critical point of fracture within feminism. The power of some women over others contradicts any general conception of shared subordination.

In addition, strategies for emancipation can be clouded by varied cultural conceptions of rights and duties, progress and freedom that differ in their conceptions of agency, inequality and oppression. To take emancipation as the outcome of decision-making by rational individuals contradicts the notion of emancipation as requiring massive social transformation of interlinked forms of oppression (including systems of production).

Emancipation presupposes some constraining bond or bonds from which the oppressed ought to be set free. But the notion of 'ought' derives from concepts of justice and rights – some notion of what a person is entitled to. A humanist notion of justice implies that somewhere there are rules that determine women's rights in universal terms. There is a considerable philosophical literature on the problems that such a view of justice raises (Hampshire 1999) and the ways these have been taken up in feminist moral theory (Hekman 1995), but for feminists the problems have always also been practical. Since feminism offers no authoritative centre to define what is or is not just for whom, feminist notions of justice are complicated by political, religious and cultural differences between women on how justice, rights and the person may be identified and what may be considered unjust. (For example, what are the rights of Kosovan Albanian women versus those of Kosovan Serbian women, or the rights of citizens versus the rights of 'illegal immigrants'?) The goal of emancipation is critical to the production of feminist knowledge, but what constitutes progress in this respect, and who envisages what should be transformed for whom, remain contested and often confused and contradictory.[4]

Feminist notions of social transformation or emancipation do not make sense without a claim to some common situation of oppression, and some notion of a common humanity with universal human rights for a common category of 'women'. In practice, however, feminists do not have a universal right to specify general rules that determine justice universally. Feminists cannot define in general what a feminist ideal of justice is (although they can investigate what definitions people actually use, and what conditions they actually live under). It is an inherent contradiction in feminism that some common ideal of justice is integral to feminist notions of methodology.

> To begin with, how could a feminist theory completely take leave of Enlightenment assumptions and still remain feminist? The critics are right that feminism must at

least in part stand on Enlightenment ground. Most obviously, feminist Postmodernists join those they criticize in believing that social progress is desirable and possible and that improved theories about ourselves and the world around us will contribute to that progress. Their own writings, whether or not they overtly dispute these Enlightenment claims, in fact enact them. They debate what those theories should say, whether science and epistemology projects will in fact lead to better conditions for women, and who should get to define what counts as social progress. (Harding 1991: 186)

Feminism has not been able simply to abandon notions of progress and emancipation. This is a contradiction that feminist researchers live with, and one reason why feminist methodology has been unable wholly to escape its Enlightenment and humanist roots.

The long shadow of the Enlightenment: challenges and contradictions at the roots of modern feminist methodology

The concerns of the Enlightenment, and the politics of modern humanism, still affect feminist social investigation. The status of scientific knowledge as superior knowledge, although contested, is part of the common sense of western thought, and is built into formal education more generally. Scientists, and philosophers of science, however, have always debated whether, or how, connections can be sought between ideas, experiences and any underlying reality, and whether reality has some essential existence or can only be known in terms of predictable regularities that can be observed (Keller 1992). Philosophers, including Nietzsche and Wittgenstein, have produced decisive rejections of any possibility of telling 'the truth', in the sense of actually connecting ideas and experiences with a real natural (or social) world, since all 'truths' are mediated by the language in which they are expressed. These disputes, and the politics of truth they entail, are significant influences on feminist thought. It is in this political arena that struggles have developed over what counts as authoritative knowledge, how power is exercised in the production of knowledge, and what is meant by a 'knowing subject'.[5]

Feminists have had to consider what ways of thinking about gender are most adequate, on what grounds, and with what moral and political implications. As challenges to Enlightenment conceptions of science and knowledge have developed, feminists have responded by exploring differing approaches to producing knowledge of gender. Here we indicate briefly key discomforts with Enlightenment thought that have influenced the feminist debates on methodology that we take up in the rest of this book.

Challenges to reason and scientific method

Enlightenment thought generated tensions between seeking mastery over nature and living in harmony with nature, but the development of science and technology was increasingly intended as mastery through the discovery of nature's hidden truths. This raises a number of difficulties. Challenging supposedly rational, neutral and authoritative patriarchal knowledge entails challenging the impartiality of scientists and their institutional hierarchies. Identifying science as ideas and social practices influenced by male dominance, and practised by people with emotions and political interests, challenges ways of connecting ideas of gender, women's experience and the possible realities of gendered lives.[6] Feminists have struggled to expose scientific knowledge as knowledge produced by particular male selves in particular social locations. Unmasking the subject of humanism reveals the imperial, western male masquerading as humanity, and transforms the 'rational' male into an emotional patriarch defending his illegitimate privileges.

The human subject is someone in particular whose invisibility is now showing. As modern scientific professions developed into specialist, male-dominated areas, they operated with patriarchal ideas and exclusionary practices that positioned women at worst as naturally subordinate to, at best as complementary to, men. The everyday activities and values of science reproduced male superiority and dominance by actively situating women outside specialist knowledge, skills and abilities (although with variations). Women could collude with their social positioning (for example, in efforts to be nice girls, respectable wives, good mothers, feminine workers) but they also resisted in various ways, in their workplaces, in their homes, and in their efforts to access income and education. Women struggled both to enter male-dominated areas and to transform how science, politics and philosophy might be understood and practised. Feminist responses to male-centred science were part of a much more general assault on the masculinism and male domination of knowledge, and the supposed separation of emotion and reason (Hochschild 1985; Keller 1992). Profound disagreements persist over what constitutes adequate and valid knowledge and how connections may or may not be made between ideas and reality.

In many respects, feminist research has been in tension with different conceptions of scientific method, rather than wholly rejecting them. There have been feminist debates over whether feminists can, or should, attempt to produce scientific knowledge, and feminists have tried to revalue nature, emotions and more holistic ways of knowing (Harding 1986; Keller and Longino 1996). In general, however, feminists have wanted to distinguish between better and worse accounts of gendered lives, and so have needed to justify some form of systematic investigation, reasoned argument and rules of method. This area has been a particular focus for debate over feminist methodology.

Challenges to the knowing self

The idea of a knowing self with epistemological, moral and political agency has been a critical and continuing problem for feminism. Feminists have questioned the ethical and political implications of a knowing self that produces male-centred knowledge with the authority of a male voice of reason. But notions of 'Women's Liberation' in the 1970s were generally humanist in conceiving women as rational human subjects with agency who could empower women in general by producing knowledge of subordination, and thus liberate women's true selves from patriarchal oppression (Feminist Anthology Collective 1981). This humanist position has attracted feminist criticism (Young 1985), but feminist approaches to knowledge production do not entirely escape it. Feminists have also maintained a moral link between the theorist and the theorized that has methodological and political implications for feminist research practice (Ransom 1993). Feminists have questioned in particular to whom the knowing self is accountable for the knowledge it produces.

Challenges to universalism and exclusionary practices

Feminist researchers have had problems in understanding how power is exercised in the production of feminist knowledge. There are also problems in conceptualizing and identifying power relations in other ways of knowing. Since feminist methodology has roots in Enlightenment notions of scientific method, it has been difficult for feminists, especially privileged academic feminists, to avoid just replicating existing power relations. But it is possible for even emancipatory projects to perpetuate relations of dominance and subordination by normalizing the invisibility of what is marginalized or excluded. Feminism thus came under pressure to throw off its humanism and to reflect more carefully on differences between women, on feminist exclusionary practices, and on power relations. Sensitivity to power relations, and the difficulties of deconstructing them, have been central to feminist debates on methodology, but those power relations closest to home are the most difficult to see.

While feminists expose gender-partiality rather than gender-neutrality in scientific knowledge, practice and organization, comparable challenges have been made to feminists. Patriarchal thought constitutes women as extraneous to authoritative knowledge production, and feminists have challenged this marginalization through political practice, and by fighting their way into academic institutions. But where feminists are privileged over others (for example, by class, racism, heterosexism, ablebodiedness, colonialism), feminist knowledge and practices can serve to produce or reproduce power relations and social inequalities (hooks 1994; Lather 1991). This has been a critical challenge to the development of feminist methodology and a central political struggle in the production of feminist knowledge.

Where feminists draw on assumptions of universal humanity to identify 'women' as a unified category, and assume that a shared female gender means shared female experience, they attract accusations of dominating other women (Spelman 1990). Where feminists appropriate Eurocentrism, and humanist universalism, they reproduce exclusion and the invisibility of power relations. Western feminism was clearly grounded in the thinking of the beneficiaries of slavery, imperialism and colonialism, despite its opposition to the patriarchal impulse of this thinking (Mohanty 1988). These accusations come in part from challenges to humanist assumptions of universalism and emancipation, in part from dissension around justice and moral agency, and in part from experiences of social divisions and power relations. As academic feminist knowledge emerges as authoritative, other forms of feminism or other women's lives can be rendered extraneous to feminist concerns.

Attention to difference and power relations does not in itself address the difficulties of accounting for what gendered lives are like, or the contradictions of treating women as a category. Recognition of power relations between women has transformed feminism, especially since the 1960s. But this recognition has also promoted an enormous range of research, 'speaking out', acting on and writing about the material conditions of women's lives, their relations with men, the state, each other, their bodies, subjectivities and identities, their children, their histories. Although this knowledge may be resisted or ridiculed, and does not unproblematically convey knowledge of reality, feminist claims to authoritative knowledge have led to considerable social change – despite extensive resistance, continuing inequalities and the entanglement of gender relations in other forms of power.

Conclusion

Feminists continue to challenge the adequacy of knowledge of gender relations produced by the authoritative voices of male-centred science and social science. They counter masculinist claims about the nature of gender and the capabilities of women. They open up the methodological, political and ethical implications of claiming connections between ideas, experience and reality. This has made relations between knowledge and power a critical area in considering how best to decide between competing knowledge claims, but has not given feminists new tools for thinking with. Feminism has moved on from the Enlightenment in making gender, politics, emotions and exclusionary practices visible in knowledge production, but not in any simple or consensual manner.

Feminism in the twentieth century did not immediately develop a new methodology that was distinct from other approaches to investigation of social relations. Feminists drew on existing conceptions of methodology and research methods, but not uncritically. They inherited Enlightenment notions of science, reason and progress (and so conflicting conceptions of epistemology) that positioned feminist knowledge in relation to existing notions of validity and authority. They could not, however, simply adopt these assumptions and conventions, because these did not produce the knowledge that they sought. Feminist approaches to methodology grew initially out of challenges to male-dominated knowledge, and from varying struggles to produce well-grounded and authoritative knowledge of women's lives. Feminist attempts to develop new thinking on methodology have been widely ignored, or have aroused considerable criticism, but if feminist challenges are taken seriously, they have implications for social research much more generally.

In the remainder of Part I we look at struggles to reposition feminist knowledge of gender in relation to notions of scientific method, and the problems of claiming valid knowledge.

Notes

1. Definitions and further information can be found, for example, on the Stanford Encyclopaedia of Philosophy website, and the Feminism and Philosophy website, and in Williams and May 1996.

2. Karl Marx, in the nineteenth century, and from a different methodological stance, also used this example to explain why he offers a scientific theory that goes beyond what appears to be the case in finding the underlying truth of the capitalist system. 'A scientific analysis of competition is possible only if we can grasp the inner nature of capital, just as the apparent motions of the heavenly bodies are intelligible only to someone who is acquainted with their real motions, which are not perceptible to the senses' (1976: 433).

3. Although women activists took a variety of positions on other contemporary struggles, they often had little interest in, for example, class, slavery and the impact of European trade and conquest.

4. There is no clear feminist line on abortion, for example, since there is no general feminist judgement on how justice to the mother and justice to the foetus can be arbitrated. Some feminists take the extreme position that a woman carrying an embryo or foetus in her body has an absolute right to abortion on demand. Others may use religious notions of rights to determine when independent life begins, or, at the other extreme, grant an absolute right to life from conception, making any abortion unjust. Other feminists make pragmatic compromises that balance the rights of the mother against the rights of the foetus (and, more problematically, the rights of the father, or community) when these are in conflict, and take into account different stages of pregnancy and states of medical technology. These compromises raise further complex issues of rights and quality of life, since a pregnant woman's right to life is rather different from her right to life without a child produced by rape, or without an additional mouth to feed, or without a disabled child, or without a girl when boys are of more value.

5. In their critical encounters with western philosophy, feminists differ in their interpretations, criticisms and responses depending on their own conceptions of feminism and its values, and their epistemological positions (Witt 1996).

6. Emmanuel Chukwudi Eze (1997) comments on the quantity of influential writing on race as well as gender during the Enlightenment. While the racist and sexist assumptions of great men have been played down in recent years, the 'age of reason' sanctioned notions of natural or justifiable hierarchies of race and gender that were legitimated by science. Recent introductory texts on western philosophy generally ignore the writings of philosophers on racial or gender hierarchy, or treat these as personal aberrations that can be overlooked in great thinkers (for example, Kenny 1997; Magee 1987; Russell 1996).

3

Can feminists tell the truth?

Challenges of scientific method

Introduction

The modern and humanist thought that feminists inherited situates feminist researchers as knowing subjects producing knowledge of a real social world in order to specify how gendered social life is organized, structured and made meaningful. This has led to various forms of engagement between feminist thought and conceptions of scientific method. Although feminist researchers are generally very critical of male-centred knowledge of gender relations, they took on the methodological problem of situating their own knowledge in relation to dominant conceptions of scientific method in social research. This does not mean that feminists necessarily want to behave like scientists, or agree on what is meant by science or method. It does mean that if they ignore the authority of scientific method, their own knowledge claims can be challenged as unscientific, subjective, political and generally untrue. If feminist knowledge is untrue, it need not be acted upon.

One reason why feminist researchers have taken different approaches to methodology is that they take different decisions on the possibilities of producing valid knowledge (including the possibility that the sort of truths that feminists seek, such as knowledge of child abuse, are never simply black or white, but 'complex, grey and almost always disputable' [Wise 1999: 1.11]). We argued in Chapter 1 that methodologies vary in how the possibilities of making connections between ideas, experiences and reality are conceived. Feminists (like other social researchers) are always methodologically vulnerable when they claim that direct connections can be made. Claiming that feminists can tell a better story of gendered realities than can others means claiming that specific connections can be established between feminist knowledge and some reality that it represents. This form of the pursuit of truth opens up a thorny path for any social researcher. In this chapter we look at the challenges to feminist knowledge posed by notions of truth and objectivity in the conventions of modern social research.

Feminist research as a quest for valid knowledge of social realities by a knowing subject

The attraction of a systematic scientific method in social research is that it apparently offers grounds for claiming authoritative knowledge of social reality. Commitment to rules of method implies some notion of an actual, real, material world (in the sense of being available to the senses, or existing independently of the observer) that can be investigated and represented (although there are differing approaches to scientific method [Fee 1983]).[1] Claims to knowledge can then be established, tested and evaluated according to known rules.

It is critical for the authority of feminist knowledge that researchers can, for example, claim 'domestic violence' or 'the subordination of women' to be both real and unjustified, rather than leaving these claims to be dismissed as subjective, irrational or the product of political bias. A poem or painting expressing an experience of violence is different from a reasoned general theory of violence, or systematic evidence of the extent of violence according to this theory, or claims to general knowledge of the reality of violence based on specific criteria. Feminists have a political responsibility to tell accurate stories of the nature of violence, why it exists in the forms that it does, and how its various forms are made meaningful, have effects and interact with other social factors. It makes a difference to people's lives if one story is believed rather than another. Accuracy, evidence and valid knowledge are needed in order to provide a foundation for practical political responses to the injustices and abuses of power. It is precisely these requirements, however, that researchers have difficulty in justifying.

Knowledge of domestic violence, for example, entails a theory of domestic violence, voicing of experience, and also judgements about what is right, about what constitutes evidence, about how meanings can best be interpreted. It can never be simply factual – a matter of amassing evidence – since every knowledge claim can be challenged by asking how evidence is constituted and what it represents. This challenge requires either some clear connection between evidence and reality, or some other conception of how knowledge can be grounded in evidence, experience or reasoning. Methodology is always problematic because no rule of method can ensure a direct connection between knowledge and reality. Even if such connection is thought to be possible, there are problems in how connections can be conceived and established. Feminists generally take the whole process of knowledge production to be a social process, and so one in which power relations are inherent. Like other modern social researchers they have acute problems in justifying the connections they claim between theory, experience and reality. It is precisely the attempt to specify these connections that postmodern thought disrupts, and we will examine this disruption in Part II.

Within modern thought, however, feminists are left to struggle with some form of the pursuit of truth.

Some feminists have been characterized as rigid (and rather stupid) 'foundationalists' who claim unreasonable knowledge of exactly what reality is (for example, Grant 1993). A foundationalist in this sense is someone who believes that knowledge is true when it accurately mirrors a concrete reality.[2] True knowledge, in this view, is produced by following rules that specify how to make direct connections between reality, experience and ideas. This would imply that domestic violence really 'is' in some unchangeable and absolute sense. Many feminists deny that they are engaged in a pursuit of truth at all because they see truth as narrowly confined to this sense of having to mirror reality. We argue in Chapter 4 that this notion of truth is an extreme position within modern thought, rather than the only one available. It is a general problem for social research that rules of method cannot in practice ensure validity in this sense. This limited sense of truth has, however, infected other uses of the term.

Feminist knowledge of domestic violence, for example, has produced a dramatic shift in general knowledge because of the attention researchers and activists have given to women's voices and women's experiences. But experiences are always interpreted, expressed in language and given meanings, and so cannot neutrally connect ideas (conceptions of violence) and reality (what actually happens) to produce one certain truth. These interconnections are complex and variously interpreted. Stories of domestic violence are culturally and historically specific, rather than timeless. In the UK, for example, feminist knowledge of domestic violence has moved from initial accounts of 'battered wives', to increasingly complex, qualified and diverse accounts, as more voices are heard, and as investigations have proceeded across varied experiences and relationships, and across generations, states and cultures. Around the world, stories of domestic violence have developed and changed as feminist knowledge takes account of a diversity of theory and a wide range of similar and different experiences. Since there is always more than one version of social life, any claim to knowledge of domestic violence can be contested both in terms of what is experienced and why, and in terms of what experiences are taken to mean and how they become meaningful.

Patriarchal authorities were aware, for example, of physical violence between partners, and of violent and sexual relations between adults and children. Feminists produced new knowledge by reinterpreting the experience and meaning of these behaviours within a new normative framework, by conceptualizing them as harmful and unjustified. They have made domestic violence matter personally and politically in new ways. By grounding knowledge in people's experiences and emotions and, simultaneously, connecting these with new ideas about what is happening, a new sense of what is 'real' is constructed, with new political responses and effects.

In the UK, a more specific example is the problematic issue of young women coerced into marriage against their will. This has conventionally been treated as a private matter of conformity to the custom of 'arranged marriage' in minority ethnic or religious cultures, and so as an issue that does not concern the state or other communities. It is now being suggested, through the constitution of a UK government unit based in the Foreign Office, that 'forced marriage' must be differentiated from 'arranged marriage' (BBC News 2000). This differentiation is produced by reconceptualizing specific 'traditional' behaviour as 'force', through the gendered language of domestic violence, rape and child abuse, and through the ungendered, liberal language of citizenship and individual rights (Ward 2000). These reconceptualizations constitute a shift in ideas, and are grounded in how the young women concerned voice their experience. Their pleas for help are variously interpreted through feminist, liberal and anti-racist theory. This shifts knowledge of the legitimate and justified 'disciplining of undutiful daughters' into knowledge of an illegitimate and unjustified 'abuse of power'. Changing the 'truth' of the 'reality' of 'forced' marriages, in these reconceptualizations of young women's experiences, entails ethical judgements about justice, rights, duties, and responsibility for change.[3]

Valid general knowledge of gendered lives would only be possible if the knowing self could reliably distinguish truth from falsity. Feminist researchers have turned to various versions of scientific methods of social investigation in their efforts to establish general and authoritative knowledge of gendered social realities that everyone can believe. But the simplest of feminist questions (are women oppressed? are some marriages forced?) raise in practice a series of problems about how to judge between different claims of what is 'really' the case. If feminists want to argue that a story of 'forced marriage' is 'truer' than a story of 'undutiful daughters', it follows not only that this claim to knowledge needs to be justified, but also that there have to be clear and general criteria for judging between competing knowledge claims and value systems (just as Russian and American scientists have to agree on the truths of the natural world in order to effect a docking procedure for their respective spacecraft). *It is the misfortune of social researchers that these criteria do not exist in any neutral or general way.*

The conceptualization and documentation of domestic and sexual violence has been one area of success in feminist knowledge production, bringing real changes in consciousness, politics and policing, even though violence continues, experiences and meanings vary, seeking justice can be a fruitless ordeal, and stories can be contested. The power of this general knowledge has also put pressure on feminists to take account of the related, but politically uncomfortable, issues of female violence, male victims of rape and child abuse, female collusion in male dominance, and the interaction of gendered power with other power relations and social divisions. Successful feminist knowledge claims have not come primarily from feminist commitment to scientific method, and feminists have had to reflect on the tensions between feminist research and the applications of scientific methods to social research.

Feminist objections to scientific method in social research

Many thinkers have criticized the claims made for scientific research methods on the grounds that science itself is a social product, that scientists are socially situated human beings with partial vision, and that no scientific method ensures access to some incontrovertible 'truth' (Chalmers 1982; Haraway

1989; Kuhn 1970; Latour 1993; Woolgar 1988). In the 1970s and 1980s, feminists made specific complaints about the domination of scientific methods by
a patriarchal consciousness that only permitted certain questions to be asked,
in certain ways, within male-centred frameworks of explanation (Comer 1974;
Dinny 1981; Morgan 1978; Women and Science Group 1981). These criticisms
are grounded in women's personal experiences of challenging scientific
expertise, of interacting with professionals claiming scientific authority (especially medical professionals) and of making sense of their own lives. Making
sense of women's experiences, absences and silences through feminist theory
enabled feminist critics to target the sexist practices and patriarchal ideas
that have shaped the social and political contexts within which scientific goals
have been prioritized and set. Women scientists also identified and questioned the hierarchical and patriarchal institutions within which authoritative
knowledge production has been financed and organized (Bleier 1984; Keller
1985).

Feminists have specifically queried the ability of patriarchal consciousness to
'discover' the nature of social reality. Patriarchal theory does not enable
researchers to ask whether, or how, women are politically situated in relation to
men because it does not provide appropriate theory and concepts. Ruth Bleier
comments:

> [P]atriarchal consciousness is our conceptual prison. But if we are born into it and it is
> *all* we know, how do we comprehend it as a prison, let alone destroy it for a vision of
> freedom that is not inherently apparent? The fashioning of our own tools, like the find-
> ing of women lost to history, has become our feminist task. (1984: 199)

A change of consciousness enables feminists to claim that the whole edifice of
professional science and its knowledge is socially constituted.

While scientific methodologies and practices vary, a specific target for feminists has not been scientific method in general, but a particular application of
scientific method, loosely known as positivism. Positivist approaches to
methodology bring a particular conception of scientific method to bear on the
study of social life, with the claim that reality is directly accessible given the
correct methods. Positivism is a very general and disputed term, but the particular aspect targeted by feminists has been the claim that rigorous rules of
knowledge production can prevent connections between knowledge and reality being contaminated by the researcher's values. In this respect, feminists
join other critics who have long questioned the possibility that knowledge
can be free of the researcher's values. There is some confusion in the literature
when specific aspects of positivist methodology are presented as those of science in general.[4] Sandra Harding, for example, characterizes 'science's
method' in general in terms of the characteristics of a particular version of
positivism.

> [S]cientific knowledge-seeking is supposed to be value-neutral, objective, dispassion-
> ate, disinterested, and so forth. It is supposed to be protected from political interests,
> goals and desires (such as feminist ones) by the norms of science. In particular, sci-
> ence's 'method' is supposed to protect the results of research from the social values of
> the researchers. (1987b: 182)

Ruth Bleier also characterizes science as asserting the superiority of facts over values and objectivity over subjectivity. She challenges these claims on the grounds that this is not how actual scientists behave.

> This book has shown that science is *not* the neutral, dispassionate, value-free pursuit of Truth; that scientists are not objective, disinterested or culturally disengaged from the questions they ask of nature or the methods they use to frame their answers. It is, furthermore, impossible for science or scientists to be otherwise, since science is a social activity and a cultural product created by persons who live in the world of science as well as in the societies that bred them. (1984: 193)

A casual scan of the mass media can produce numerous current examples of scientists being challenged by lay people and also disagreeing with each other (for example, over the safety of mobile phones, infant vaccinations, genetically modified foods, breast implants, or the causes of global warming) as well as social researchers disagreeing over the nature and causes of crime, uneven development, racism, the 'crisis' of masculinity, the effects of childcare, and so on. Donna Haraway observes that 'official ideologies about objectivity and scientific method are particularly bad guides to how scientific knowledge is actually *made*. Just as for the rest of us, what scientists believe or say they do and what they really do have a very loose fit' (1991: 184).

Scientists do not engage just in rational argument, but also in struggles over access to information and resources, the pursuit of profit, state regulation and intervention, international controls, and so on (Kuhn 1970). Harding concludes that male-dominated claims to value-neutrality have not been effective in actually controlling biases (1987b: 184). The problem for feminists (as for any other social researchers) is that they too cannot be free of their social positions, their access to resources, their ambitions, their grounded and gendered experiences, their political commitments and the limits of their languages.

Across the sciences and social sciences, positivism has been a dominant methodology, but it has never been the only one available. Since the Enlightenment, and especially since the later nineteenth century, thinkers have debated the numerous problems of trying to apply the methods of the natural sciences to the study of social life, and have offered various conceptions of scientific method for examining relations between knowledge, experience and reality. Social research has been extensively influenced by those who argue that the methods of the natural sciences cannot be applied to the study of social life because human subjectivity and social relationships inevitably enter into the study of humanity. This is a further difficulty in making claims to valid knowledge.

Feminists are in a contradictory position. They have to make patriarchal consciousness visible in order to think differently and to make different sense of women's experiences. But they have still tried to produce valid, general knowledge of the nature of gendered social life. Elizabeth Fee, for example, in criticizing science, makes her own claim to knowledge.

> We have been used to a virtual male monopoly of the production of scientific knowledge and discourses about science, its history and meaning. In response to the current possibility of transforming the social relations between the sexes, a conservative

ideological movement within science *has mobilized to defend inequality, protect the status quo, and create barriers to change.* (1986: 43, our emphasis)

In this claim about the reality of political mobilization, Fee is remaking connections between ideas, experience and reality, and implying a particular relationship between knowledge and power.

If feminist researchers want to produce knowledge of what gender relations actually are (as a basis for emancipatory action) that is in some way 'truer' than pre-existing partial, patriarchal or male-centred knowledge, they still confront the problem (faced by all social researchers) of finding general criteria for making their knowledge believable. Elizabeth Grosz (1990) cites Jacques Derrida's mocking of feminists' attempts to produce knowledge of gendered social life by making statements about social reality. 'Feminism is nothing but the operation of a woman who aspires to be like a man. And in order to resemble the masculine dogmatic philosopher this woman lays claim – just as much claim as he – to truth, science and objectivity in all their castrated delusions of virility [. . .]' (Derrida in Grosz 1990: 103).

All feminist researchers face problems in producing and justifying better knowledge of gendered social life. They are not able to adopt the position that failure to do so does not matter. It is politically necessary for feminists to be able to judge between knowledge claims, and so feminist researchers have looked for solutions in varying ways. They have adopted differing theories and ontologies (different ideas of what social realities essentially are), and differing epistemologies (different rules for how knowledge of gender should be produced). This gives feminists varying relationships to methodology, and positions them in different ways of thinking about knowledge and validity within modern frameworks of thought. While feminists have struggled to escape from the limits of these positions (and we consider these struggles in later chapters), in the rest of this chapter, we lay out the problematic relations between truth and objectivity that Derrida derides.

Objectivity, subjectivity, relativism: competing paths to truth

In order to clarify feminists' varying responses to the problems posed by claiming knowledge of real experiences in a real social world, it is helpful to clarify the methodological distinction between *objective knowledge, subjective knowledge*, and the *lack of any such dualism*. This separation between objectivity, subjectivity and relativism in modern thought goes back to reasoning based on Cartesian dualisms (see Chapter 2).

Those feminists who take modern feminist research to be a quest for 'better' knowledge of social realities by a knowing subject have a choice between three main positions on connecting knowledge and reality. We consider these positions here as logical possibilities, rather than examining actual practices (since individual feminists are not necessarily methodologically consistent), in order to clarify the implications of choosing one position rather than another. We consider relativism as a fourth possible methodological position, but one that rejects reliance on scientific method.

Position 1: objectivity as separate from, and superior to, subjectivity

To be objective the researcher's findings must be impartial, general and free from personal and political biases. The popular notions that 'facts' can be gathered independently of 'values', and that careful observers can be 'impartial', depend on objectivity in this sense being achievable. In this position, reason can be used to control subjectivity in order to produce objective knowledge – a direct connection to reality.

From the perspective of Cartesian dualisms, objectivity and subjectivity are seen as separable, and reason as neutral. Subjectivity contaminates the quest for truth and must be rationally controlled. If feminists could produce objective knowledge, this would give them good grounds for claiming that their knowledge is valid. Objectivity implies that the researcher can control the research process so as to produce neutral knowledge of social reality that is external to the researcher and independent of the observer's observations – just as the world turns whether we know it or not. A relationship is implied between objective knowledge and truth.

Since the Enlightenment, there have been numerous debates over whether objectivity is desirable or achievable, but the consequence of distinguishing between objectivity and subjectivity as separate ways of knowing has been to target the researcher's subjectivity as a problem for scientific method. Subjectivity, with its personal limits, partiality and lack of balance, is taken as muddying the waters of clean, clear, objective knowledge. Objective knowledge of, for example, 'domestic violence', 'forced marriage', 'homophobic bullying', 'good mothering', would require accurate definition to enable evidence to be impartially gathered, compared and tested. From this position, it would be critical to the validation of feminist knowledge that feminine subjectivity could be controlled through the rigour and rationality of scientific method. This position is most clearly expressed in positivist methodology, but the notion that research should not be biased is a wider one.

Hammersley (1992) and Hammersley and Gomm (1997), for example, note that although social researchers can no longer appeal to a neutral notion of 'science', they still have the problem of justifying what is 'true'.

> While the abandonment of foundationalism requires us to recognize that research will inevitably be affected by the personal and social characteristics of the researcher, and that this can be of positive value as well as a source of systematic error, it does not require us to give up the guiding principle of objectivity. [. . .] While they [researchers] need to take account of ethical and strategic considerations that relate to other values, truth is the only value that constitutes the goal of research. (Hammersley and Gomm 1997: 4.12)

Hammersley and Gomm argue that the notion that 'the pursuit of scientific knowledge' should be free from bias depends on various conceptions of 'bias'. This enables them to label feminist research as biased in ways that the proper pursuit of truth should not be since they claim that feminist political advocacy can interfere with the discovery of truth (1997: 4.14). They want to protect the pursuit of truth from contamination by the pursuit of political ends. Politics and the pursuit of truth have different goals and so different rational strategies to achieve them. Hammersley claims that discovering which conclusions are 'sound' is more rational and ethical than pursuing political ends (1994: 294). Hammersley and Gomm (1997) identify unbiased research as ultimately validated in a liberal and rational academic community that is apparently uncontaminated by practical or political causes. In contrast, feminism (along with Marxism) is a form of 'emancipatory research' that carries overt political motives. If researchers with emancipatory goals take the aim of their research to be the promotion of their cause, they introduce sources of bias that must be resisted by defenders of truth (Hammersley and Gomm 1997: 5.4). Feminist research can be rational, but is nevertheless a dogmatic pursuit of political goals, rather than the pursuit of truth.

It can be argued against Hammersley and Gomm that objectivity, in the sense of reaching the truth by controlling bias, is not a reasonable aim for social science. Rationality does not ensure validity or escape its social constitution. For feminists, the relationship between the pursuit of truth and the reality of our biases, experiences, power relations and bodies is always problematic (Gelsthorpe 1992; Humphries 1997; Ramazanoğlu 1992b; Temple 1997). From a feminist perspective, Hammersley and Gomm can be conceived as embedded in a 'masculinist' position that identifies its own value system and politics as rational and superior, ignores men's appropriation of reason, and treats power struggles over the authorization of knowledge as struggles over validity. From the feminist (as from the Marxist) perspective, it seems more rational to assume that all research incorporates subjectivity, partiality, bias and political commitment. It is hard to see that adjudication on the soundness of knowledge in a male-dominated academic community could produce knowledge of the 'truths' of subordinated women's experiences. The problem for feminism is to make the politics of knowledge production as evident as possible, rather than to claim that bias can be reliably controlled. Feminists can be reasonable, logical and systematic in their research, without treating reason as a neutralizing force. They can (problematically) pursue truth in the sense of claiming a 'better story', but they cannot claim to be objective.

Claims to objective or unbiased knowledge of social issues are always expressed in culturally specific and emotionally and politically loaded terms. Notions of 'rights', 'coercion', 'assault', like notions of 'tradition', 'family', 'religious community', carry meanings that defy neutrality. The supposed objectivity, neutrality and rationality of scientific method allow the production of patriarchal knowledge and work against knowledge of the realities of gender relations. Linda Birke asks whether a feminist science should still pursue objectivity given that there is no absolute means of validating different types of knowledge (1986: 144). In answer she quotes Evelyn Fox Keller, who argues that 'an adherence to an objectivist epistemology, in which truth is measured by its distance from the subjective, has to be re-examined when it emerges that, by this definition, truth itself has become genderized' (cited in Birke 1986: 152).

Few feminists have, therefore, tried to adopt an explicit commitment to reason as productive of objective, or unbiased, knowledge, or as the basis for claiming feminist knowledge as true. A political commitment to research *for* women precludes claims to detachment or neutrality but does not preclude any claim to valid knowledge. Sandra Harding comments that 'it is obvious to all that many claims which clearly have been generated through research guided by feminist concerns, nevertheless appear more plausible (better supported, more reliable, less false, more likely to be confirmed by evidence, etc.) than the beliefs they replace' (1987b: 182). Unfortunately for Harding there is nothing about issues such as domestic violence, racism or child abuse that is 'obvious to all'. The lack of shared meanings and experiences is a practical issue confronted by feminists epistemologically, personally and politically. The pursuit of objectivity (in the hope that this will enable feminists to see more of 'the truth') seems to have little to offer feminist researchers who do not see reason as neutral but still need to justify the knowledge they produce.

The objectivity debates: what is 'strong objectivity'?

In order to clarify the grounds on which feminists can make knowledge claims, a clear distinction is needed between objectivity (in the sense of knowledge that is free from bias, subjectivity or the personal) and validity (in the sense of telling a better story of women's experiences, and specifying connections between ideas, experience and reality). There is a considerable area of confusion here, particularly in what have been termed the American objectivity debates (Haraway 1991; Harding 1991, 1993). This has given rise to particular problems of terminology in which objectivity has become increasingly confused with validity, or the pursuit of truth, just at the point where the differences between them need clarifying. Harding asks how feminist knowledge can be 'truer' than male-centred knowledge while feminist researchers are openly politically committed (1993: 49–50).

Harding clearly wants feminists to be able to produce valid knowledge – she takes from Donna Haraway the bottom line of a 'no-nonsense commitment to faithful accounts of a "real" world' (Harding 1993: 50). But she is also grappling with the problem that feminists cannot simply state what the social world is really like – they have to be able to justify the knowledge of 'reality' that they produce. The problem is to find general criteria with which to justify knowledge claims. Harding tries to escape having to choose between subjective knowledge, or objective knowledge, or taking a relativist stance (seeing all knowledge claims as relative to their conditions of production) as paths to truth. Her solution is to find ways of making feminist knowledge 'more objective' by making objectivity more rigorous and powerful (Harding 1993: 51). In her terms, feminists should be attempting to 'maximize strong objectivity' (Harding 1993). It is in this notion of 'strong objectivity' that the differentiation between objectivity and validity becomes confused.

Harding (1993) does not give a concise definition of what she means by 'strong objectivity'. Instead she offers 'standards for maximizing strong objectivity'. Knowledge that is 'strongly objective' is 'less partial and distorted' than existing (male-centred) knowledge (Harding 1993: 68). Harding suggests six steps to maximizing strong objectivity.

1   *The knowledge-production process is included in the research.* This means reflecting critically (reflexively) on who is producing knowledge for whom, with

what funding, by what means, in what social situation. 'Strong objectivity requires that the subject of knowledge be placed on the same critical causal plane as the objects of knowledge. Thus strong objectivity requires what we can think of as "strong reflexivity"' (Harding 1993: 69).

2 *The agendas for research questions should be grounded in the experiences of those who are ignored in dominant beliefs and activities.* 'From the standpoint of the marginalized, dominant truths are not objective' (Harding 1993: 54). Those who are socially dominant dominate the production of knowledge. (This is how knowledge of, for example, 'male power', or 'domestic violence', can remain unconceptualized in knowledge of 'family life'.)

3 *Strong objectivity resists relativism,* since feminists need to be able to judge whether some knowledge claims offer 'better' accounts of reality than others.

4 *Strong objectivity means treating the researcher and the subjects of knowledge as embodied and visible, and also as socially heterogeneous.* Feminist knowledge has to be grounded in the diversity and contradictions of women's lives, and the logic of multiple subjects.

5 *Feminist knowledge is located within an explicit, historically specific community –* a political and epistemic community of women – rather than being produced by an individual knowing feminist.

6 *Strong objectivity entails a commitment to liberatory knowledge.*

Harding's 'strong objectivity' is not an accommodation to Hammersley and Gomm's control of bias. Rather it is an attempt to escape a Cartesian opposition between subject and object, to use reflexivity as a resource rather than a threat, and to abandon false claims to value-freedom (Harding 1993: 73–4). However, since she retains the notion of objectivity as superior to falsity, partiality and distortion, while abandoning its neutrality, she leaves some perplexity in her wake. It is not clear how strong objectivity can make feminist knowledge 'truer'.

Despite her efforts, Harding does not effectively rescue feminists from the chains of the Cartesian dualism that so powerfully distinguishes objectivity from subjectivity. She recognizes that 'objectivity' carries unwanted implications, but she is reluctant to abandon it altogether because she wants feminists to be able to distinguish between different claims to truth, including the ability to challenge other feminists.

> Finally, the appeal to objectivity is an issue not only between feminist and prefeminist science and knowledge projects but also within each feminist and other emancipatory research agenda. There are many feminisms, some of which result in claims that distort the racial, class, sexuality, and gender relationships in society. Which ones generate less or more partial and distorted accounts of nature and social life? The notion of objectivity is useful in providing a way to think about the gap that should exist between how any individual or group wants the world to be and how in fact it is. (Harding 1993: 72)

This is the critical issue in Harding's attempt to clean up objectivity in the service of feminism. She sees some version of objectivity as essential for establishing the validity and authority of feminist knowledge through connecting this knowledge with social reality. But she lacks clear criteria for supporting these connections and so tries to strengthen objectivity in the service of validity. This leaves attempts to claim validity for feminist knowledge in confusion.

A clearer resolution of Harding's problem can be reached by going back to the point she takes from Donna Haraway – that feminists want to be critically conscious of the research process and their place in it, but still tell 'truer' stories about a 'real' social world. Like Haraway, Harding takes the view that 'one story is not as good as another', and that feminist stories of social reality are not all equally valid (Haraway 1989: 348).

Although Haraway (1991) takes up Harding's concern with objectivity, she shifts feminist problems in producing knowledge of a social reality from those of validity within scientific method, to those of politics – how telling the 'truth' occurs, rather than how to be more or less objective. In Chapter 4, we come back to Haraway's (1991) attempt to escape from the constraints of objectivity and its trailing Cartesian dualism, through her notion of 'situated knowledges' and the 'privilege of partial perspective'.

Position 2: subjectivity as separate from, and superior to objectivity

Some radical feminists, especially in the 1970s, were accused of reversing the relationship between subjectivity and objectivity, without seriously challenging the Cartesian dualism that assumes subjectivity and objectivity to be mutually exclusive. Having claimed that 'objectivity' and 'rationality' express not neutrality, but male interests, subjective or 'feminine' knowledge could logically be seen as a productive alternative for subordinated women (Daly 1978).

Within dualistic thinking, subjective knowledge can be taken as inferior to objective knowledge but as offering its own limited truths. *Subjectivity implies partial, personal, intuitive knowledge that comes from the consciousness of a knowing subject situated in a specific social context.* While few adopted an explicit privileging of subjectivity, feminism did empower women to think differently, to ask new questions, make new connections, to value their intuitions and skills, to think about their bodies and to value their own experiences. This allowed for revaluing feminine ways of knowing and sources of knowledge that had been devalued by the dominance of claims to rationality and objectivity (Ruddick 1980). Rita Arditti comments:

> Since science does not progress only by analytical inductive knowledge, the importance of imagination and emotion in the creative process should be obvious. The role of intuition in science is consistently undervalued in a science which is exploited for corporate, military and political reasons. A feminist perspective would re-introduce and re-legitimize the intuitive approach. (1982: 144)

Drawing on personal knowledge, in the light of feminist theory, allows women to express their experiences of living gendered lives in conditions of social inequality.

> I can make no claim to any scientific background. [...] My credentials are simply those of having been a Lesbian as long as I can consciously remember and having

spent my adult life working in this field in an effort to obtain civil, moral, legal, religious [. . .] *total* rights for Lesbians. (Damon 1970: 339)

I think if you're a Black woman, you've got to begin with racism. It's not a choice, it's a necessity. There are few Black women around now, who don't want to deal with that reality and prefer sitting around talking about their sexual preferences or concentrating on strictly women's issues like male violence. But the majority of Black women would see those kinds of things as 'luxury' issues. What's the point of taking on male violence if you haven't dealt with state violence? Or rape, when you can see Black people's bodies and lands being raped every day by the system? (Bryan et al. 1997: 44)

Challenges to the objectivity of patriarchal knowledge arose in the context of attempts to escape from patriarchal consciousness. Mary Daly, for example, explains her method of research by opposing it to 'the male method' of claiming that a disinterested observer can arrive at objective knowledge of reality (1977: 7), that is, to an extreme version of male-centred positivism. She identifies the political and social context of male method as defining the goals and procedures of research so that only certain areas of knowledge can be authorized. She claims that the 'new consciousness of women is not mere "knowledge about", but an emotional-intellectual-volitional rebirth' (1977: 200). For this rebirth it is necessary to reinterpret 'method' (1977: 8). She aims to move beyond the 'tyranny of methodolatry' (1977: 11) that has wiped out women's questions about the social world, and argues that 'the right word will have the power of reality in it' (1977: 12). Finding the 'right word' and establishing its rightness, though, is less simple. The difficulties of making reasonable arguments while challenging rationality remain.

There are some arguments that female subjectivity and women's close relationship with their bodies (through menstruation, childbearing, breast feeding) give women feminine powers of thought – sources of knowledge uniquely available to female persons. This view is very generally criticized as impracticably essentialist.[5] The valuing of personal experience, however, is not the same as subjectivity being separate from, or superior to, objectivity. Although radical feminists have been widely criticized for favouring subjective knowledge, it is difficult in practice to find feminists actually defending the privileging of subjectivity as the means to general knowledge of social reality (Jackson 1997; Richardson 1996). In particular, many feminists accused of such essentialism explicitly reject the charge (Dworkin 1988; rhodes and McNeill 1985: 7). It is more common to find them valuing subjectivity, emotions, embodied and experiential knowledge, while being aware that subjectivity cannot be neutralized (Attar 1987; Bell and Klein 1996).

The position of subjective privilege is a logical possibility in western thought, but it has not been systematically developed as a feminist methodological position. A dramatic and productive period of feminist research came from grounding knowledge in a wide range of women's experiences, looking for voices and ideas that had been excluded from history and the public domain, and turning a critical feminist gaze on representations of women in art, literature and mass media. But this starting point commonly led to questioning the value of thinking through Cartesian dualisms at all, and to proposals for abandoning dualistic or binary thinking rather than embracing subjectivity. Barbara du Bois's (1983) notion of 'passionate scholarship', for example, suggests abandoning science's dualities, but she still proposes rigorous and reflexive approaches to social research. Modern feminists were very much aware that they were under pressure to justify the accounts of reality that they proposed, and to explain the gendered lives and relationships that they conceptualized and experienced.

Position 3: objectivity/subjectivity as inseparable

When feminists attempted to move beyond thinking in terms of the separability of objectivity and subjectivity, an influential methodological model was already available. This was Marxist methodology (the method of materialist dialectics). Marx's materialist dialectics comes from a strand of Enlightenment thought in which subjectivity and objectivity are taken as problematically inseparable. The aim is to discover the truth, rather than to be objective. *In this view, all attempts to produce knowledge of social life are political but the politically committed can still be scientific in the sense of connecting ideas and experience to underlying realities.* Theory and accountability are critical, but attempts to be objective misconceive and mystify real relationships between knowledge and power.

Marx (1976) could be openly outraged by the immorality of capitalism and its 'bloodsucking' capitalists, with his prejudices clearly showing, and yet claim to produce 'better' knowledge of the 'truths' of the capitalist system than those of existing political economists. This was not because he was objective, but because he told a 'better story' about the real nature of the capitalist system of production. He conceptualized actual connections between observations of workers' lives, his theory of the exploitation of workers and the underlying necessity of profit-making in capitalism.[6]

Marx's claims were restricted to the kinds of power relations that he examined. Bringing in experiences of nationalism, heterosexism or racism, for example, shows the limitations of his theory in taking account of the interaction of capitalism with other aspects of power. (Just as anti-racist theory can lack awareness of heterosexism, or feminist theory awareness of racism, and so on.) Variations in personal experiences, political consciousness and attention to the voices of others help shape any area of knowledge production, in addition to the power of theory.

The notion that political commitment is an inextricable part of the process of social investigation, and is compatible with knowledge of social realities, even if this knowledge is partial, is central to feminist methodology: 'detachment is not a condition of science' (Smith 1988: 177). In this view, all researchers are politically engaged, have personal biases and limited experiences, and are situated in particular cultures, locations and languages. Feminists can aim to be reasonable without claiming that reason either requires or produces detachment.

If feminists abandon any quest for objectivity, however strong, this leaves them with considerable problems in claiming any connection between knowledge and social realities, and in judging between competing knowledge claims. The pursuit of truth is profoundly changed if power relations are always implicated in the rational production and evaluation of knowledge (J. Rose 1984). Some feminists have been influenced by Marx's method, in particular through adopting a feminist standpoint (see Chapter 4). Others have turned to poststructuralism and postmodernism (see Part II). One possible escape route within modern thinking, however, comes from the perspective of relativism, with its explicit rejection of modern scientific method.

Position 4: relativism: truth as relative to its conditions of production

From a relativist position there are no general rules or criteria of validity that can establish a direct relationship between knowledge claims, experience and actual social reality. From this position, valid knowledge of an external social world is neither directly nor indirectly accessible. All that can be known is already interpreted within a particular language of knowing. There are always competing claims to truth, but no general rules for judging between them (Woolgar 1988).

Absolute and consistent relativism is always a problematic position in social research, and rarely adopted at all. Relativists accept the multiplicity of 'truths', but their position becomes increasingly contradictory as they assert their own truth claims. Assertions, for example, that there really are multiple truths, or that particular subjects are socially constituted or that particular claims to truth have particular effects, begin to construct claims to valid knowledge of how the social world is actually constituted. Querying how truth is constructed or challenging how we know what we know is not the same as adopting a consistently relativist position. It is not absolute relativism that has significantly challenged feminist methodology, rather it is the problem that absolute truth is unattainable.

Relativism might seem to offer feminist researchers a way out of their methodological difficulties by abandoning any attempt to connect knowledge and reality. Feminists can still produce knowledge, but they (like other social researchers) will produce multiple truths and need not try to choose between them. For example, they need not seek a direct relationship between 'reality' and the claim that a particular experience is a form of 'domestic violence'. From a relativist perspective, 'domestic violence' is one version of 'reality' that competes with others (for example, that 'victims' subconsciously bring violence upon themselves, or that the incident in question is not 'violent' at all). 'Domestic violence' does not exist in a real world independently of the people concerned, the researcher and the researcher's theory and language. The logic of relativism accepts that multiple truths are produced within different ways of knowing and so provide varied ways of making sense of the social world.

Since relativists cannot connect different accounts of reality with some actual reality, no account can be deemed truer (better connected) than others. Violent incidents may really occur, but they can only be known as violent through the medium of language and culture. Knowledge is, therefore, relative to particular ways of thinking and how these are organized and given meaning.

Relativists logically reject the right to judge between cultures, and so reject the universality implicit in modern, humanist feminism. From a relativist perspective, young British women who are kidnapped by their relatives and coerced into marriage cannot simply be deemed to be 'victims' of 'forced marriage', as if this judgement represented a single reality. The notion of 'forced marriage' is contingent on (relative to) prior notions of individual human and civil rights and the judgement that a religious community or kinship group does not have greater rights over the individual than these. A problem of 'forced marriage' can be alternatively conceived as a problem of 'undutiful daughters' if daughters are seen as having communal and family duties rather than individual rights. Relativist accounts of the social world in terms of multiple and contingent truths can claim to be reasonable, but are not dependent on rules of method that specify connections between these truths and some independent reality. Multiple 'readings' can be made of social life, just as they can of literature, art or popular culture.

A relativist acceptance of multiple accounts of inaccessible 'realities' offers a direct challenge to modern feminism. First, feminist notions of liberation do tend to imply specific conceptions of individual human rights; second, feminists are under moral and political pressure to choose between competing accounts of reality. The feminist who takes a story of 'forced marriage' to be truer than a story of 'undutiful daughters' may stand in the uncomfortable political position of passing judgement on one culture from the standpoint of another. In the case of 'forced' marriage in the UK, this discomfort is complicated by the political relations of colonialism and migration, differences of class and culture between minority communities, and the unequal coexistence of majority and minority cultures.

An 'undutiful daughter' who accepts consensual arranged marriage, but resists coercion, is also making a judgement if she conceptualizes her customs and religion as inappropriately dominated by men (Gedalof 1999; Hussain 1984). Changing dominant accounts of reality (turning a community's 'undutiful daughters' into individual 'injured citizens') signals an anti-relativist stance. The rejection of relativism, however, requires that feminists specify grounds for judging between different accounts of reality. We return to this point in Chapter 7, but it is a requirement that has given feminists, like other social researchers, considerable cause for concern, and has no agreed solution.

Relativists have a strong argument for denying the existence of general rules that can apply across all stories. In this view, feminists lose any grounds for invoking universal rules on how to judge between knowledge claims, and so any certain or general means of distinguishing what is true from what is false. When feminism loses a claim to universal criteria of validity, it also loses its universal knowing subject – the knowing feminist, and the object of her knowledge claims, the universal 'woman'.

In some respects both feminists and their critics have welcomed these deconstructions. The universalism of western feminists pronouncing on what is right and good for gender relations in other societies and cultures, or of privileged women making general claims to knowledge for others that ignores their own social location, is replaced by multiple voices. But feminists resist relativism when they require judgements to be made between different accounts of social reality. Hearing the pleas of young women resisting 'forced marriage' in terms of assault, kidnap or coercion, rather than neglected duty, does not fix a connection between knowledge and reality, but does tell a 'better' story from a feminist perspective. Multiple voices can make different knowledge claims but these need not be treated equally.

Patti Lather (1991) contends that relativism's multiple truths are productive for feminism, because feminists cannot specify universal criteria for judging between competing knowledges of gendered lives. She claims (Lather 1991: 115) that relativism is only a problem for those whose 'modern minds' are locked into claiming one site of knowing as privileged. But, having taken a relativist stance, she is then unable to define emancipation and injustice, and so the point of feminism (1991: 164). Relativism cannot offer feminists a solution to the problems of needing connections between ideas, experience and reality in order to achieve valid knowledge as a basis for effective emancipatory action. A wholly relativist position is inconsistent with feminist politics and ethics. It matters which accounts of reality are believed and acted on; it matters who has the power to determine what counts as authoritative knowledge; it matters how knowledge claims are expressed and what weight they carry. Feminism is politically dismembered by relativism.

Conclusion

At the heart of all methodologies of social research is the critical problem that no one can actually establish for sure what social reality is, how it connects to knowledge and experience, or the exact relations between knowledge and power. Feminists have had to abandon claims that they can specify direct connections between feminist ideas and the realities of people's gendered lives. Social researchers cannot in practice specify some universal criteria for ascertaining what is true – for establishing 'the validity of criteria of validity across the confines of a single theoretical system' (Benton 1978: 196). Modern feminist approaches to social investigation responded to the devaluing of women's abilities, and the disparaging of feminist knowledge, with efforts to produce authoritative knowledge. But modern thought did not provide solutions to the problems of making authoritative connections between the knowledge feminists could produce and what this was knowledge of. Feminists want to understand actual power relations and the nature of persistent inequalities so that people can work to transform these effectively. Disagreements in feminist debates on science and objectivity make it clear that general knowledge of a real social world is not simply available.

Modern humanist feminism held on to concepts of reason and the need to validate knowledge of gendered social life, but not without problems. Feminists have not abandoned the project of being reasonable, but they have looked critically at the meanings and consequences of claims made for reason and science, since making knowledge claims is a social and political process that is dependent on its conditions of production. There can never be one enduring truth about the nature of social reality that is independent of how knowledge of it is produced, so feminists need other ways of thinking. 'Succinctly, feminist theorists have moved from the "reactive" stance of the feminist critique of social science, and into the realms of exploring what "feminist knowledge" could conceivably look like' (Stanley and Wise 1990: 37). As male-centred and patriarchal knowledge is exposed as partial, political and unreasonable (rather than general, neutral and rational), feminists can reasonably claim that 'reason', 'truth', 'reality' and the 'knowing self' are themselves specific social productions. While feminists have taken different positions on whether some knowledge claims are better founded than others, they have tried to resituate issues of validity by grounding feminist knowledge in women's experience.

If feminists seek knowledge that is 'truer' than any prior knowledge, and that identifies real power relations, in order to change them, they still face the problem of validating their knowledge. Feminists can accept relativist arguments that knowledge is contingent on its conditions of production, but this does not justify telling any story of reality that they like. The stories of gender that feminists tell have to make sense of the diversity of people's experience. In any social research it is extremely problematic to claim a relationship between socially produced knowledge and the realities of people's lives. It is questionable whether telling the truth is at issue at all.

In Chapter 4, we consider feminist attempts to develop and justify a distinctive methodological stance within modern thought, before looking, in Part II, at the consequences for feminist methodology of challenges from postmodern thought.

Notes

1. Since Enlightenment thought, and subsequent developments, generated varied and often conflicting conceptions of scientific method, different conceptions of science and validity have been available to feminists. Claims that direct connections can be specified between ideas, experience and reality have always been contested in social research.

2. Foundationalism is a (generally critical) label for an epistemological position that specifies rules of method for establishing a foundation of scientific knowledge that is built on more or less certain connections between knowledge and reality. Reality exists independently of the knowing subject, and knowledge of reality can be progressively accumulated. Any knowing subject using the same rules should be able to produce the same knowledge. Foundationalism is sometimes taken, inaccurately, to characterize all modern and feminist approaches to epistemology.

3. For discussion of forced marriage in the UK by some of those involved, see BBC News 1999. Little attention has been given to the experiences of 'undutiful sons'.

4. Feminists who take positivism to represent scientific method in general ignore the many criticisms of this methodology from other approaches to social research that are more concerned with the constitution of consciousness, meanings and understandings, such as hermeneutics, ethnomethodology, phenomenology (Williams and May 1996).

5. Essentialism is used as a criticism of feminist theory when feminists claim particular connections between knowledge, reality and experience as due to inherent qualities of femininity or masculinity. In particular, it targets claims that there are essences given in nature (for example, an innate female nature, an essence of femininity, or innate racial characteristics) and that these essences can explain social relationships such as those of gender or race.

6. Marx was able to observe the same daily life, and read the same official reports, statistics and evidence that his critics read, but to read this information differently from those who did not share his theory and method. Marx's claims to truth came from the

power of his theory to identify hidden social, economic and power relations that really exist whether people are conscious of them or not. How people make sense of their experiences of these relations depends on their conceptions of them. His notion of theory is grounded in the reality of the experiences and relationships of the subordinated. Theory is necessary to conceptualize actual experiences in relation to hidden power relations, but knowledge is never independent of experience and the conditions that give rise to it. It is impossible to determine that one precedes or causes the other (Marx 1971).

4

From truth/reality to knowledge/power

Taking a feminist standpoint

Introduction

Feminists have taken different paths in responding to the challenges of scientific methods, and the difficulties of speaking for women-in-general. Since there are no universal criteria for judging between competing claims to knowledge, they have debated how best to seek connections between feminist theories, women's experiences and knowledge of gendered realities. Differences in the conditions of women's lives pose a considerable challenge to feminist attempts to produce general knowledge of gender. In this chapter, we look at the idea of a feminist standpoint as a significant area of debate on the possibilities of connecting feminist knowledge and women's diverse experiences to the realities of gendered social relations.

While it is difficult to generalize across the various conceptions of feminist standpoint, it can tentatively be said that the notion of standpoint is a way of taking women's experience as fundamental to knowledge of political relations between women and men (of which people may or may not be aware). Taking a standpoint means being able to produce the best current understanding of how knowledge of gender is interrelated with women's experiences and the realities of gender. Knowledge can be produced from a feminist standpoint wherever women live in unequal gendered social relationships, and can develop a feminist political consciousness. It is a way of exploring (as opposed to assuming) how women experience life differently from men, or intersexuals, or others, because they live in specific social relationships to the exercise of male power.

Before examining how a feminist standpoint can serve to move feminist methodology beyond debates on objectivity, and what problems standpoint theorists encounter, we locate the notion of standpoint at the limits of modern thinking.

The knowing feminist at the limits of modern methodology

Donna Haraway (1991) provides a useful metaphor of feminists trying to climb a greased pole while holding on to both ends. The point of climbing the pole is to produce valid knowledge of gendered social life. With one hand, the feminist researcher holds on to feminism's inheritance of commitment to science and reason, in order to provide knowledge of what gendered lives are really like, and to compete successfully with patriarchal knowledge. Feminists do want 'enforceable, reliable accounts of things' (Haraway 1991: 188). With the other hand, she is unwilling to let go of the relativist claim that the 'knowing feminist', the 'reality' she 'discovers', and the 'truths' she tells are all socially constituted in particular situations, cultures and ways of thinking. It is difficult for feminists wholly to abandon the pull of either relativism or reality, and so they tend to slip around, or feel forced to choose between them.[1]

Haraway's solution is to abandon the attempt to connect ideas, experience and truth in this way (since you cannot climb a pole while holding both ends) and to explore instead the notion of partial visions and situated knowledges. 'The constraints that interest her are those imposed by politics, by the play of power among those who seek knowledge' (Longino and Hammonds 1990: 171). It is worth looking back at this slippery pursuit of truth/reality, however, before moving on. First, the greasy pole clarifies particular difficulties in claiming that feminist knowledge is better than, say, patriarchal knowledge, and in judging some feminist accounts to be better than others. Second, it makes it clearer to students of feminist methodology why feminist approaches to methodology vary. Third, it lays out the contradictions of modern methodology that feminist standpoint theorists attempt to escape.

A methodological continuum: slipping and sliding on Haraway's greasy pole

The pursuit of truth is slippery because feminist knowledge claims cannot directly specify connections to reality, and 'truths' are socially constituted within male-dominated disciplines and academies. The grease persists, because there are no absolute solutions (Haraway 1991: 184–5). All modern social research that entails empirical investigation of the social world as a means of connecting knowledge and reality is sliding around on this methodological pole whether researchers recognize this or not.

The line of the continuum illustrated in Figure 1 marks logical possibilities open to modern social researchers between the two polar positions that have been indicated in Chapter 3. At the pole marked X, rational application of rules of scientific method can discover The Truth and so claim valid knowledge of an external reality that is independent of the researcher. The extreme position of this Archimedean point, or God's-eye view, implies an all-knowing observer, external to, and independent of, what is being observed. From this point, connections can be 'seen' that specify relationships between knowledge and reality (Haraway 1991: 193). Feminists cannot reasonably occupy the X position on the continuum because they have exposed the impossibility of objectivity in practice. In the intermediate positions that slide toward the X point, feminist researchers retain some notion of a knowing subject producing valid knowledge that adds to the general stock of truth.

Figure 1 *Scientific method: a methodological continuum*

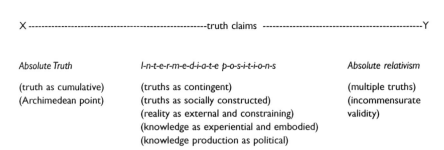

X --truth claims --Y

Absolute Truth	I-n-t-e-r-m-e-d-i-a-t-e p-o-s-i-t-i-o-n-s	Absolute relativism
(truth as cumulative)	(truths as contingent)	(multiple truths)
(Archimedean point)	(truths as socially constructed)	(incommensurate
	(reality as external and constraining)	validity)
	(knowledge as experiential and embodied)	
	(knowledge production as political)	

At the pole marked Y is absolute relativism. In this position there is no way (except in terms of local rules and local truths) of adjudicating between different versions of 'truth'. No relationship can be claimed between knowledge and some external, independent reality. Toward the Y point, feminist researchers, as knowing subjects, are deconstructed, unstable and diverse. Their knowledge of social reality is constituted in language, so that feminism cannot produce generally valid knowledge, and feminists have more than one standpoint from which to produce their partial knowledges.

Adopting either of the polar positions provides clear grounds for justifying the knowledge that is produced and for specifying how general or specific it is. However, the logic of each of these polar positions has been heavily criticized. Feminists are under pressure to locate their methodological solutions in intermediate positions, none of which provide certain knowledge or can fully justify their position. It is this range of intermediate positions, plus the problems of sliding between them, that make it impossible to squeeze all feminist methodology into a single way of thinking. It is not surprising that feminists (and their critics) disagree on whether or not feminist research is a rational, generalizing project, grounded in evidence, rather than relativist constructions of diverse stories and cultural/political interests. Other approaches to methodology in social research also occupy and attempt to justify intermediate positions, so there is considerable overlap between feminist and other modern modes of thinking, at the level of methodology. All claims to knowledge of social life remain vulnerable to contestation and require critical examination of their claims to authority.

Sandra Harding's notion of 'strong objectivity' (see Chapter 3) can now be seen as an attempt to keep feminist methodology away from the Y position, in order to claim that some stories are 'less false' than others. Relativism is incompatible with feminist politics and a feminist quest for knowledge of actual power relations. But Harding is also caught in a slippery struggle to avoid sliding into the X position, where notions of truth and objectivity are too rigid (Harding 1993, 1997: 388).

The confusions of Harding's position in deeming some knowledge claims more objective or 'less false' than others, without 'invoking the notion of truth and reality in the conventional senses of these terms' (Harding 1997: 383), becomes clearer if she can be seen to be struggling between the X and Y positions. She limits 'truth' to the rigid notion that there can be only one true story that 'has, now and forever, already been identified and that as far as the truth claimant is concerned, the matter is closed, *fini*, ended' (Harding 1997: 383). Her notion of 'less false' then relies on a contingent notion of objective knowledge being located in some intermediate position between X and Y, where claims to knowledge rest on evidence that has (so far) survived tests made against it (Harding 1997: 387–8). This argument lacks any general criteria for establishing how evidence can be tested and knowledge claims authorized so that more or less 'false' can be determined. A critical connection between evidence and 'reality' remains unclear.

The frustrations of this kind of pursuit of truth led some feminists into thinking about feminist knowledge through the notion of a feminist standpoint. Feminist standpoint theory expresses various attempts to refuse any intermediate position between X and Y that would pressure feminist researchers into a primary focus on justifying their criteria of validity, and so specifying a relationship between feminist knowledge and truth/reality. Instead, taking a feminist standpoint implies examining how knowledge and power are connected, and so making visible both the hidden power relations of knowledge production and the 'underpinnings of gender' (Smith 1997: 395).

What is a feminist standpoint?

Feminist standpoint theorists explore the difficulties of establishing relationships between knowledge and power without abandoning the hope of telling better stories about gendered lives. There are, however, different ways of thinking about taking a feminist standpoint (including disagreements over whether it is theory or epistemology, both or neither). It is impossible to offer a brief summary that can adequately accommodate all versions. It is perhaps more useful to see these debates as specific struggles to challenge authoritative knowledge of gender within the constraints of modern thinking. Rather than feminists producing a common conception of a feminist standpoint, struggles to improve on feminism's Enlightenment inheritance result in variations in conceptualizing experience, ideas and reality, and possible connections between them.

A feminist standpoint requires some theory of gender and power, a conception of feminist knowledge and conceptions of experience and reality. This entails adopting some epistemological position in providing grounds for deciding what constitutes adequate knowledge of gendered social existence. Approaches to taking a feminist standpoint vary because there is more than one feminist theory and more than one feminist epistemological position. The notion of standpoint is often unified, simplified and dismissed as inadequate by critics who treat standpoint theory 'as a general category of analysis with no names attached' (Hartsock 1998: 227). However, since different scholars have produced different versions of feminist standpoint, based on different epistemological assumptions, some clarification is required of what this disputed idea is meant to achieve.

Variations in conceptions of a feminist standpoint, and how this moves feminist knowledge beyond modern concerns with objectivity and validity, are usefully brought out in a debate in the journal *Signs* in 1997 (Hartsock 1997), even though this does not cover every version of standpoint theory. Susan Hekman (1997a) gives a relatively sympathetic, but also critical, review of contributions to a feminist standpoint. She argues that standpoint theory is now 'frequently regarded as a quaint relic of feminism's less sophisticated past' (1997a: 341) because its reliance on Marxist theory has made it unable to meet either the challenge of difference or that of postmodern and poststructuralist thought.

Nevertheless Hekman is sympathetic to standpoint theory in the sense that she accepts that 'politics and epistemology are inseparable' (1997b: 399). She says:

> My purpose in writing this article was to trace the way in which feminist standpoint theory, a theory that emerged out of the Enlightenment tradition, deconstructed (if you will) that tradition. *Women speaking their truth* had the effect of transforming truth, knowledge, and power as the Enlightenment defined them. (1997b: 401, our emphasis)

The notion that 'women speaking their truth' results in new knowledge of gendered social lives, grounded in women's experience, is a central theme of conceptions of a feminist standpoint, but this is not a simple or agreed notion. The editors of *Signs* asked four feminist scholars whom Hekman identifies as 'feminist standpoint theorists' to comment on her article. These authors respond to Hekman's criticisms, and comment on their earlier work (in part in the light of more recent accommodations between feminism, poststructuralism and postmodernism) (Collins 1997; Harding 1997; Hartsock 1997; Smith 1997).

Dorothy Smith explains that those whom Sandra Harding (1986) initially grouped together as 'feminist standpoint theorists' were feminist scholars working independently on problems of 'locating knowledge or inquiry in women's standpoint or in women's experience' (Smith 1997: 392). Smith says that in a sense Harding created what has come to be known as 'feminist standpoint theory' through producing this classification. While the people she grouped together had some assumptions and concerns in common, Harding's label served to distract attention from how these scholars were working in different intellectual locations and with varying concerns. Nevertheless, Hekman's critique and the responses to it bring out five key characteristics of a feminist standpoint:

1   *A feminist standpoint explores relations between knowledge and power.* This is in opposition to a modern, foundationalist project of scientific method (and its greasy pole) that seeks direct connections between knowledge and reality. A feminist standpoint assumes the inseparability of politics, theory and epistemology. It problematizes the nature of relationships between ideas, experience and social reality. Women 'speaking their truth' are situated in relation to forms of power: that shape their lives; that they can (variably) exercise; that constitute what counts as knowledge; that determine whose voice can be heard.

2   *A feminist standpoint deconstructs the 'knowing feminist'.* The idea of 'the feminist' as a socially constituted knowing self is opposed to an individualized, stable, Cartesian, knowing self, or one with a fixed identity (for example, a 'class', a 'gender' a 'race', a 'sexual orientation'). The feminist researcher 'knows' from a specific and partial social location, and so is socially constituted as a 'knowing self' in particular ways of thinking and authorizing knowledge. Questioning the 'knowing self' makes the specificity of the researcher visible, just as feminists expose the actual men behind the apparent neutrality of patriarchal knowledge. Making the researcher visible makes power relations between women a critical feature of understanding the complexity and variety of gendered power relations. This raises two problems: first, what it means to have multiple subjects of feminist knowledge; second, whether the feminist intellectual (through access to feminist theory) somehow gains superior knowledge of women's experience that ordinary women do not have. This implies a further question of whether there is a difference between a feminist standpoint and a woman's standpoint and whether, indeed, either standpoint is possible.

3   *A feminist standpoint is (albeit problematically) grounded in women's experience, including emotions and embodiment.* Taking a feminist standpoint entails women voicing their experience. This grounding raises particularly contentious issues about: how experience can be known; how connections can be claimed between experience, knowledge and reality; and what social relations exist between the experiencing object of knowledge and the knowing feminist. There is considerable variation among contributors to this debate in how experience is conceived and how experience, knowledge and the knowing feminist are thought to be connected.

4   *A feminist standpoint has to take account of diversity in women's experiences and the interconnecting power relations between women.* Recognizing the numerous differences in women's (and men's and intersexuals') experiences fragments 'woman'/'man' as universal categories. Acknowledging difference leaves 'women' as the object of feminist knowledge but puts this object in tension with deconstructed 'woman' (see Chapter 1). Establishing what is the same and what is different about women's experience also requires knowledge of

specific gender relations in specific social locations. Investigations of gendered social life encounter the inseparability of people's lives from their constitution in relation to power. This requires empirical investigation of specific forms of power, social situations, relationships and the specificity of their interconnections, and cannot be known in general, or prior to investigation.

5 *Knowledge from a feminist standpoint is always partial knowledge.* Knowledge is partial both in the sense of being 'not-total' and in the sense of being 'not-impartial'. In different ways standpoint theorists try to avoid claiming that their knowledge is generally true, or true for 'women'. Dorothy Smith comments:

> The women's movement and its methodology of working from experience began to unearth the tacit underpinnings of gender. But at the very moment when experience is summoned by what women can find they have in common, it is being translated into the universalizing discourse of a movement making political claims across a variety of fronts. It has seemed to be that in the women's movement, some women have wanted to be able to go directly from what we know by virtue of how we participate in social relations to claims to knowledge at the level of a universalizing discourse. The critique of 'essentialism' aims at this move. (1997: 395)

It is not that knowledge from a feminist standpoint cannot ever be general, but that exactly how general any knowledge claim can be, needs to be established. There can be grounds for local, regional or global knowledge, but not for 'universalizing discourse'.

While these five issues are raised in differing versions of standpoint theory, they do not add up to a common position. What is striking about the responses to Hekman's article by Hartsock, Harding, Collins and Smith is their claims that Hekman has misunderstood at least some aspects of their work and that she subverts the radical purpose of taking a feminist standpoint. While 'my critics don't understand me' might be a common complaint among academic writers, it is significant for our purposes that Hekman is accused, in effect, of trying to locate standpoint theory as the knowledge claim of a knowing feminist self who is pursuing truth from a shared, intermediate position on Haraway's greasy pole. In their responses, her four critics flatly reject this positioning. They emphasize instead how taking a feminist standpoint is an attempt to escape the constraints of seeking direct connections between experience and reality. Their differing views aim to develop more radical and productive ways of knowing within their critiques of modern knowledge production.

Patricia Hill Collins argues that

> standpoint theory never was designed to be argued as a theory of truth or method. Hekman's article simply misses the point of standpoint theory overall. By decontextualizing standpoint theory from its initial moorings in a knowledge/power framework while simultaneously recontextualizing it in an apolitical discussion of feminist truth and method, Hekman essentially depoliticizes the potentially radical context of standpoint theory. (1997: 375)

Sandra Harding (who is perhaps primarily a commentator on standpoint theory, rather than a feminist standpoint theorist) protests that while some writers on feminist standpoint (particularly those influenced by Marxist theory) do draw on the language of truth and reality, 'Hekman distorts the central project of standpoint theorists when she characterizes it as one of figuring out how to justify the truth of feminist claims to more accurate accounts of reality. Rather it is the relations between power and knowledge that concern these thinkers' (1997: 382–3). Hartsock comments that in some respects, Hekman 'reads standpoint theories through a kind of American pluralism that prefers to speak not about power and justice but, rather, about knowledge and epistemology' (1997: 367).

Collins, Harding and Hartsock clearly want to distinguish between foundationalist thought (towards the X pole) that treats reality as discoverable through neutral scientific method, and their own understandings of standpoint theory. They use the expression 'feminist standpoint *theory*', rather than 'feminist standpoint *epistemology*', because they appear to identify epistemology with attempts to claim neutrality and certainty for knowledge of external reality. Dorothy Smith proposes taking a 'women's perspective' as a 'method of inquiry' since: 'what I do as theory is not really an epistemology, although it must wrestle with epistemological problems' (1997: 396). Smith claims that a 'women's standpoint' requires new concepts for expressing women's experience in terms of gendered power and 'relations of ruling' (1989: 36). But it is also more than theory in that it confronts the contradictions of method and epistemology that the Enlightenment has bequeathed to feminism.

In our view, the notion of a feminist standpoint is theoretical and political, but does entail some epistemological position because feminist standpoint theorists assume the inseparability of politics and epistemology. However, this does not avoid theoretical and epistemological differences between them. There are particular differences, for example, between those influenced by realism, those influenced by empiricism, and those who consider the possibility of relativism (in multiple standpoints). The notion of a standpoint is epistemological in the following senses: first, 'standpoint feminists' think about how people think about gender; second, they think about how people know what they know of gender; third, they make statements about actual gendered power relations; fourth, they need to be able to identify whether taking a feminist or women's standpoint produces 'better' knowledge than other theoretical/epistemological positions. Feminist knowledge still needs to be justified if feminist research is to make sense of actual 'relations of ruling' (Smith 1989: 36) and to grasp the diversity of gendered experience.

These critical responses to Hekman's characterization of a feminist standpoint usefully clarify the rather different elements of Enlightenment inheritance on which standpoint theorists have drawn and to which they pose a radical challenge. There are significant differences in how contributors to these debates think about the relations between the knowing feminist, the knowledge she produces, the social/gendered world she produces knowledge of, and the experiences and relationships that people have. In order to see the logic of the modern humanist thinking and the radical responses to it in which standpoint theory is rooted, it is useful to compare Nancy Hartsock's specification of 'a feminist standpoint' with Dorothy Smith's notion of 'women's standpoint'.

Nancy Hartsock: achieving a feminist standpoint as a vantage point on male supremacy

Nancy Hartsock (1983a, 1983b) draws explicitly on Marxist thought in order to specify how women are better positioned than men, through their experiences of gender subordination, to see the social world of gender relations as socially and inequitably constructed. She models her notion of a feminist standpoint on the Marxist idea that in capitalist systems workers stand in a relationship to capital that gives them (potentially) knowledge of capitalism (as an exploitative system) that differs from the dominant 'truth' that capitalism is a natural or wealth-producing system (Lukács 1971; Marx 1976). She characterizes a feminist standpoint as a 'vantage point on male supremacy', and suggests that this vantage point is 'privileged' in the sense that it is both grounded in women's lives, and serves 'as an epistemological device' (1983b: 284).

> [T]he criteria for privileging some knowledges over others are ethical and political rather than purely 'epistemological'. The quotation marks here are to indicate that I see ethical and political concepts such as power involving epistemological claims on the one hand and ideas of what is to count as knowledge involving profoundly important political and ethical stakes on the other. Hekman is right that I want to privilege some knowledges over others because they seem to me to offer possibilities for envisioning more just social relations. (Hartsock 1997: 372–3)

A feminist standpoint is possible, in Hartsock's view, if women generally *experience* life *differently* from men because they live in *different social relationships to men's exercise of power*, and if they experience *material differences* in gendered conditions of life. She does not claim that women actually have privileged knowledge of power relations, or privileged ways of accessing 'reality', as a result of being female. Women can understand the social world from a feminist standpoint insofar as they share a common material situation (gender subordination) and develop a common political consciousness (feminism).

A key point that Hartsock adapts from Marxist theory is that a patriarchal vision of gender serves to structure the material relations of gender in which both men and women are forced to participate. Patriarchal knowledge is, therefore, powerful and cannot be dismissed as simply false. She is clear that the vision of power relations available to women does not come naturally, so a feminist standpoint must be struggled for (Hartsock 1983a: 232). It represents an achievement of political consciousness that requires, first, that feminist theory can conceptualize the essential relations of gender beneath patriarchal visions of gender relations, and, second, that political consciousness can grow in struggles to change those relations. The adoption of a feminist standpoint is a way of exposing real relations of gender subordination as unjust, and so has a liberatory role.

The use of 'essential' here is realist rather than essentialist. It implies *not* that 'women' have a fixed, essentially female nature, but rather that real relations of gender can exist of which people are normally unaware because they do not think with feminist concepts or political consciousness. Despite Hartsock's clear statement of this point, many of her critics ignore the Marxist theory that underlies it, and accuse her of essentialism (Hartsock 1998). She identifies a level of real, material relations of gender subordination that are essential in the sense of being necessary to the operation of patriarchy. These are normally hidden by patriarchical ideology and can only be 'discovered' by accurately conceptualizing patriarchy and its operation. These essential relations of patriarchy are contrasted with apparent relations – what appears to be the case – for example, the patriarchal view that male dominance is natural and proper. This is the level of appearances to which essential relations give rise. Hartsock's claim to know from a feminist standpoint cannot be dismissed as essentialist since taking this standpoint is not an attribute of a female body or nature, or even of living as a woman.

This notion of standpoint assumes that there are specific social locations (being a woman or a man) grounded in material conditions (different actual experiences of living as a woman or a man) from which real relations of power (male domination) can be best conceptualized. Since not all feminist researchers draw on this realist/materialist/Marxist logic, Hartsock's version of feminist standpoint is not compatible with all approaches to feminist methodology. Marx saw knowledge as political, and the knowing self as socially constituted, but theory and epistemology also played a critical role in differentiating between what Marx and 'bourgeois intellectuals' made of the same evidence.

There is a careful differentiation between Hartsock's version of standpoint and what she calls a 'modernist/Enlightenment' version of truth. Like Harding, she confines this version of 'truth' to an extreme position on Haraway's greasy pole.

> In the modernist/Enlightenment version, truth has to do with discovering a preexisting external something that, if it meets some criteria, can be labelled as true. Moreover, it must be discovered from nowhere in particular so that Truth can retain its pristine qualities. [. . .] The Marxian project, then, changes the criteria for what counts as knowledge. (Hartsock 1997: 369–70)

Hartsock takes from Marxism the ideas that 'truth' is historically specific, that the search for knowledge is a human activity, and that the knowing self is socially constituted. The truths that get established in divided societies tend to be those of the dominant groups. She argues that the point of Marx's project is to understand power relations in order to change them, rather than the pursuit of truth in a positivist or empiricist sense: 'And to this end, Marx's categories move and flow and enact the fluidity that many postmodernist theorists insist on' (Hartsock 1997: 370).

Since a feminist standpoint is not what is seen from a fixed social place, or from a female identity, or from a woman's body, it must be grounded in experience of gender subordination and constituted as feminist theory. Hartsock proposes a critical connection between the potential for standpoint and women's experience. A standpoint is a relational concept in that it is knowledge that has to be struggled for, and so could be struggled for by anyone (whether male, female, intersexual or other) who is politically committed to transforming unjust gender relations (just as a bourgeois could take a proletarian standpoint in understanding capitalism). Donna Haraway comments on Hartsock's logic:

> Perhaps being born into, or finding yourself in, certain situations produces a *potential* for standpoint, but the achievement of standpoint is the achievement of a critical take, and a *collective* critical take. Standpoint is crafted out of struggle, out of engagement, and then becomes a powerful possibility for fuelling a different kind of knowledge in the world [. . .] a way of producing – of materializing – the world differently. (Bhavnani and Haraway 1994: 37)

Where Hartsock favours a realist epistemology, in assuming that essential power relations (such as racialized or male dominance, compulsory heterosexuality) really affect people's lives, whether people think with these concepts or not, Haraway suggests a more fluid relation between knowledge and its materializing power.

Achieving a feminist standpoint in this sense is politically empowering, because it provides knowledge of how gender relationships work in actual situations, and so offers a basis for transforming them. Although Dorothy Smith's concept of standpoint differs from that of Hartsock, she provides an illustration of how her experiences as a mother, secretary and then sociologist were illuminated by an alternative and critical consciousness of power relations gained through feminism (Smith 1989: 36-7).

It is not the case that in practice all women actually experience male power in the same way, and there can be different standpoints in relation to different forms of power (for example, those of class, gender, racism). Hartsock acknowledges that her work on standpoint may have the effect of excluding the specific experience of lesbians and women of colour, since her initial focus was on what women have in common in 'western class societies' (1983a: 234).

Patricia Hill Collins (1990) draws on Hartsock's conception of standpoint, but explores the specificity of African American women's experience through the conception of black feminist thought. Black feminist thought is grounded in the specificity of black women's experience of intersecting inequalities, including their marginalization from authoritative knowledge production. This requires black feminist theory to make sense of black women's experience (1990: 22). Collins emphasizes that knowledge does not arise simply from experience, and that experience is not simply individual.

> Hekman clearly identifies the very construct of standpoint with the idea of individual perspective or point of view. This assumption allows her to collapse the individual and group as units of analysis and proceed to reason that *individuals and collectivities* undergo similar processes. [. . .] By omitting a discussion of group-based realities grounded in an equally central notion of group-based oppression, we move into the sterile ground of a discussion of how effectively standpoint theory serves as an epistemology of truth. (1997: 376)

Collins suggests that in societies characterized by the sort of racial inequalities prevalent in the USA, disadvantaged groups can seek strength in collective action based on common experiences of subjugation (1997: 380). Privileged groups, in contrast, can think of themselves as individuals, and so obscure the privileges they gain from group membership. bell hooks illustrates this claim by looking at white privilege in the USA through what she terms a critical black gaze (which can be compared with the notion of standpoint) (1992: 167–8). This critical gaze serves, first, to identify whiteness as a privileged social identity, and, second, to make explicit that this privilege is part of an institutionalized system of racialized inequality that situates people in racialized relationships to each other.[2]

Hartsock's view that those who share gender subordination can share a potential vantage point on otherwise hidden power relations depends on a realist conception of relations between power and knowledge. This position has been particularly targeted by postmodern and poststructuralist critics. While grounded in women's experience, Dorothy Smith's conception of standpoint is somewhat different.

Dorothy Smith: taking women's standpoint; beginning in experience

Dorothy Smith does not adopt Hartsock's clearly realist epistemology, and this makes her position on reality and its relation to women's experience harder to understand, but it is a position that she defends strongly against Hekman's interpretation of it. She quotes Hekman:

> Despite their significant differences, all of these accounts share the conviction that the feminist standpoint is rooted in a 'reality' that is the opposite of the abstract conceptual world inhabited by men, particularly the men of the ruling class, and that in this reality lies the truth of the human condition. (Hekman 1997a: 348)

Smith complains that 'Hekman goes beyond Harding to constitute us as a common theoretical position, indeed as a foundationalist theory justifying feminist theory as knowledge. A coherence is invented for us' (1997: 393). It is this version of being 'rooted in reality' that Smith rejects.

Hekman (1997a) does note that there is more than one version of standpoint theory, but infuriates Smith by trying to fit her earlier work on 'women's perspective' (Smith 1974) and 'standpoint of women' (Smith 1988), into a common feminist standpoint project on connecting truth and reality. This misses the point of Smith's distinctive attempt to reflect critically on the problems of claiming connections between experience and knowledge of reality. It also misses the significant differences between Hartsock's direct indebtedness to a particular Marxist/realist position, and Smith's claim that 'the social is always *being brought into being* in the concerting of people's local activities. It is never already there' (1997: 395). While Smith and Hartsock both see women's experience as critical to the production of knowledge of male power, they tackle the problems of connecting ideas, experience and reality somewhat differently (Smith 1974, 1988, 1989, 1998).

Smith indignantly repudiates Hekman's opposition of theory and reality in her interpretation of Smith's work:

> First, I am not proposing a *feminist standpoint* at all; taking up women's standpoint as I have developed it is not at all the same thing and has nothing to do with justifying feminist knowledge. Second, I am not arguing that women's standpoint is

rooted in a reality of any kind. Rather, I am arguing that women's standpoint returns us to the actualities of our lives as we live them in the local particularities of the everyday/everynight worlds in which our bodily being anchors us. (Smith 1997: 393)

It is Smith's interweaving of standpoint and everyday living/being/embodiment that Hekman finds difficult. Hekman comments: 'Our disagreement hinges on my claim that [Smith] roots women's standpoint in the reality of women's experience and that this results in the (in my view, futile) attempt to replace concepts with brute reality/experience' (1997b: 401).

Smith insists that she does not embrace reality and reject concepts as Hekman suggests, since she does not see concepts (people's consciousness) and reality (actual relations of ruling) as two equivalent or opposing regions. Rather, her point is that when women speak from their experiences of subordination, they produce knowledge that does not exist in dominant discourses (Smith 1997: 394). For Smith, a woman's standpoint is not rooted in some reality that is independent of knowledge of it. Reality and conceptions of reality are both constituted through 'people's socially organized practices in the actual locations of their lives' (Smith 1997: 393). A woman's standpoint also opens the women's movement to criticism from those who experience the marginalization and silencing of women's practices of, for example, racism or heterosexism (Smith 1997: 393).

For Smith, the knowledge that can be told from experience is local knowledge of everyday life, 'the secret underpinning of everything we do' (1997: 395). A women's standpoint begins to 'unearth the tacit underpinnings of gender', but experiential knowledge cannot simply establish a direct connection to reality, since it has to be expressed in some general discourse. Unlike Hartsock, Smith does not grant women any epistemological privilege, but she does see starting from people's experience of everyday lives, and moving beyond the limits of individual experience, as productive of knowledge of power relations.

Smith's concept of 'actuality' differs both from Hekman's notion of reality versus concepts, and from Hartsock's notion of essential relations. Smith locates a women's standpoint in a complex social process of knowledge construction. The feminist knowledge that results is actively situated in living and knowing. What women know and experience as 'reality' is socially produced. Reality exists independently of people's consciousness of it, but the connections between what is real, what is thought and what is experienced cannot easily be disentangled. This makes Smith's notion of 'actuality' and its constitution hard to pin down.

> The notion of 'actual' in my writing is like the arrow on the map of the mall saying 'You are here', that points in the text to a beyond-the-text in which the text, its reading, its reader, and its concepts also *are*. It is, so to speak, where we live and where discourse happens and does its constituting of 'reality'. (Smith 1997: 393)

In this, as in Hartsock's view, theory cannot be separated from experience. Smith stresses that 'concepts are also in actuality and that the objectifications of what I early on described as the relations of ruling are themselves people's socially organized practices in the actual locations of their lives' (1997: 393). Concepts and theories play an active role in organizing actual social relations. Smith's notion of women's standpoint 'folds concepts, theory, discourse *into actuality* as people's actual practices or activities' (1997: 393). She acknowledges that this is 'a bit tricky to grasp' (1997: 393 – and Hekman [1997b: 401] declares frankly that she does not grasp it).

Liz Stanley and Sue Wise, who are generally sympathetic to Smith's approach, make a comparable critique of realist standpoint theory. While people have different interpretations of what really goes on in the social world, Stanley and Wise 'don't accept that there is something "really" there for these to be interpretations of' (1993: 132). Liz Stanley (1992) recognizes material differences between women, since women can gain and exercise power, but, from a more phenomenological position, she rejects the view of an unproblematic reality 'out there' waiting to be discovered. This does not mean that nothing is real, since there are 'the structured and repetitive regularities and inequalities of social life' (Stanley 1992: 31) that have real effects on people. Stanley claims that 'there is a social reality, one which members of society construct as having objective existence above and beyond competing constructions and interpretations of it' (1992: 32), but this reality cannot be directly accessed except as competing conceptualizations of it.

A woman's standpoint, in Smith's view, emerges from a women's movement, 'beginning in women's experiences, told in women's words. [. . .] [T]aking women's standpoint and beginning in experience gives access to a knowledge of what is tacit, known in the doing, and often not yet discursively appropriated (and often seen as uninteresting, unimportant, and routine)' (1997: 394–5). These interconnections of standpoint and experience enable the emergence of new knowledge: 'When we assembled *as* "women" and spoke together *as* "women", constituting "women" as a category of political mobilization, we discovered dimensions of "our" experience that had no prior discursive definition' (Smith 1997: 394). Smith also specifies that she uses 'women' here as a category whose boundaries are subject to 'the disruption of women who enter speaking from a different experience as well as an experience of difference' (1997: 394).

Smith's anger with Hekman illustrates the importance of the political as well as the intellectual differences between them. This is the difference between the view attributed to Smith (that reality, experience and theory are separated and so require connections to be made by the theorist), and the position taken by Smith (that real power relations, and their effects, are organized in everyday social practices and ideas). Hartsock and Smith also differ both in how they understand the nature of reality, and in how they think about the connections between knowledge, experience and reality. What Smith's and Hartsock's notions of standpoint have in common is a dependence on women actually sharing some common experiences of subordination and exclusion from knowledge production across their differences. In any given case, what exactly is held in common is a matter of investigation, and so cannot simply be assumed. Knowledge from any standpoint is open to challenge and disruption.

What problems remain?

Debates on taking a feminist standpoint are constrained by the modern and humanist legacy of the Enlightenment, which has been particularly targeted by postmodern thought. But it seems premature to dismiss standpoint theories and epistemologies as wholly having failed. These attempts to resist essentialism and foundationalism and to value women's experience of real relations of power have been productive. They encounter numerous problems in trying to specify connections between knowledge and power, and between knowledge, experience and reality, but feminist standpoint theorists do attend to the epistemological problems of the knowing subject and its visions, and the political problems of empowering subjugated voices. Nevertheless, attempts by feminist standpoint theorists to tackle productive ways of researching gendered social life at the limits of modern thinking have attracted numerous criticisms.

One area of criticism assumes standpoint theory and epistemology to be a single position, flawed by aspects of modern thinking such as humanism, foundationalism, essentialism, conceptions of fixed identities, inappropriate claims to privileged knowledge or assertions of totalizing theory. There can be grounds for such criticisms where actual examples are found in particular accounts of standpoint theory (as opposed to sweeping dismissals of all standpoint theory). But the connections between knowledge and power remain open to debate, reconsideration and testing in practice. (What standpoint theorist for example, explicitly depends on essential or fixed identities in defending their work?[3]) Such dismissals miss the challenges and dramas feminists experience both in slipping and sliding on Haraway's greasy pole, and in their varied attempts to leap off. These dramas explode patriarchal knowledge *as* patriarchal, find ethnocentrism, racism and other exclusionary practices in feminism, and produce new knowledge of material power relations. Critics can miss the critical role of resistance in feminist thought, the significance of methodological and political struggles between feminists, and the inherent tension in feminist methodology between a political need to identify the power relations that shape knowledge production, and acceptance that knowledge and the knower are multiply socially constituted and situated.

There are also criticisms of standpoint theory from within feminist debate. These are in part influenced by postmodern thinking in identifying points of weakness in modern theory, but they also raise more specific problems about claiming connections between knowledge and experience. We review these briefly here to indicate the limits of modern thinking and the challenges to feminist thought that are taken up in Part II.

The problem of how the knowing self is socially constituted

It is one thing to claim that a knowing self is historically situated and socially constituted. It is another to know what is constituted, how and why. Feminists have recognized the problem that 'woman' is not a fixed self. But this leaves the processes that give rise both to 'woman', and to the particular power relations that affect gendered lives, as further problems to be investigated. The knowing subject who can (through struggle) produce knowledge from a feminist standpoint cannot be taken for granted. Efforts to claim a feminist standpoint raise questions about what it means to have multiple feminist subjects, and what follows from claiming that the knowing self is not an individual. These problems are illuminated by the efforts of postmodern and poststructuralist thinkers to deconstruct the subject and consider how particular 'knowing subjects' are constituted.

The problem of claiming epistemological privilege

Standpoint theories raise the problem of whether those with experiences of gender subordination can 'see' power relations and their material situations better than can those who dominate. This is the question of whether the oppressed have special access to the nature of oppression, and whether taking a feminist standpoint implies that ordinary people suffer from false consciousness, in the sense that they see what appears to be the case (for example, that masculinity and femininity are natural states), while the feminist theorist claims superior knowledge (for example, in claiming that masculinity and femininity are socially constituted). Standpoint theorists have taken various positions in relation to this problem, with Hartsock's Marxist-influenced position being more open to criticism on this point than Smith's. Maureen Cain (1990), commenting on Hartsock's notion of privileged standpoint, asks whether if women lost their subordinate position they would also lose their double vision. (The experience of wealthy and socially successful women by the end of the twentieth century suggests that this is indeed the case.)

Cain argues that since feminist theory has to incorporate the diversity of women's experience, a feminist standpoint does not need to claim epistemological privilege. Knowing from a feminist standpoint is a political process and potentially transformative. However, the feminist knower relies on concepts and knowledge historically available to her from a particular social situation, language and theory (Cain 1986: 260). This social situation is also, and simultaneously, constituted by underlying power relationships that really exist.

The problem of difference

Standpoint epistemology has been criticized because women are not a unified category but are divided by, for example, real relations of racialized power, heterosexism, globalization or ablebodiedism. These can exert powerful, and often violent, effects both on people's lives and on processes of knowledge production. Feminist theory has recognized diversity in women's material conditions of existence, but has been shaped in part by western ethnocentrism and the social divisions of particular societies. Difference has been struggled over, and the marginalization of disadvantaged groups made explicit by these socially constituted as 'other' (for example, Collins 1990). Privileged feminist researchers can silence ontological differences in women's experiences and fail to acknowledge the social processes that effect the constitution of 'otherness'. Standpoint theory addresses difference primarily through the limits of shared experiences of subordination.

The problem of how knowledge can be grounded in experience

The grounding of a feminist standpoint or a women's standpoint or multiple standpoints 'in experience' is central to standpoint theory, but remains problematic in practice. The notion of experience does not have consistent meanings across all versions of standpoint. There are epistemological and ontological differences in how connections are conceived. Dorothy Smith emphasizes that the 'authority of experience is foundational to the women's movement (which is not to say that experience is foundational to knowledge) and has been and is at once explosive and fruitful' (1997: 394). Smith denies that experience is foundational to knowledge in order to avoid the position that there is one true reality in 'women's experience' from which feminist knowledge can flow. Beverley Skeggs gives a generally negative appraisal of standpoint theory, but does recognize its achievements in putting 'women' at the centre of knowledge production (1997: 24–8). This leaves making sense of 'experience' as an unresolved issue, but one that cannot be abandoned.

The problem of conceptualizing material reality

Feminists have wanted some material conception of power in order to identify and resist unjust relations of power. Standpoint feminists try to make sense of the contradictory nature of women's experience and conflicting accounts of reality, but they do not agree epistemologically on how to make connections between ideas, experience and entrenched hierarchies of power, or hidden power relations. Liz Stanley and Sue Wise (1990), for example, are critical of what gets silenced in materialist notions of standpoint, particularly the notion of multiple feminist standpoints. Feminists do need to understand the material foundations of, for example, male dominance, sexualized racism, compulsory heterosexuality, and their diverse interconnections.

The problem that knowledges are multiple, partial, contingent and situated

Claims to know from a feminist standpoint raise the (unresolved) problem, fundamental to all debates on feminist methodology, of whether/how some accounts of gender relations can be taken to be 'better founded', 'truer' or 'less partial' than others. Donna Haraway jumps off her greasy pole by abandoning privileged knowledge in favour of partial visions and socially situated knowledges, but she is still caught in the dilemma that partial visions are not all equal (1991: 188).

There is no single feminist standpoint because our maps require too many dimensions
for that metaphor to ground our visions. But the feminist standpoint theorists' goal of
an epistemology and politics of engaged, accountable positioning remains eminently
potent. The goal is better accounts of the world, that is, 'science'. (1991: 196)

Haraway's notion of 'vision' is of partial, embodied, situated, knowledges
produced from multiple and partial perspectives. But since she hangs on to the
feminist claim that some partial visions are 'truer' than others, she leaves the criteria of 'science' or validity as politically and epistemologically problematic.
However, she departs from a realist notion of standpoint, and so from Hartsock's
position, in arguing that the fact that people can see from subjugated positions
does not mean that these visions are necessarily trustworthy or innocent (1991:
190): 'The positionings of the subjugated are not exempt from critical re-exami-
nation' (Haraway 1991: 191). She adds: 'Subjugation is not grounds for an
ontology [. . .] there are no immediate visions from the standpoints of the subjugated' (1991: 193). Seeing from below is not then a solution, since it still leaves
feminists with the problem of making sense of what is seen. While Haraway
appears to reject realism, she also resists relativism. The differences between partial knowledges do matter – just any partial perspective will not do (Haraway
1991: 192). Her attempt to claim that some stories of power are 'better' than
others, without being able to specify any general criteria for establishing what
constitutes 'truer' or 'better', indicates a continuing tension over validity, and
between epistemology and politics.

The problems of accountability, alliances and empowerment

Maureen Cain (1990) suggests opening up the concept of a feminist standpoint
to multiplicity through choices that involve a politics, a theory and theoretical
self-reflection on one's own historicity. The standpoint theorist can make
alliances and she can be accountable for the knowledge she produces. Political
strategies then depend on whom you share a standpoint with, which in turn
depends on whom you share experiences, interests and power relations with.
This has given feminists problems both in conceptualizing and acting on differences between women, and in relating to, for example, male victims of violence
or the agency of powerful women.

The strategy of making alliances across women's social and political divisions
has brought sharp encounters between competing understandings of reality.
Maureen Cain (1990) says she was criticized for saying (in Cain 1986) that you
could not produce knowledge from two standpoints (for example, those of class,
race or gender) at the same time. She suggests that connections have to be
worked out in specific sites. (Perhaps you can know from two or more sites
simultaneously, but this would not produce the same knowledge.) Haraway
(1991) considers that knowledge-producers have to be accountable for the pat-
terning of reality that they 'see'. This allows for people's agency as objects of
feminist knowledge as well as the agency of the knowing feminist. This conception of agency, political choice and political alliances is firmly grounded in

feminism's radical modern humanism, and the notion of consciousness as political education.

Conclusion

The notion of a feminist standpoint has been extensively criticized and accused of suffering from some, if not all, of the failings of modern social science and foundationalist epistemology. At best, critics find standpoint theorists stuck in feminism's modern foundations. At worst, standpoint theory is (inaccurately) identified as simplistic, uniform and essentialist.

Sandra Harding suggests that feminist standpoint is a case of an epistemology in transition, in which participants are engaged in struggle and development (1987b: 187). Standpoint debate moves on from attempts to claim clear connections between feminist knowledge and women's realities, to attempts to explore the relations between knowledge and power. But this leaves feminists divided on how to make knowledge claims authoritative, how to understand power, how to judge between competing knowledge claims, and how feminist knowledge can be grounded in women's experiences and differences.

The growing challenges from postmodern thought, especially since the 1980s, appear to offer some ways out of these dilemmas. In Part II we move on to look at what sort of challenge postmodern thought poses to feminist knowledge production, and how far it can offer some resolution to problems of investigating connections between ideas, experience and reality. The issues addressed in Chapter 5 open up new paths for feminist thought, but they do not resolve all the difficulties of feminist methodology. In the course of Chapters 6 and 7, we come back to a number of problems – of differences between women; of the grounding of feminist knowledge in experience; of the materiality of power relations; and of validity – that are raised in choosing between competing knowledges.

Notes

1. Haraway states that feminists do want reliable knowledge.

> This point applies whether we are talking about genes, social classes, elementary particles, genders, races, or texts; the point applies to the exact, natural, social and human sciences, despite the slippery ambiguities of the words *objectivity* and *science* as we slide around the discursive terrain. In our efforts to climb the greased pole leading to a usable doctrine of objectivity, I and most other feminists in the objectivity debates have alternately, or even simultaneously, held on to both ends of the dichotomy, which Harding describes in terms of successor science projects versus postmodernist accounts of difference and I have sketched in this chapter as radical constructivism versus feminist critical empiricism. It is, of course, hard to climb when you are holding on to both ends of a pole, simultaneously or alternately. (1991: 188)

2. The shock of seeing whiteness through a black gaze is also evident in the reactions of white South African feminists to being faced with their privileges during the early

1990s (Bazilli 1991; Pethu 1992; Thompson 1992). These accounts echo earlier encounters in the UK and the US (Carby 1982; Lorde 1983; Ros 1984; Shah 1984). The invisibility of whiteness as a power relation can allow white women to think themselves innocent of white privilege (Frankenberg 1993; Lewis and Ramazanoğlu 1999). Susan Holland-Muter claims that what is obvious about white privileges to those excluded from them is obscure to people who 'see the world from a white standpoint' (1994: 58). She says that white feminists in South Africa (including those opposed to apartheid and engaged in anti-racist activities) experience fear and anger in being personally identified as racist. 'For example, we have talked about "blackness", but I have never taken part in a forum where "whiteness" and "privilege" have been discussed' (Holland-Muter 1994: 60).

3. Paul Gilroy is sympathetic to Patricia Hill Collins' (1990) critical project on the marginalization of black women from western knowledge production, and accepts her argument that feminist knowledge does not flow from essentially feminine experience (Gilroy 1993: 2–3). But he criticizes Collins' version of a black feminist standpoint for failing to distinguish between black 'woman' and black 'feminist' (in a comparable manner to Hartsock's distinction between 'woman' and 'feminist'). Gilroy accuses Collins of using the term 'black' to cover both *knowing* (as a black feminist) and *being* (as a black woman). Gilroy concludes to his own satisfaction that Collins' black women's standpoint is grounded in a humanist and 'thoroughly Cartesian racial subject', and thus depends on fixed and stable identities, rather than 'incorporating the problem of the formation of the knowing subject into both epistemological and political practice' (1993: 53). While Collins, like other standpoint theorists, does encounter problems of subject formation within modern thought, there is a considerable difference between the way she opens up problems about the relations between power, knowledge and experience, and any systematic defence of fixed identities.

PART II

FREEDOM, FRAGMENTATION AND RESISTANCE

5

Escape from epistemology?

The impact of postmodern thought on feminist methodology

Introduction

In their pursuit of better knowledge, feminist researchers carry what Jane Flax calls 'Enlightenment dreams' (1992: 448). These are dreams not only of achieving knowledge, but also of commitment to justice, emancipation and progress. At the centre of these dreams is the knowing feminist attempting to make new connections between ideas of gender, experiences of gender and realities of gender. Despite these deep roots in modern thought and scientific method, debates on rationality, objectivity, validity and standpoint show feminists struggling with their methodological legacy, challenging the certainties of patriarchal knowledge, confronting difference, developing critiques of the modern subject, foundationalist epistemology, and knowledge based on these foundations.

While feminists were working on how to move beyond their contradictory inheritance, powerful critiques of Enlightenment thought, humanism and epistemology were being developed in poststructuralist and postmodern thought. In this chapter, we consider the challenges and opportunities that postmodern thinkers offer to feminists in thinking differently about knowledge production and the nature of gender.

Postmodern thought

Postmodernism as a general term has been applied to three main areas (in each of which it has a long and complex history): (1) a movement in art and architecture; (2) the poststructuralist writings of French theorists and philosophers such as Foucault, Derrida, Deleuze and Guattari; and (3) more general theories of late capitalism in which society is designated 'post-industrial', 'post-Fordist' or 'postmodern'. The poststructuralist strand has been further developed by thinkers labelled with the more general term 'postmodern' (for example, Lyotard, Baudrillard, Rorty).

An impact on feminist methodology has come primarily from the second area. There are significant differences between poststructuralism and postmodernism (as well as within each of these areas of thought), and we do not attempt to characterize the diversity of this field. We consider the implications for feminist social research of 'postmodern thought', in which we loosely group poststructuralism and postmodernism as postmodern.

Postmodern thought in this loose sense, is difficult to pin down:[1]

> [T]here is no unified postmodern theory, or even a coherent set of positions. Rather, one is struck by the diversities between theories often lumped together as 'postmodern' and the plurality – often conflictual – of postmodern positions. One is also struck by the inadequate and undertheorized notion of the 'postmodern' in the theories which adopt, or are identified in, such terms. (Best and Kellner 1991: 2)

Our concern is with the impact of particular aspects of this thought on feminist attempts to connect ideas, experience and reality, and on understandings of relations between knowledge and power. Although standpoint feminists struggled to extricate their methodology from its Enlightenment and humanist inheritance, postmodern thought has produced radical criticisms and different concerns. Postmodern thought targets modern and humanist attempts to produce valid knowledge as misguided, and has been used to dramatic effect in criticizing feminist knowledge. In particular it challenges any unified conception of 'women' or 'feminism' or 'knowing feminist' and undercuts the notion of feminist knowledge as grounded in the experience of women. In this sense, postmodern thought challenges the authority of feminist knowledge of or for women.

The (mostly male) exponents of postmodern thought have largely ignored feminist struggles with science and humanism. Their arguments have been brought into debates on feminism largely by feminists.[2] Postmodern thought is potentially radical in that: first, it questions how feminist knowledge claims become constituted and established; second, it abandons the idea that direct connections between experience, knowledge and reality can be achieved through rational, scientific method or from a feminist standpoint; third, it challenges humanist conceptions of self, agency, power and emancipation.

Feminism's encounters with postmodernism, however, need not be taken as negative. Michèle Barrett and Zygmunt Bauman drain some of the danger from the prefix 'post-'. Barrett argues that 'post-' carries two different emphases, meaning either 'that we are now decisively *beyond* the substantive noun, or that we have come *from* it' (2000: 50). While this ambiguity can create controversy, she argues that it is important to hold on to both meanings. Bauman (1988) notes that modern thought is not what *preceded* postmodernism. Rather, postmodern thinkers have conceptualized modernism in opposition to postmodernism. In this view, postmodern thought provides a productive release from the critical constraints and insufficiencies of modern thought. It is this potentially positive relationship that has been picked up by feminists who find postmodern thought liberating, or go further in merging revived and improved feminisms with postmodern thought.

While we have had to simplify postmodern thought here, feminists cannot either simply embrace it as solving all feminism's methodological problems or dismiss it as unwarranted or inconvenient. Postmodern thinkers can produce facile and inadequate criticisms of feminism, suppressing its internal differences, just as feminists can of postmodern thought. Any simple contrast between unified modern and unified postmodern ways of knowing is not very enlightening. Postmodern critics cannot reasonably reduce feminist approaches to methodology to a simple 'modern foundation', since the foundations of modern thought were always contested (Morawski 1996: 98). We have indicated in Part I the existence of diversity, debate and contradiction within modern feminist thought.

Feminist critics of postmodernism too cannot reduce the complexities of postmodernism and poststructuralism to a few simple claims that can be rejected. Those influenced by postmodernism have noted the problems of trying to treat varied versions of postmodernism as unified (Butler 1992: 5). Jane Flax comments: 'By even speaking of "postmodernism" I run the risk of violating some of its central values – heterogeneity, multiplicity and difference' (1990: 188). We do not have space to attend to detailed differences here, so have picked out how elements of postmodern thought have presented both problems and opportunities for feminist research.

Some feminists argue that feminism *is* in some respects a postmodern theory (Flax 1987; Weedon 1997), or at least that it should be (Hekman 1992; Nash 1994), but they make this argument with qualifications. Postmodern thought is attractive in enabling feminists to look imaginatively at power, selves and knowledge production and, in particular, at *how* the power of language and representation operates (Hall 1997a; McRobbie 1997; Skeggs 1995a). But feminists have also raised a number of problems about treating feminism *as* a version of postmodern thought (Bordo 1990; Fraser 1989). Feminists were already making 'gender trouble' in their accounts of the social nature of gender and sexuality, but postmodern thought produced more radical trouble that questions the very terms of feminist debate and thinking (Butler 1990). While standpoint feminists shake the foundations of male-centred western knowledge, postmodern thought takes these foundations apart to show what is taken for granted in their constituent elements and processes (rationality, the knowing subject, scientific method, truth, reality) and how knowledge is produced and made powerful. These deconstructions uncouple knowledge, power and reality in order to examine how various connections between them have been produced, and with what effects.

In our own work, we have found aspects of postmodern thought critical and productive, and this has influenced our research and thinking (for example, Holland et al. 1998), and our presentation of the issues raised in Part II. The concerns of postmodern thought and of feminist research, however, remain different. Postmodern thought can be politically conservative while being intellectually radical, and some feminist engagement with liberal and Marxist thought is still potentially productive. In the second part of this chapter we argue that feminism should retain some distinctive elements in its approaches to social investigation as much else is swept away.

We look first at postmodern thought as a positive challenge to feminist methodology, and at how feminism's modern defects might be remedied through a postmodern anti-humanism. We then indicate how this leaves feminists defending aspects of feminism's radical humanism.

Postmodern freedoms: sweeping away the foundations of feminist methodology

We consider seven ways (see summary of chapter subheadings above) in which postmodernism offers feminism both freedom *from* the grip of modern, humanist thought and the constraints of scientific method, and freedom *to* open up fresh ways of thinking about gender.

Freedom from scientific method: questioning connections between knowledge, rationality and truth/reality

Postmodern thought challenges feminism by denying the possibility that scholars can specify a particular relationship between human knowledge and some underlying reality. It follows that the boundaries between specialist disciplines are no longer real boundaries, but effects of particular decisions about how to tell truths, and what counts as truth. Literature, sciences, social sciences, cultural studies, history and feminism are all ways of producing 'texts' that audiences can 'read' in different ways. The boundaries between 'fact' and 'fiction' collapse, opening up new possibilities for subjugated voices, stories about experience, autobiography, memories. We can question how some forms of knowledge become more authoritative than others. Since science is but one way of thinking/talking, the authoritative status of rationality and scientific knowledge needs new explanation. Once any direct connection between truths produced by scientific methods and some true, external reality are denied, feminist knowledges, like any other claims to knowledge of social life, are just political fictions that cannot have a testable relationship with an external, real world. The collapse of this relationship also transforms the notion of history as narrating a chronological sequence of events, and of modernity as an advance on what came before. New conceptions of history offer creative opportunities for thinking about events, space and time, but also fragment any relationship of linear progression between modernity, science and progress (Adam 1996; Bauman 1990; Glucksman 1998).[3]

Standpoint feminists identify problems with the masculinism of science, and the supposed neutrality of rational scientific methods. Postmodern thought goes much further in abandoning any model of rational scientific method as a means of connecting knowledge and social realities, and any chance of certainty. Rationality and science (as a distinctive mode of inquiry opposed to, for example, dreams, magic, custom, religion, fiction) are reconceptualized as particular ways of thinking. The relations between social reality, material conditions, ideas and experience are no longer seen as validated through scientific method and the rules of epistemology that shape modern social science. Efforts in modern feminism to discover the realities of gender simply express one mode of thought. Feminist knowledge cannot then have general validity; the researcher is left in a relativist position, unable to judge whether some knowledge claims are better than others.

Michel Foucault avoids feminism's dilemma of deciding between what can truly or falsely be said about gender by posing the problem differently. He asks *why* there are different claims to knowledge of what is true, for example in different discourses of sexuality (Foucault 1984a). Feminist knowledge can then be seen as a discourse (a way of specifying what counts as knowledge). Scientific discourses operate as sets of rules that specify at a particular moment what is or is not the case. Foucault's approach examines not what is or is not true, but how each discourse operates, its history and effects, and the connections between different discourses. He shows how ways of distinguishing between what counts as scientific, true or reliable are themselves consequences of how scientific discourses are constituted in a particular way of thinking that decides what counts as knowledge (Foucault 1980b: 197).[4]

Foucault is not concerned with establishing the validity of his own claims to knowledge. He argues that the reality of, say, 'normal sexuality' cannot be discovered (for example, by connecting theories of sexuality, experiences of sexuality and the realities of sexuality). Particular forms of 'sexuality' are only real in the sense that they are constituted in discourses. These discourses specify through authoritative channels (for example, formal education, law, medicine, psychiatry) what sexuality is. With their accompanying practices, they bring into being normal and deviant sexuality (for example, the 'good husband', 'the frigid wife', the 'straight guy', the 'pervert') as objects of the discourse. The nature of 'normal sexuality' or 'perversion' can be seen as discursive constructs, produced in language and in authorizing practices, rather than as underlying realities waiting to be found. Discourses of normal and deviant sexuality can then have powerful effects on people's lives.

Validity, rationality and scientific method (as means of establishing the authority of particular forms of knowledge through connecting ideas, experience and reality) are also taken to be discursively constituted in particular ways of thinking. Foucault's claims can of course be contested, but he does not seek to establish a body of data. Rather, he unsettles what is taken for granted in existing ways of thinking so that people are free (or at least freer) to recognize how authoritative knowledge is socially constituted (for example, 'you are a bad mother', 'homosexuality is an illness') and so can be resisted.

In Foucault's theory, the 'reality' of sexuality cannot be accessed, but researchers can examine how the 'truths' of, say, 'normal heterosexuality' come to be constituted and with what effects. Normality or perversion cannot be found by making the correct connections between ideas, experience and reality. New discourses can establish what is normal and to be aspired to, and what must be denigrated, controlled, punished or otherwise disciplined. But they can also be challenged and changed (for example, by the 'gay man', the 'desiring woman', the 'new man'). Feminists have found much that is empowering and illuminating in this approach, for example in asking how particular versions of 'heterosexuality' come to be constructed in particular ways of thinking (Helliwell 2000; Holland et al. 1998; Jackson 1995; Smart 1996; Wilkinson and Kitzinger 1993).

Freedom from scientific method offers feminists relief from the problems of taking up a standpoint, and the intractable problems of connecting ideas, experience and reality through the competing paths of realism, materialism and empiricism, and so on. In asking how multiple truths and multiple knowledges are produced, any direct connection between knowledge, experience and the extra-discursive (realities that exist outside discourses, and so cannot be known) is abandoned. In some respects, Foucault's theory serves to legitimate ways in which feminists were already trying to connect knowledge and power. But freedom from scientific method also challenges the foundations of feminism by claiming the end of epistemology, and so of feminist methodology. The end of epistemology shifts the focus of empirical investigation onto how discourses are constituted, the varying ways in which texts/evidence can be read, and what effects particular forms of knowledge have.

Freedom from binary thinking: deconstructing oppositional categories

A key postmodern concept that feminists have been drawn to as a tool for analysis is deconstruction (Nash 1994). Spurred by the ideas of Jacques Derrida (1970), deconstruction critically analyses the binary oppositions through which western philosophy and culture are thought. We take deconstruction (more simply than Derrida) as reflecting on, questioning and unsettling existing assumptions, meanings and methods. Deconstruction in this sense exposes binary thinking and questions how ways of thinking, telling truths, reading texts, and so on, have been socially constituted in particular contexts.[5]

Derrida suggests that meaning in western philosophy is produced and understood through opposition and differentiation (see the discussion of Cartesian dualisms in Chapter 1). In order to analyse meaning in language, these oppositions must be made explicit. The process of deconstruction reveals both the interdependence of pairs of categories, and the hierarchy of binary oppositions that gives primacy to one of the pair over the other: masculine/feminine, reason/nature, mind/body, civilized/primitive, objective/subjective, human/animal. This deconstruction (and further deconstruction of deconstructions) brings out 'the implications of the historical sedimentation of language which we use' (Derrida 1970: 271). Feminists have also worked on reconceptualizing the binary logic of western thought and its oppositional categories (particularly the masculine/feminine opposition and its relationship of superior/inferior). Susan Hekman, for example, welcomes Derrida's inscription of difference in non-oppositional terms to reveal the multiplicity of differences that cross and re-cross the boundaries between the masculine and the feminine (Hekman 1992: 174–5).[6]

Deconstruction serves to wrench meanings from their taken-for-granted contexts and identify their effects. This can transform assumptions about natural or necessary binary oppositions of class, gender, race, bodies, into new and fluid possibilities for multiplicity, difference and resistance. The notion of hybridity (slippage, for example, across the socially constituted boundaries that define racial and ethnic groups) questions how oppositions are made, what power is exercised in making them, and offers opportunities for subversion in constituting them differently (Bhabha 1995).

Donna Haraway offers alternatives to binary thinking, first, in her history of primatology (1989) and, second, in her notion of the cyborg (1991). She points out that in discourses of, for example, Japanese primatology, the rigidity of western binary thinking about the boundaries between people and primates does not prevail. Primatology is not then the neutral accumulation of scientific knowledge by impartial scientists (in the sense of discovering an independent reality). Rather, it is a series of contested narratives that can construct primate nature into the dualisms of western scientific discourses or into quite different objects of knowledge in other systems of thought.

In Haraway's notion of the cyborg, a hybrid of machine and organism, the Enlightenment binaries (animal/human, organism/machine, material/non-material) are both disrupted by changes in thought, and transformed by changes in technology. Haraway (1991) argues that by the late twentieth century, we (humans) were all cyborgs, and so 'woman' loses its myth of original unity. In the absence of some natural unity between women, feminist alliances have to be built rather than assumed. Cyborg politics are struggles not over what reality is, but over what gets to count as knowledge (Haraway 1991). Deconstructing binary categories allows feminists to explore the power relations within the binaries, to open ways of thinking and modes of resistance through non-oppositional categories, and to recognize the fragility and permeability of socially constituted boundaries.

Freedom from the knowing self: decentring the subject

Postmodern thought opposes the various Enlightenment and humanist approaches to truth being discovered by individual, autonomous subjects. This is not only by arguing, as feminists have (see Chapters 3 and 4), that there is no one truth, no view from nowhere, no knowledge that is separable from the specific location of its production and the power relations within which it is produced. More radically, postmodernists are held to have brought about the death of the subject, in the sense that the 'knowing subject' was an Enlightenment notion that cannot be justified outside that way of thinking.

In postmodern thought, the subject need not be dead in the sense that there is no knowing subject, but only in the sense that no human subject really exists across differences in knowledge production. Foucault makes this point in a critical methodological shift away from the study of 'man' towards 'genealogy':

> One has to dispense with the constituent subject, to get rid of the subject itself, that's to say, to arrive at an analysis which can account for the constitution of the subject within a historical framework. And this is what I would call genealogy, that is, a form of history which can account for the constitution of knowledges, discourses, domains of objects etc., without having to make reference to a subject which is either transcendental in relation to the field of events or runs in its empty sameness throughout the course of history. (1980a: 117)

The knowing feminist cannot be essentially, naturally or authentically a woman, because she is historically variable and socially constituted. In this view, feminine or masculine natures are not something people are born with. They are produced through the discourses of femininity and masculinity of a given way of thinking, and the effects of these discourses. This brings about not so much the death, as the deconstruction, or decentring, of particular subjects and their specific histories.

Foucault and Deleuze and Guattari (despite some divergence in their theories) all decentre and multiply the subject rather than do away with it. They

> reject the modernist notion of a unified, rational, and expressive subject and attempt to make possible the emergence of new types of decentred subjects, liberated from what they see to be the terror of fixed and unified identities, free to become dispersed and multiple, reconstituted as new types of subjectivities and bodies. (Best and Kellner 1991: 78)

Foucault criticizes the humanist discourses that place the knowing subject at the centre of knowledge production. He questions how we become particular kinds of subjects who produce particular kinds of knowledge of the world. He asks: how we are constituted as subjects of our own knowledge; how we are subjects who exercise or submit to power relations; how we are moral subjects of our own actions (Foucault 1984b: 49).

Judith Butler (1990) argues that gender comes into existence through the way people perform it. She states that gender is produced not by subjects with agency, but by 'a process of reiteration by which both "subjects" and "acts" come to appear at all. There is no power that acts, but only a reiterated acting that is power in its persistence and instability' (Butler 1993: 9). A subject, such as the 'knowing feminist', is constituted not once and for all, but again and again, and in this process, procedures of inclusion and exclusion operate (Butler 1992: 8). Butler criticizes theories of the social or cultural construction of gender that propose a prior subject, or any force, such as discourse, language or the social, that acts like a subject in doing the constructing (1993: 6–9).

Many feminists see deconstructions of the knowing subject as undermining the political project of feminism, removing the possibility of feminist researchers working in the interests of 'women', and producing knowledge about and for 'women'. Rosi Braidotti argues that in order to announce the death of the subject one must first have gained the right to speak as one (1991: 122). Butler responds to these fears with both a challenge and a promise. She wants to know who gets constituted as the feminist theorist who knows, and who is excluded and constituted as *not* the knowing feminist (1992: 14), thus raising the issue of differences between feminists. What may be wrong with the knowing feminist for Butler is not that she is a knowing subject, but the insidious kind of subject she may be constituted as – especially the knowing 'woman' who claims to speak for all 'women' (1992: 13).

Butler retrieves a decentred subject by arguing that 'the critique of the subject is not a negation or repudiation of the subject, but rather a way of interrogating its construction as a pregiven or foundationalist premise' (1992: 9). She draws a distinction between questioning how particular subjects come to be constituted (interrogating the subject) and pronouncing the death of the subject.

> To take the construction of the subject as a political problematic is not the same as doing away with the subject; to deconstruct the subject is not to negate or throw away the concept; on the contrary, deconstruction implies only that we suspend all commitments to that which the term 'the subject,' refers, and that we consider the linguistic functions it serves in the consolidation and concealment of authority. To deconstruct is not to negate or dismiss, but to call into question and, perhaps most importantly, to open up a term, like the subject to a reusage or redeployment that previously has not been authorized. (1992: 15)

Questioning the authority of feminists to speak as subjects with specialist knowledge of gender relations and female experience, or struggling over how far knowledge is appropriate, ethical or general, is not the same as invalidating the knowing feminist and her knowledge. But it does raise problems about who gets constituted as the knowledgeable feminist, whom the feminist speaks for, what the feminist speaks of, and who and what gets excluded. Just as feminists challenge the invisible knower of patriarchal 'truths', so critics of feminism, and those excluded from sites of authoritative knowledge, can deconstruct the academic feminist as a very particular knowing self, constituted in particular relations of privilege. Feminists can also challenge the knowing subjects who challenge feminist knowledge by examining how these subjects come into existence and claim authority to speak. To pronounce the death of the subject raises questions about which subject died, and who carries on speaking after the subject is dead (Butler 1992: 14). Postmodern thought establishes knowing feminists, and their critics, as particular subjects, with particular histories, and as engaged in particular struggles around claims to authoritative knowledge.

Freedom from essential identities: celebrating multiplicity, fragmentation and flux

Postmodern thought directs critical attention to the powerful consequences of particular ways of telling the 'truth' about our selves. Feminists have had considerable difficulties in retaining 'women' as the focus of feminist thought while rejecting 'woman' as a fixed or essential identity, defined in relation to 'man' (Riley 1988). It has been difficult for feminists to avoid the suggestion that their understandings of gendered identities are essentialist (although most of them strenuously deny the charge). Postmodern thinkers claim that modern notions of social identity, such as gender, race or class, are too fixed, static and ahistorical to be able to grasp how people's powers of producing multiple identities are actually exercised. There is considerable confusion in these criticisms between general challenges to essentialism (which are also well developed in feminism) and more clearly targeted challenges that examine the difficulties of wholly escaping essentialism while retaining a political commitment to 'women' (Fuss 1989; hooks 1994).

Postmodern thought has been particularly influential in exploring how diverse, variable and unstable identities can be. The notion that people are socially located by social class, gender, sexual orientation, race, ethnicity, or any other social category, gives way to claims that multiple and shifting identities are produced through how what is 'true' is established and struggled over. Like the knowing subject, each identity has a particular history in a particular culture; it is a state of *becoming*, rather than one of *being* (Brah 1992; Hall 1990). Subjectivity itself can be conceived as an effect of language. Discourses of identity can be examined to see how, for example, what is 'properly' feminine/masculine, what is a 'good' sexual reputation, whether one may be intersexual, is established in particular cultures, and how these identities can shift and change.[7]

The ways identities are performed, established and regulated have powerful effects on people's lives but these are socially organized and so may be resisted. This is not a one-way process as the subordinated can also contribute to the meanings of dominance and distinctiveness. Gayatri Spivak (1987) has suggested the notion of strategic essentialism to indicate the mobilization of identities for political purposes by subordinated groups.

A postmodern approach need not demand that identities such as woman/man, Hindu/Muslim, black/white, gay/straight, have to be abandoned, but does insist that, like the knowing self, they should be interrogated. Interrogation means that their histories should be questioned, the constitution and crossings of their boundaries examined, and their multiplicities enabled, in order to show what makes some identities powerful in relation to others, and how this power is exercised. Such processes of interrogation, however, are not neutral; they do not escape the power relations that shape processes of knowledge production and political mobilization more generally.

Freedom from universality and ethnocentrism: playing language games with local truths

Postmodern thought takes claims to universality, such as the claim that 'women' want or need 'liberation', as expressions of western ethnocentrism. Derrida suggests that, 'If one had to answer, therefore, the general question of what is deconstruction a deconstruction of, the answer would be, of the concept, the authority, and assumed primacy of the category of "the West"' (cited in Young 1990: 19). Feminist approaches to method have been caught up in this assumed primacy.

Jean-François Lyotard (1984) attacks the legitimacy of 'modern' (and so feminist) claims to general knowledge on the grounds that these are dependent on grand narratives of emancipation, science and progress. Feminism's grand narrative is women's liberation. This tells a story (metadiscourse) of patriarchy that is legitimated through reference to a dream of universal emancipation to which all women should subscribe. Grand or metanarratives are totalizing and universalizing social theories that claim to stand for all time and, presumably, places. 'A metanarrative is a story that wants to be more than just a story, that is to say, one which claims to have achieved an omniscient standpoint above and beyond all the other stories that people have told so far' (Norris 2000: 28). Feminism can be easily dismissed if critics use Lyotard to ignore its diversity, and characterize it as a monolithic, modern metanarrative (of patriarchy), trapped in essentialist assumptions and confined to foundationalist epistemology.

In place of claims to universal knowledge, Lyotard argues that all 'truths' are local rather than general because they are produced within the rules of particular, limited, language games. The rules of each game (or way of producing knowledge claims) produce particular ways of authorizing what counts as knowledge (Lyotard 1984: 60). In this view, feminist methodology is one language game among others, with its own rules for deciding what counts as authoritative knowledge. The 'truth' of 'women's subordination' cannot then hold good in other ways of thinking with other rules (for example, across patriarchal sciences, or across cultures). This is a critical challenge to feminism. The language of modern feminism is linked to a language of rights, ethics and politics that assumes a common humanity, and some shared interests between women, but it is this connection that Lyotard specifically disrupts (1984: 7).

Since Lyotard denies any universal standard that allows judgements to be made between 'truths' produced in different language games, he does not allow feminists to judge some stories as truer, or better founded in experience, than others. Viewed through his requirement of incredulity towards grand narratives, feminism is illegitimately caught up in a 'totalizing obsession' in its struggle against male domination (Lyotard 1993: 7). Feminism can be seen not only as humanist and universalizing, but also as terrorizing, in imposing a dream of emancipation on 'women'.

One implication of Lyotard's ideas is that while feminist knowledges may be 'true' within the rules of a feminist methodology, *it does not matter* that there is no position from which one 'truth' can be judged against another. Lyotard's postmodern researcher does not discover 'the truth', but simply tells stories – though there is a duty to verify them within the terms of the relevant language game (Lyotard 1984: 60). Relativists can embrace this position, but feminist politics requires judgement between claims to knowledge in order to identify unjust power relations and provide accurate understandings of what might be changed. Even when feminists welcome postmodern theory, a sense emerges from the literature that the separation of general claims of justice and morality from limited knowledge claims is somehow to be resisted (Hekman 1992: 189-90; McNay 1992). The freedom from universalizing theory that postmodern theory offers is salutary, but also politically, ethically and practically problematic.

Freedom from material embodiment: regarding the body and sexuality as socially constituted

The deconstruction of essentialist and binary categories frees up thinking, not only about gender, but also about how sexuality and bodies are socially produced. A central tension in feminist debates has long been over whether, or how far, sexuality, gender and reproduction are cultural rather than bodily states, and how embodiment can be understood (Caplan 1987; Jackson and Scott 1996). The ever-present threat of slipping into essentialism means that postmodern theories of the body can offer relief. Postmodern thinkers acknowledge that the body has a material existence – we cannot prevent ageing and death – but they treat material existence as socially constituted and given meaning. Judith Butler, for example, argues that the materiality of bodies does not tell us anything about how they are also social (1993: x–xi). Bodies are matter, but not matter with some sort of independent existence.

If meaning is given *to* the body rather than residing *in* the body (for example, constituting pregnancy as a medical problem, or as a mark of adult womanhood), new questions can be asked about how the truths of bodies are told, what sexual difference means and whether or not the body ends at the skin (Bordo 1993; Grosz 1994; Haraway 1991; Martin 1989; Shildrick 1997).

Foucault's analysis of the disciplining and regulation of bodies, the normalization of regulation, and the production of 'docile bodies' (1984a, 1991a) does not ask what the truth of the material body is, but how meaning is mapped onto the body, and what sort of bodies are socially constituted in different situations. Carol Smart (1992) draws on Foucault to argue that in Britain the constitution of women in bodily terms, with its corollary of male mental superiority, has been very powerful. In the nineteenth century, 'discourses of law, combined with medicine and social science, brought into being a problematic feminine subject who, at the moment of her constitution, "self-evidently" required regulation' (Smart 1992: 30–1). Around terms such as 'prostitute' or 'motherhood' arose associations, terms and conditions which defined 'natural' realities that justified interventions. The discourses that constructed women's bodies as unruly and in need of disciplining were powerful, but they could be resisted in 'stark struggles over meaning' (as continuing struggles over abortion, contraception, childcare and sexuality indicate) (Smart 1992: 31). However, the 'feminine' had already been produced as problematic and naturally in need of regulation (Smart 1992: 32).

Alongside feminist work, postmodern thought has been particularly productive in showing how sexuality and embodiment can be made to appear
natural and material through the way truths are told; and through how binary
categories (such as masculine/feminine) are related to each other. For feminists,
however, the materiality of the body is potentially a significant site of gendered
difference, and this remains a sensitive and disputed issue.

Freedom from power as a possession: understanding power as productive

Feminism's general theory of male power, patriarchy, has taken a knock in postmodern attacks on totalizing metanarratives. Feminist ideas of emancipation
emerged from the binary thinking and humanism of modern thought, from
women's experiences of living in male-dominated societies, and from the possibility of women having collective interests. Postmodern thought offers escape
from seeing women as oppressed by male power, and undercuts any general
political project of emancipation and empowerment for women. Judith Butler,
for example, allows that feminists can question the conditions under which
agency becomes possible, but that agency itself is part of the workings of power
that it opposes (1995: 136–7). Emancipation, in her view, cannot transcend
power. Postmodern thinkers reject the idea of the human subject bringing about
progress through rational, purposive action.

Some feminists gratefully, if critically, turn to Foucault's theory of power as
more productive than notions of emancipation for understanding male power
(Ramazanoğlu 1993).[8] A major theme running through Foucault's work is the
need to examine relationships between knowledge and power, and he argues
that these cannot be assumed without investigation.

> I know that as far as the general public is concerned, I am the guy who said that
> knowledge merged with power. [. . .] If I had said, or meant, that knowledge was
> power I would have said so, and having said so, I would have had nothing more to
> say, since, having made them identical, I don't see why I would have taken the trou-
> ble to show the different relations between them. (Foucault 1988b: 264)

Foucault did study domination and physical power (in studies of prisons
and madness, for example), but he moved increasingly to a position that denied
that power was a repressive force, was located in particular institutions, or came
from a dominating class, gender or race. While feminists draw on women's
experiences to theorize men's power as dominating and institutionalized, or as
violent, repressive and illegitimate, Foucault defined power as productive in the
sense of producing knowledge, rather than repression. 'In general terms, I
would say that the interdiction, the refusal, the prohibition, far from being essential forms of power, are only its limits, power in its frustrated or extreme forms.
The relations of power are, above all, productive' (Foucault 1988a: 118).

He suggests that this productive power is everywhere in society, like blood
running through capillaries. Power struggles are about the deployment of
power; how truths are told and power is exercised. Women and men are socially

constituted in relation to each other in discourses, with all the trappings of practices, laws, interventions, that this brings. Foucault argues that people are much freer than they feel because they can tap into the power to deconstruct the socially constituted 'truths' within which their sexual or other identities are constrained (Martin 1988: 10). Female subordination can be transformed through the production of new discourses of sexuality (for example, allowing women to have positive feminine desires beyond those of motherhood and satisfying men). This enables researchers to see women's collusion in the exercise of power, and opens up the fields of masculinity studies and queer theory.

Foucault's research method of genealogy explores not who has power, but rather the patterns of the exercise of power through the interplay of discourses. He traces particular examples of how power is produced, exercised and made legitimate at particular historical moments, looking at how different forms of knowledge can run through similar institutional structures (Foucault 1988b: 265). His particular focus is on the micropolitics of power, rather any broader institutional or societal congealing of power. This positions feminists as asking the wrong questions in seeking a specific source of power (men) and a system of repressive power (patriarchy).

If Foucault is right, this relieves feminists of having to explain where men's power lies and why it is so hard to shift institutionalized power structures, since no dominant group simply possesses power (Foucault 1984a). Male power, or class power, or white power, or ablebodied power is then constituted in dominant discourses of natural superiority that have real effects on social relations and practices by specifying and authorizing what counts as truly superior/inferior.

Postmodern thought has been very productive in enabling feminism to escape the limitations of its modernist roots and think differently and imaginatively about sexuality, gender and power. But in discussing the freedoms it offers we have also suggested some of the problematic implications for feminism, and so points of resistance to merging feminism into postmodernism.

Thus far but no further? Feminist resistance to postmodern thought

Postmodern thought itself can be seen a specific form of knowledge, emerging at a particular time, telling particular truths, and constituting a particular version of modernity to which it is opposed. Feminists can make their own deconstructions of the historical specificity of postmodern ways of thinking and their effects (Bauman 1988; Mouzelis 1995). Some feminists ask why it is just at the point when feminists are staking claims to knowledge, defining female subjectivity and seeking women's emancipation that a particular academic constituency deconstructs epistemology and the knowing subject, and flees into versions of relativism that preclude justifying political action on emancipation (Braidotti 1991; Lovibond 1989). Christine Di Stefano claims that 'postmodernism expresses the claims and needs of a constituency (white, privileged men of the industrialized West) that has already had an Enlightenment for itself and that is now ready and willing to subject that legacy to critical scrutiny' (1990: 75).

Feminism is undermined by postmodern thought if feminists are lured into an academic agenda of male-centred philosophy, relativist deconstructions and abstracted theory in male-dominated institutions. This agenda disparages methodology with its knowing subject as an outmoded, humanist, modern way of thinking, yet still regulates how feminists may think about thinking. This constrains how knowledge is authorized, what questions can be asked about material relations of power, and so what feminists may or may not legitimately say about gendered social existence. Despite the potential productivity of deconstructing how we think, what is deconstructed can remain largely abstracted from everyday experience. Moira Gatens states that 'writing, speaking and thinking about alternative ways of understanding human being, sexual difference and socio-political life are themselves forms of political struggle' (1991: 136). But she argues that there are also struggles around economic, legal, social and political arrangements that are crucial to social change. Postmodern theorists have been accused of depoliticizing feminism, but postmodernism is not apolitical. The effects of pluralism and relativism on feminism fragment feminist politics and can allow accommodation to existing power relations rather than insisting on subversion.

Feminist researchers have to consider how political struggles around subjectivity, writing, speaking, thinking and producing/interpreting texts are incorporated into methods of social investigation (Lury 1995). They can grasp the advantages offered by postmodern thinkers, whilst appraising their limitations in making connections between ideas, experience and the realities of people's lives. The problem is how best to strike a balance between empirical investigations of embodied and material differences, power relations and inequalities, and critical reflections on how knowledge is produced. In striking this balance, feminists have identified a number of sticking points that mark reluctance to abandon the entire legacy of humanism and scientific method. These sticking points produce divergence between feminists as they respond to them in differing ways, and also divergence between postmodernists, so a clear line of battle cannot be drawn. In the rest of this chapter we note points of tension affecting the survival of feminist methodology in struggles around the knowing subject, embodiment, institutionalized inequalities, emancipation and the connections between politics, ethics and epistemology.

The knowing subject, agency and epistemology

Deconstructions of the knowing subject undermine the knowing feminist/woman, indeed undermine the category 'woman' as the subject and agent of feminist politics. But, just as postmodern thinkers can decentre rather than kill off the knowing subject, feminism need not abandon 'women' as a political category. Denise Riley comments that although instability in the designation 'women' is something that feminists must face, 'it would be wildly perverse to deny that there can be any progressive deployments of "women" – all the achievements of emancipation and campaigning would be obliterated in that denial' (1988: 98). Judith Butler argues that difficulties in establishing what 'woman' means does not mean the category of 'women' should not be used politically (1992: 15–16). She does not contest the political necessity within feminism 'to speak as and for *women*'; the problem is how to connect this political position with knowledge claims about women – the constituency for whom feminism speaks (Butler 1992: 15).

Feminists can both deconstruct the subjects who produce postmodern knowledge, and the political effects of this knowledge, and also move on from deconstruction in actively constituting new knowing subjects. Nancy Hartsock draws on Marxism to suggest that the subordinated can 'engage in the historical, political and theoretical process of constituting ourselves as subjects as well as objects of history' (1990: 170). This engagement enables feminists both to retain some notion of people's ability to shape their own future (as socially constituted moral agents with the capacity to conceptualize and resist domination), and (albeit problematically) to retain the notion of 'women-insofar-as-they-share-common-experience-and-interests' as the constituency for feminist knowledge.

From a feminist perspective, postmodern thought need not be seen as beyond epistemology. Postmodern thinkers themselves make knowledge claims, some of which seem to have become established as general truths. Rather than feminists being required, for example, to take on trust that power is everywhere and cannot be possessed, that gender is performative, or that hybridity is powerful, these knowledge claims can be investigated, qualified and contested, and their knowing subjects deconstructed. Since postmodern thinkers produce knowledge, they have an implicit epistemological stance on what counts as knowledge, though their epistemologies differ from those of modernity. They deconstruct rationality, but continue to propose reasoned arguments.

Foucault argues that it does not matter who is speaking (who produces knowledge), because what matters is what rules authorize what is said and what effects knowledge has (1991b: 72).[9] Janet Ransom (1993) responds that it does matter who is speaking because feminists have to struggle with the boundaries of what women share and do not share. These struggles cannot be resolved at the level of theory or discourse analysis since they require knowledge of women's diverse experiences and the structures of social divisions. She claims that 'feminism requires the development of a methodology which acknowledges the presence of the speaker in what is spoken' (Ransom 1993: 144). The postmodern intellectual is not a voice from nowhere, and postmodern analyses do not escape their own political effects.

Donna Haraway argues that epistemology remains part of the solution to judging between competing knowledge claims, and that criticism of the failings of humanist feminism should not leave feminists 'lapsing into boundless difference and giving up on the confusing task of making partial, real connection. Some differences are playful; some are poles of world historical systems of domination. "Epistemology" is about knowing the difference' (1991: 161).

For feminist researchers, the nature of relationships between people and how these are constituted, structured, investigated and understood remains a central political, ethical and epistemological concern.

Embodiment and emotions

The freedom from essentialism offered by postmodernism still leaves a problem of how to understand bodily differences and control of people's bodies, and what difference bodies and emotions make to gendered social life. Feminism differs from postmodern thought in starting from how it feels to be subordinated. This feeling is emotional rather than intellectual and may lack expression in existing language. Maureen Cain argues that Foucault's 'concern for the suppressed discourses has been shared in feminist work' (1993: 94). But she argues that feminist epistemology must reach beyond Foucault in order to allow for realities that people experience (which could include 'sexual harassment', 'forced marriage', 'ethnic cleansing') before they have been constituted as such in particular discourses. People may have no name for what they feel, or may feel traumatic experiences more sharply than everyday subordination (Berlant 2000: 42).

Feminists struggle to find useful ways of recognizing both that social lives are lived in material bodies, and also that bodies and emotions are, in significant respects, socially produced and culturally variable. The subordination of women is a matter not only of the meanings of gender, sexuality and bodies, but also of actual bodily experiences. Discourses of menstruation, childbirth, illness, ageing and disability, for example, vary over time and between cultures, affecting how these events are experienced, defined, regulated and valued. But pregnancy, illness, disability or assault are not just consequences of how meanings and social resources are managed. These are also bodily experiences that exist in part outside their social constitution. Postmodern thought has been very productive in analysing how embodiment is produced in language, and with what consequences, but bodily impairment, ageing and sexual and reproductive differences are not wholly matters of language.

Moira Gatens suggests that while bodies do get discursively constituted, inequalities of power would be illuminated by 'addressing politics from the standpoint of entrenched bodily differences such as sexual difference' (1991: 138). Feminists should still be able to ask whether the enormous success of male power over women, throughout much of history and across very many societies, has any connection to embodied differences (Ramazanoğlu 1995). Such questions need not entail prior essentialist assumptions, and can enable the exploration of discourses of embodiment as well as investigation of embodied existence. To explore what material embodiment contributes to gendered existence is not to claim that people are their bodies, nor does it dispute the claim that people can model their bodies into what they believe to be natural, desirable or status-conferring states. The contribution of bodies to gendered existence remains particularly difficult to grasp (and is likely to be further complicated by developments in genetics, neuroscience and reproductive technology).

Material reality and persistent institutionalized inequalities

Postmodern thinkers do not deny their own material embodiment, or that they live in a material world, but postmodern thought cannot specify connections between experience and material realities. Judith Butler (1993), for example, rejects the view that gender can be freely chosen, but her theory of gender as performative is not able to explain why gender gets performed and institutionalized in some ways rather than others, or the extent and persistence of male domination. Her approach could show, for example, how western women who lose their hair through illness, ageing or medical treatment can perform 'baldness', thus creating new and positive feminine identities for bald women, rather than wearing scarves, hats or wigs to perform more conventional femininity. But deconstructions of what is performed and how positive baldness can be empowering do not include analysis of the materiality of disease, or of structural and institutionalized relations of inequality (for example, differential access to resources for obtaining wigs).

The effects of taking on one identity (bald and proud) rather than another (bald and embarrassed, or bewigged and feminine), or shifting between multiple differences, have compelling consequences in terms of social exclusion and inclusion. But people are not free to become any identity. Young people in the UK have produced positive identities as 'Black British' or British Asian', in much the same way as 'Hyphenated Americans', but they cannot choose to be white. The poor cannot choose to be wealthy. Femininity, masculinity, intersexuality, being ill, can be performed in different ways, but shifting sex requires chemical and surgical intervention; transformations of reproductive capacity are still limited, policies of social inclusion require transformations of production systems and the distribution of resources. Postmodern thought conflicts with feminism where a focus on processes of becoming, and on the subtle possibilities of multiplicity and instability, ignores the cruel constraints on choice that limit so many lives, the ubiquitous structures and institutions of inequality that vary life expectancy, quality of life and experience more generally. Benita Parry argues for knowledge of the oppositional violence that is actually experienced: 'Those who have been or still are engaged in colonial struggles against contemporary forms of imperialism could well read the theorizing of discourse analysts with considerable disbelief at the construction this puts on the situation they are fighting against and the contest in which they are engaged' (1995: 43).

Connections between power, resistance and emancipation

Discomfort with women's complicity in the exercise of power (through treating their privileges as natural, merited, innocent or unquestioned) unravels any simple focus on women's subordination to men. Feminism thus loses any clear project of resisting male power in order to achieve women's emancipation. In investigating a postmodern, liberatory research practice, for example, Patti Lather celebrates the freeing of emancipatory intentions from the constraints of modern binary thinking and its aims of mastery. She comments that postmodern thought serves to 'celebrate the dispersion and fragmentation that has displaced the ideal of a global, totalizing project of emancipation' (1991: 164). However, practical questions remain about the nature of gendered inequalities, actual structures of domination and how unjust power can effectively be opposed. In commenting on Lather's warnings about the dangers of feminism's emancipatory practices, Mary Maynard warns that the 'anti-totalising totalisations of post-modern discourse may, ironically, degenerate into new regimes of truth' (1993: 329).

Foucault's theory of power as productive has been helpful for feminists, but was not intended to explain the institutionalization of domination, inequalities of resistance, and so actual gendered power relations. He has written on knowing sex, but not on knowing gender (Bartky 1990: 65). Postmodern thought does not explain why men still dominate so many areas of political and economic life, why women's empowerment has proved so limited, and why feminism's vigorous counter-discourses are so often disempowered. Foucault's theory, for example, does not deny that men are privileged by hidden relations of power, and that these are hard to discover, but he does not enable a researcher to establish why power becomes institutionalized in some ways rather than others, why some 'truths' become discursively constituted as authoritative and powerful while others do not, or how to challenge male power effectively. Bartky (1990) concludes that even though Foucault's critique of power sounds a liberatory note, he still reproduces the sexism of western political theory.

Jean Grimshaw (1993) suggests that since Foucault sees power as everywhere, it is difficult for him to distinguish between malign and benign forms of power, which inhibits an adequate theory of women's resistance to power. Feminists approach this difficulty differently by being reluctant to abandon a moral commitment to women. This leaves them with responsibility for general social criticism and for judging some power to be malign. They are then vulnerable to criticisms that their universalizing justifications are improperly ethnocentric and dominating (Lather 1991; Sawicki 1991). Pauline Johnson argues that feminism still has to grapple with the contradiction in modern humanism between the universalism of its ideals and the particularistic viewpoints from which this universalism is expressed (1994: 22). Since humanism is not innocent (Johnson 1994: 135), feminists face practical problems about how emancipatory goals can be set and met, how differences can be addressed, and how different voices can be heard.

But while many feminists are happy to say goodbye to a grand theory of patriarchy or emancipation that ignores divisions between women in favour of recognizing difference, saying goodbye to their own emancipation is a different matter: 'How can anyone ask me to say goodbye to "emancipatory metanarratives" when my own emancipation is still such a patchy, hit-and-miss affair?' (Lovibond 1989: 12).

Feminists have had a limited impact on practical transformations of male domination of public life and production systems, rigid gender categories, sexualized racism, nationalist conflicts, corruption, interpersonal violence and war more generally. Successful resistance requires access to resources, countering partiality in policing and judicial practices, and having effective influence in the public sphere. New truths and positive new identities can still be marginalized, disparaged or silenced (as the identity of 'feminist' has been). Violence, or the threat of violence, in every area of society from the bedroom to the state is still a common and everyday means of regulation in most of the world.

Connections between politics, ethics and epistemology

Even when feminists welcome postmodernism, there is criticism of the political and ethical implications of postmodern thought, and resistance to the separation of justice, morality and politics from knowledge claims (Hekman 1992: 189-90). Feminists need not argue that postmodern thinkers are uninterested in ethics, but can investigate how, or whether, localized and contingent knowledges actually escape male-centredness and ethnocentrism, or the various sites of privilege from which postmodern thinkers speak. Postmodern thought offers feminists understanding of the limits of feminist thought rather than means of transcending them.

In identifying what is unjust and should be transformed, feminists draw on general criteria of judgement that should apply universally, but which can only be justified in particular political and ethical schemes (Ramazanoğlu 1998). Feminists are in the contradictory position of being confined to local truths, but living in a world shaped by global interrelationships. They need valid knowledge of the range, diversity and interconnections of gendered social life in order to judge what power relations are and how/whether they should be changed. They can neither prescribe a common ethical programme across women's differing value systems, nor leave moral judgements as abstract and ethical practices as local.

Feminist methodology implies a connection between politics, ethics and epistemology, whether researchers like this or not. The alternative seems to be 'an open-ended commitment to a plurality of values that cannot be determined in advance' (Shildrick 1997: 211), and so the fragmentation of feminism. Shildrick suggests that feminists should offer 'radical openness to multiple possibilities of becoming' (1997: 212). This leaves them in the contradictory position of thinking (as does Shildrick) that some behaviours *are* better than others, but of losing any general moral criteria against which to judge them. Since this contradiction cannot be resolved, feminists can only be pragmatic about choosing their ethical positions and political identities, making these explicit, making themselves accountable for the knowledge they produce, and interrogating their own constitution as knowing subjects.

Conclusion

While postmodern thinkers do not speak with one voice, the various freedoms that they offer beckon feminism away from any lingering modern humanism. In its place feminism can fragment into a plurality of feminisms, with a shifting interplay of rules, truths, selves, localities, communities, histories, discourses and ways of exercising power. Feminist methodology has no postmodern grounds for continued existence across these fragments. If fragmentation is accepted, feminist efforts to connect knowledge, experience and reality must be judged defective and ineffective. Attempts to improve on feminist methodology through postmodern thought can transform feminist research into critical interrogations of the social constitution of selves, knowledges, identities, subjectivities, desires, realities and their effects. This can threaten an endless questioning of deconstructions, and deconstructions of questioning (Elam 1994).

Feminist researchers can, however, keep their moral agency and emancipatory impulse in exploring what 'women' do and do not have in common. Feminist knowledge encompasses movement between partial knowledges, limited experiences and specific social locations, and justifiable, accountable, reasonable knowledge of social interaction, experiences, meanings, relations and structures. The rules of postmodern thought do not generally allow this movement, and so render feminist hopes of political transformation incompatible with postmodern thinking. But feminists do not have to play postmodern games by their rules. Feminist researchers can choose not to abandon investigation by knowing subjects of specific power relations, their intersections, histories, materiality, morality and effects, and can dispute claims that these are unknowable.

Feminists need not reject postmodern thought, or ignore criticisms of modern notions of methodology. But taking up the productive freedoms that postmodernism offers does not escape epistemology or dispense with the problems of what connections are made or refused between knowledge and power, or between ideas, experience and reality. Feminist and postmodern thinkers continue to have different concerns, because of the centrality in feminist knowledge of women's experience, of the normative framework that justifies feminist resistance, and of the goal of political alliances and emancipation. These concerns also divide women, but remain integral to the politics and methodology of feminist research.

Postmodern thought has had a considerable impact on English-speaking social theory, but often in ways that undermine or devalue investigation of the social relations of everyday life in favour of questioning culture, and deconstructing texts, representations, discourses and performances.[10] There is a danger of distancing practical empirical investigations from critical questioning of modes of thinking. Much feminist engagement with postmodern thought has tended towards an abstracted and theoretical level. If connections between politics, ethics and epistemology are to be taken seriously, feminist researchers cannot avoid critical reflection on ideas, theories, abstractions, how these are constituted, and with what effects. But they can also confront the problems of understanding real social divisions, of grasping the diversity of women's (and men's and others') everyday experiences, and the factors that shape and constrain them. In Chapters 6 and 7, we consider the problems that remain for feminist social researchers in empirical investigations of gender.

Notes

1. For a clear and critical exposition of key elements of poststructural and postmodern thought as postmodern theory see Best and Kellner 1991, and for a general introduction, Sarup 1993.

2. There are numerous accounts of encounters between feminism and postmodern and poststructural thought, e.g. Barrett and Phillips 1992; Benhabib 1992; Braidotti 1991; Buchanan and Colebrook 1999; Feder et al. 1997; Griffiths 1995; Hekman 1992, 1996;

Holland 1997; McNay 1992; Nicholson 1990; Ramazanoğlu 1993; Waugh 1992; Weedon 1997.

3. Linda Tuhiwai Smith (1998) points out that Maori women, when asked for their life histories, did not proceed in a western chronological order or with a sense of themselves as an individual. They started by situating themselves in their current genealogical relationships with others and in their community's history.

4. Foucault calls a particular way of thinking of this sort an 'episteme'. This is the 'discursive apparatus' (as opposed to science's accompanying practices and institutions) that regulates what is to count as scientific knowledge. The notion of episteme enables Foucault to show discontinuities in thought (rather than a steady accumulation of scientific truths) and how powerful discourses can be. Science and rationality themselves are particular ways of expressing and authorizing knowledge in a particular episteme (Foucault 1991b).

5. We do not have space to address the complexity of Derrida's notion of deconstruction or whether or not he resists pinning down any consistent meaning or method as deconstruction (Derrida 1987; Norris 1987). The version of deconstruction that we draw on does not imply that what has been socially constructed must be the outcome of some agent that does the constructing. We leave this as an issue requiring investigation in each case.

6. Hekman notes that this reading of Derrida and deconstruction is not uncontested. Some feminists have suggested that both Derrida and deconstruction attempt to erase difference and/or deny the feminine, leading to Di Stefano's notion of 'the incredible shrinking woman' (Hekman, 1992: 175). Flax (1990) suggests that Derrida still works with a binary distinction between men and women.

7. The influence of postmodern thought on the deconstruction of identities is also linked to shifting relations between feminist and psychoanalytical thought (Benjamin 1986; Brennan 1989; Grosz 1990). Subjectivity is reconceived in terms of social and historical processes, requiring new investigation of how differences are constituted, and how emancipation can be possible. Jacqueline Rose notes that feminists find in psychoanalysis one of the few places in western culture where it is recognized that women do not fit painlessly into femininity (1983: 9). She concludes (1983: 19) that feminism needs the insight that femininity is difficult for women (and presumably the corollary that masculinity can be difficult for men [Holland et al. 1998]).

8. There are variations in how postmodern thinkers conceptualize power. Best and Kellner (1991), for example, illustrate something of the detailed differences between Foucault's and Deleuze and Guattari's conceptions of power and desire. Deleuze and Guattari (1983, 1987), while conceptualizing micropolitics, and seeing subjects as produced and controlled in everyday life through desire and culture, argue that 'politics is simultaneously a macropolitics and a micropolitics' (1987: 213). They are concerned with changing capitalist society and, unlike Foucault, have a theory of the state.

9. Foucault says he has tried

> to explore scientific discourse not from the point of view of the individuals who are speaking, nor from the point of view of the formal structures of what they are saying, but from the point of view of the rules that come into play in the very existence of such discourse [...] to give it, at the time when it was written and accepted, value and practical application as scientific discourse [. . .]. (1973: xiv)

10. There are, however, productive explorations of new possibilities (for example, Hall 1997a; McRobbie 1997; Scarry 1994; Skeggs 1995a).

6

Researching 'others'

Feminist methodology and the politics
of difference

Introduction

In this chapter and the next, we return to the methodological problems confronting feminist social researchers that postmodern thought does not resolve. These come, in particular, from the contradictions of wanting to tell better stories of gendered lives across people's differences. Feminists are caught in a now familiar methodological and political dilemma. First, they cannot access the realities of gendered lives directly. Second, they have no general rules for deciding between competing accounts of gender. Nevertheless, if they want to understand and transform unjust gender relations (and the interrelations of gender with other unjust power relations), they have to be able to judge between different representations of reality. Seeking to judge some stories of gender as better than others (rather than just different) requires critical decisions in feminist research practice. Different decisions have led to some diversity in feminist methodological strategies. In this chapter we look at some aspects of the politics of difference in feminist research practice.

Any attempt to explore the lives of others through empirical social research brings feminists up personally against conflicts of interest between women, as well as involving them in conflicting ways of conceptualizing gender and difference. Problems are experienced particularly strongly in interviewing, ethnography, oral histories, focus groups and other methods of direct personal contact, since social researchers have the power to represent the lives and ideas of the researched as similar or different across any divisions between them. Making knowledge claims across differences means taking responsibility for interpreting the social existence of others, and so is normative, personal and political as well as epistemological. This responsibility also exists in constructions and deconstructions of representations and objects that produce knowledge of gendered relations (Griffin 1994). In their texts and activities feminists reproduce or contribute to knowledges that have effects on people's lives, and can identify, or ignore, hidden power relations.

Confronting difference in feminist social research

There are a number of ways of conceiving difference in feminist theory that we cannot pursue here (Barrett 1987; Felski 1997a; Scott 1990; Young 1985). Modern feminist theory uses the idea of difference to mark differences of political interest between women, men and others, and also to identify social and economic divisions between women (and so also between men and others) resulting from, for example, capitalism, racism, colonialism, heterosexism, ablebodiedism. More abstracted postmodern and psychoanalytical theories deconstruct these categories, their social constitution, effects and instabilities. Notions of difference conceptualize how people are actually situated in relation to others, and also what these differences mean and how they are constituted, regulated and experienced (Walkerdine 1997).

People do not necessarily agree on how to express their differences, and most people's lives have contradictory aspects. Most women, for example, have some emotional ties to men (brothers, fathers, other kin, partners, sons, friends), and are divided in some respects (class, ethnicity, ablebodiedness, nationality, religion) from other women. Expressions of women's diverse political interests, and of previously silenced or marginalized voices, can transform feminist debates through focus on what divides women rather than on what they have in common. Zinn and Dill comment: 'Gender differences and gender politics begin to look different if there is no essential woman at the core' (1996: 323).

In practice, interrelations of gender relations with other forms of power, and other social divisions, lead to continuing political fragmentation. As feminism has no political centre, women can make of it what they want, and can continue to disagree with each other (see, for example, Crossley and Joyce 1996). But feminist researchers can still investigate what is happening across women's differences, and why. Many feminist researchers have been cautious about the epistemological, political and ethical consequences of fragmenting feminism, and they can counter postfeminist fragmentation (see note 5) with strategies of alliance between 'women' (and between 'women' and 'others'), rather than with strategies of deconstruction or diversification.

In social research, researcher and researched always stand in some social relationship to each other, but these relationships are rarely balanced, or ones with fully shared meanings. Feminist research relationships need critical examination rather than any prior assumption of shared female identities, or of 'being women' (Spivak 1988; Wilkinson and Kitzinger 1996; Wolf 1996). Judith Stacey comments that feminists can suffer a 'delusion of alliance' (1991: 116) if they assume common interests in woman-to-woman research. Even if researchers identify politically with the people they research, they are still constituted as particular knowing selves, in particular social situations, are generally located in hierarchical relationships, and have the power to distance the researched from their experience (Smith 1989).

In any empirical social research, dealing with differences ethically and skilfully in specific situations is anything but simple. In some ways, attention to difference encourages feminists down divergent methodological paths. In other ways, the politics of difference pulls them back to a common focus on ethical issues in acknowledging and managing the exercise of power in knowledge production. Feminist knowledge is worked out in practical struggles over exactly what people do and do not share in their conditions of existence, but these are also struggles over how, or whether, connections can be conceived between ideas, experience and reality. These are not only philosophical and epistemological problems, but also practical matters of research skills and ethical practices.

Our case for feminist methodology necessitates looking at the implications of exclusionary practices in feminist research, and the power of researchers to decide what they have in common with those they research, and how difference can be represented. Making this power explicit raises uncomfortable problems about conceptualizing and managing the relationship between the researcher and researched. In the rest of this chapter we consider the pressures on feminist social researchers to respond to the politics of difference.

Being different: the constitution of 'otherness'

The researcher is in a potentially powerful position to specify what differences exist, what they mean, whether they matter, and how they should be represented in research findings. This power lies in the authority, or effective ability, to name difference and to specify the boundaries and meanings of relationships. 'Difference from' has to be conceptualized in relation to something else that is deemed 'not-different'. This is not just recognition of human diversity – to recognize, for example, that some people are settled, while others are nomadic. The binary thinking that characterizes western attributions of superiority and inferiority both differentiates between the 'self' (the same) and its 'other' (the different) and actively constitutes a social relationship privileging the 'same' who has the power to name, subordinate, exclude or silence the 'other'. This is the power, for example, to define settled people as normal, as (universally) how people should be, and to constitute nomadic people as 'other', as abnormal, as not belonging, as subordinate and as lacking rights. The 'otherness' of the nomad, viewed from the standpoint of the nomad, can identify settlers as exercising unjust power. From the standpoint of the settled population, being settled can be taken as natural, invisible and of no account. The normality and dominance of the 'settled' is constituted through its difference from the category of 'nomad'.

'Otherness' came into western feminism as a way of seeing how 'woman'/'feminine' has been socially constituted as what 'man'/masculine (the norm, humanity) is not. Woman is not only man's 'other' but is in a dualistic relationship of social subordination to man (Beauvoir 1953). Simone de Beauvoir's analysis of this dualism aims to rescue women from subordinated femininity and the female body.[1]

Various concepts of 'otherness' as constituting a structural relationship of inequality have been widely taken up within feminism.[2] Dualistic positioning of subordinated femininity is not simply a western conception, but a more widespread (though by no means universal) relationship of separation and subordination that can take differing forms in different cultures. Fatima Mernissi, who was born into an urban, domestic harem in Morocco in 1940, challenged the social frontiers of her existence when she was a small girl by asking why, if men and women had to have separate spheres, men could not be on the inside of the harem and women on the outside (Mernissi 1995). But a binary conception of man and his 'other' assumes common identities of 'woman' and 'man' that cannot be sustained across all experiences, bodies, histories, cultures, representations and relationships. Examination of how 'others' are constituted, through what relationships, and with what effects, has also been turned on feminists themselves by those whom feminists have constituted as 'other' (Hall 1997b; Mohanty 1988; Spivak 1988).

'Otherness' (or 'alterity', from the Latin word for other) sits somewhat awkwardly in English (which is why we have given it quotation marks). Here it indicates the process of constituting/being actively constituted as 'other' in relation to 'one', rather than having a fixed, authentic or essential identity or social location. The idea that 'otherness' is a fluid, socially constituted, repeatedly performed relationship, rather than a stable essence, challenges the notion of an 'other' as naturally different from, and properly subordinate to, a dominant category of normal self. This challenge has come particularly from struggles around conquest, nationalism, capitalism, globalization, gender, racism, heterosexism and ablebodiedism that identify unjustified power relationships in divisions between them/us, knower/known, inside/outside. These struggles are those not only of language and meaning, but also of material differences in quality of life, personal liberty, access to resources, state regulation, legitimated violence, and so on. Feminists do not have a unified theoretical or political position in these struggles.

The power to decide what difference is measured against, and how the 'different' shall relate to the 'same', is not equally available to researcher and researched, nor equally to all researchers. Differences between women are matters not just of theory, ideas or identities, but of historical experiences, discourses, relationships and everyday practices of social life. Struggles arise in intellectual debates on the meanings of difference and the effects of these meanings, but they are also the outcomes of experiences of the injustices and constraints of everyday experiences of 'otherness', and of resistance to being actively subordinated. Feminist researchers may be powerful in relation to particular research subjects, yet marginalized in their own academies. Struggles over who can speak, and what they can say, can be violent where dominant 'selves' exert force in keeping their 'others' subordinated.

Edward Said's conception of 'Orientalism' (Said 1978) exposes the power of the West to produce knowledge of the East (the Orient) as the subordinated 'other' of the West. Said questions how the power of knowledge production has been exercised in representing subordinated peoples against the norm of those in power. Like feminists, he makes explicit connections between ethics, politics and the study of human experience. Said sees in the power relations that constitute Orientalism a human failure to see human experience *as* human experience. Privileged western feminists cannot escape their complicity in this human failure (Afshar and Maynard 2000). Chandra Mohanty (1988) shows how, by the 1980s, many western feminist texts constituted 'third world women' as a unified, stable category of analysis. This category comes from the vantage point of the political interests of western feminists, and establishes 'third world women' as uniformly oppressed and powerless, thus leaving western feminists as the true subjects of feminist history (Mohanty 1988: 79). Mohanty adds that 'it is only in so far as "Woman/Women" and the "East" are defined as *Others*, or as peripheral, that (western) Man/Humanism can represent him/itself as the centre' (1988: 81).[3]

Feminist researchers are exposed as particular, socially constituted, knowing selves with the power to constitute their own 'others' as subordinate. This power is vested not in a free-floating feminist subject, but in specific, and so variable, powers of communities, institutions, locations or discourses in producing selves and identities, in maintaining the boundaries of privilege and dominance, and in regulating relationships between self/'other'.[4] Feminists are no more immune than other social researchers to arrogance, ignorance, complacency, academic insecurity, power hunger or limited capacities for self-knowledge, empathy or patient listening.

A politically and ethically significant impact on feminist research has come from those who personally experience the constitution of 'otherness' as oppressive, unjust and immoral, generating anger and resistance. Just as feminists feel anger at women's constitution as man's 'other', so subordinated women resist their constitution as the 'others' of privileged women. Anger at being constituted as 'other' in a relationship of subordination brings up empirical questions about how particular social relations of difference have been constituted and, consequently, about what, if anything, women actually have in common across their differences (Begum 1992; Collins 1990; Mirza 1997a; Morris 1993). The deconstruction of the category of 'woman' is not only an effect of postmodern reflections on how categories of thought are constituted, it is also a very powerful consequence of experiences of conflicts of interest between women. 'If the white [feminist] groups do not realize that they are in fact fighting capitalism and racism, we do not have common bonds [. . .] then we cannot unite with them around common grievances' (Beal 1970: 394).

Starting from personal and community experiences of violence, social exclusion, being silenced, and how these experiences feel, provides varied perspectives on the politics of gender relations. Awareness of how differences are constituted in research relationships and given meaning produces different positions on understanding the differences in gendered lives. Feminism has been shaken by the anger, pain and sense of injustice that comes from subjugated voices gaining public space, and expressing resistance to being constituted as 'other'.

Being different: experiencing and resisting 'otherness'

The potential multiplication of postfeminisms, with their celebrations of diversity, might seem to offer a painless solution to the political and methodological problems of taking account of difference.[5] There are ways of acknowledging difference that can accommodate 'otherness' through valuing cultural specificity, through diverse voices entering public spaces, and through the recovery of subordinated histories. This accommodation allows the celebration of difference as cultural specificity, and multiplies the differences that can be recognized (Smith 1999). Henrietta Moore comments that there seems to be no limit to demands for recognition of difference because this resists one self being overwhelmed by another (2000: 1132). If differences and specificities can be documented without power relations between researcher and researched being examined or taken personally, the celebration of diversity can be a relatively comfortable position for researchers to adopt. But proliferating difference need not have any radical effect on understanding or transforming critical power relations between the 'same' and its 'other'.

There is a critical distinction between, as Adele Murdolo puts it, 'difference as benign diversity and difference as disruption' (1996: 69). This is the distinction between acceptance of multiplicity and cultural diversity, and more radical political challenges to the constitution and organization of difference in practice. Much postmodern thought, like liberal humanism and patriarchy, can tolerate the existence of social and cultural multiplicity without challenging the material bases of inequality. Henrietta Moore argues that the idea that identities are matters of multiple affiliation is easier to accept philosophically than to act on politically (2000: 1130). It is more radical, but more difficult, to identify relationships of difference in terms of unjust power relations between particular people. It is open to social researchers to ignore the political significance of any relationship between the researcher and the researched, but this does not erase relationships that exist, the experience and knowledge of the researched, the power the researcher can exercise, or the moral and political implications of ignoring these.

Radical resistance (from either researcher or researched) lies in identifying power and injustice in relationships of difference. It is questioning these relationships and how they are experienced that encourages campaigns for democracy and civil rights, religious and cultural freedom, gay rights, disability rights, indigenous people's rights, and other strategic expressions of identity politics. Putting resistance into practice depends on identifying the relation between the 'one' and the 'other' as located both in discourses of otherness and in the institutionalization of power. This does not mean, though, that all those who are similarly politically positioned in categories of difference necessarily share the same consciousness or experiences, or produce the same knowledge claims, just as women need not achieve a feminist standpoint. Fatima Mernissi (1995) describes tensions between those women in her harem who accepted their position as right and proper, and those who experienced their enclosure as unjustly imposed by men and dreamed of growing wings in order to escape.

Feminist researchers can access the power to constitute themselves as 'same' and so to position themselves in relation to their 'others' in terms of powerful binary oppositions. James Clifford comments that ethnographers set out to interpret 'others', but that in practice they construct their own selves in constituting the 'others' whom they study (1986: 10). Sara Ahmed (2000) argues that when people meet strangers, these are not wholly strange. A stranger is somebody the knowing self already knows, since 'the stranger' is already constituted as 'strange' in a relationship with the familiar. Ann Laura Stoler (1995) suggests that during the European colonial period, a distinctive, gendered, European bourgeois self developed. This self emerged in the racialized and sexualized context of colonialism that generated social boundaries around what it meant to be 'truly European'. The practices and discourses of colonizing 'others' produced what was distinctive about European selves. Those constituted as 'other', however, can multiply and diversify their 'otherness', proliferate difference and actively produce confusion, hybridity and ambivalence (Bhabha 1996). Proliferating difference can unbalance and disrupt the stability of privileged selves, and so the relationship between 'self' and 'other'.

Complications of difference

Beyond abstracted categories of 'otherness', researchers face the complexity of interlocking and shifting relations of difference in practice. Stuart Hall argues, for example, that racism operates by constructing 'impassable symbolic boundaries between racially constituted categories' (1992: 255) in what Gayatri Spivak (1988) terms the 'epistemic violence' of discourses of the 'other'. But binary categories of racism are considerably complicated by ethnic categories. Ethnicity diversifies the specific histories, cultures and experiences from which people speak (Hall 1992: 258). Valerie Walkerdine's (1997) analysis of the constitution of working-class subjectivities identifies the disciplining and control of working-class femininity in complex interactions between popular representations of classed and gendered identities and people's consumption of popular culture. These various complexities are significant in social relations between researcher and researched.

Those who are collectively constituted as 'other' can be divided by multiple forms of power, and by social divisions within and between categories of identity, community and locality. This can destabilize any social location or system of boundaries. There are numerous divisions, for example, between women who are socially constituted as 'Asian' in the UK (including variation by language, regional origin, religion, ethnicity, class, sexual orientation, ablebodiedness, local politics, caste or generation). Those who are socially located in the same category can feel differently about similarities and differences. People have differing experiences of what it feels like to be socially included or excluded, successful or subordinated, vocal or silenced. Complicated interrelations of difference and 'othering' can build up since researchers and researched can be positioned in both dominant and subordinate positions in relation to varied 'selves' and 'others' (Bhopal 1997), some of which are much more rigid than others.[6]

Ien Ang (1996) notes that Homi Bhabha and other writers on postcolonialism and postmodern theory have identified a place of ambivalent existence for minority subjects who are located between the 'same' and the 'other' (for example, colonial subjects who negotiate identities with their colonizers, or privileged 'Asians' in the West). They see this space as providing the potential for hybrid identities to challenge binary oppositions. Bhabha suggests that strategies of hybridization open up spaces for negotiation where power is unequal but where, somehow, agency exists in the interstices of the exercise of power that can give new meanings to minority communities (1996: 58). Ang, however, cautions (from considering 'Asian' women in Australia) that this complexity does not necessarily confer freedom. The power of ambivalence can be limited to a space in which minority subjects are confined as well as embraced. 'Ambivalence is not only a source of power but also a trap, a predicament' (Ang 1996: 46). Varying claims about the power of ambivalence, hybrid identities and the agency of 'others' in resisting their 'othering' show the problems of making abstracted, and so general, claims to knowledge about and across differences. The power of ambiguity or hybridity in relation to boundaries of 'same'/'other' differs in different situations; it cannot simply be assumed without investigation.[7]

Since the diversity of political spaces for negotiating 'otherness' cannot be asserted in general, researchers need to examine what is similar and different in any given research situation. Different relationships of similarity and difference affect how people constitute, manage and resist particular boundaries, and with what agency and consequences. Martin and Mohanty (1986) argue that feminists should unsettle boundaries and identities to show how particular personal and political alliances can be renegotiated. If complex negotiations are facilitated in interstitial spaces, and the researched can resist their 'othering', the specificities of relationships between researcher and researched can be examined. This means that any social investigation requires skilled strategies for recognizing the potential complexity of social categories, relationships and meanings. Unfortunately, it is precisely this requirement of understanding relationships of difference and 'othering' that is so hard to manage in representing gendered lives, and has led to divergence in feminist approaches to representing 'others' across differences.

The politics of representing 'others': the privileged researcher

Much feminist discussion of the politics of representation concentrates on how to recognize and take account of the privileges and power of the feminist researcher, and how difficult this is to achieve (Wilkinson and Kitzinger 1996). It seems difficult for those who are privileged (for example, by class or material advantage, racism, heterosexism, being ablebodied) to recognize their own contributions to the maintenance and reproduction of relevant discourses and institutionalized power relations in their everyday practices. Just as men have found it difficult to see the parts they play in gender subordination through unthinking discourses and practices of masculinity, feminist researchers have found it hard to take their privileges personally.

Some feminist researchers, especially students or junior academics, may not appear to exercise much power. Others may choose to study those like themselves (Smith 1999) or more powerful than themselves (Luff 1999). All social researchers, however, can exercise power by turning people's lives into authoritative texts: by hearing some things and ignoring or excluding others; by constituting 'others' as particular sorts of research subjects; or by ruling some issues as extraneous to 'proper' knowledge (D.E. Smith 1998). While postmodern thinkers have questioned how the meanings of difference come to be constituted and with what effects, feminist social researchers experience actual and specific differences in relationships between researcher and researched. They must represent not only how difference is constituted in specific instances, but also how it is experienced, what it feels like, whether it is positive or just, and what resistance to change entails.

The complexities of difference position people in different areas of expertise on power relations, but this does not ensure that they interpret or express sameness or difference in the same way. The nature of 'otherness', as standpoint theorists argue, is potentially most firmly grasped by those with daily experiences of subordination and exclusion, but much depends on political consciousness. Rosalind Edwards (1996) provides an example of the difference that political consciousness makes. She identified herself as a lone mother and a former mature student in her studies of mothers and mature students, and so felt she had something more than gender in common with her research subjects. But she then experienced the behaviour of some black women as a problem because they not only refused her invitation to be interviewed, but collectively complained about being invited. Edwards had not seen the significance of her own powerful position that made her appear to these research subjects as 'an untrustworthy white institutional figure' (1996: 85).

Bola et al. (1998) argue that Edwards could feel her black critics had judged her wrongly because she did not see herself as a racialized subject and her whiteness as powerful. Well-intentioned identifications in terms of structural locations and aspects of identity (gender, locality, sexual orientation, race/ethnicity, class, and so on) can make knowledge claims appear authoritative and moral without ensuring critical examination of the impact of these social locations on the researcher/researched relationship. bell hooks comments that white American academics have found it easier to accept black women as needy than as powerful (1994: 107–8). Powerful black women threaten white women's unspoken privileges by making them visible and unmerited. (Privileged women in other societies can adopt similar positions in relation to their own 'others', particularly in differences between middle-class, urban women, and women in rural areas [Basu 1995; Mohanty 1988].)

Heidi Mirza comments: 'Postmodern theory has allowed the celebration of difference, the recognition of otherness, the presence of multiple and changing subjectivities. Black women, previously negated and rendered invisible by the inherent universalizing tendency of modernity, finally have a voice' (1997b: 19). bell hooks also acknowledges that postmodern theory has made a space for 'difference' and 'otherness' to be discussed by academics, but she still finds ignorance and absences. She is very critical of the power of postmodern thinkers to discuss difference without any 'critical black presence'. She charges that American writers on postmodernism 'seem not to know black women exist or even to consider the possibility that we might be somewhere writing or saying something that should be listened to' (1991: 24). The voices of the researched have a critical part to play in the production of feminist knowledge, but they may have to struggle against considerable odds to be heard, or to be heard on their own terms. If they are not heard, then knowledge production proceeds without them.[8]

Accusation or confession of unmerited privilege, without other changes, can leave relationships of difference in place (Friedman 1995). Apologizing for privilege does not change established relationships (Patai 1991). The institutionalization of privilege is not dismantled by changes in socially constituted identities, or by liberal erasure of 'otherness'. (Claiming that everyone is the same under the skin, and that there is no need to notice difference, allows the privileged to ignore institutionalized power relationships.) The interconnections between 'otherness' as abstracted theory and 'otherness' as lived experience remain morally, politically and epistemologically significant for feminism.

Leaving difference out of research without acknowledgement has implications for what knowledge feminists produce, what power relations they consider, and whom they constitute as absent. Martha McMahon (1996) comments on the difference it made to recognize childless women as absent from her study of motherhood. She saw how her theory of motherhood was affected by her own childlessness, and by perceptions of her unmarried, childless aunts as women whose lives had not been worthwhile.

There has been particular awareness of the political and epistemological significance of silence and absences in ethnographic studies, since these arose in the context of imperial and colonial conquests where subject peoples were available for study by ethnographers from dominant societies (Spivak 1988; Stacey 1991; Wolf 1996). Ethnographers are presented very directly with the task of understanding people across barriers of language, culture and meaning, as well as across barriers of the privileges constituted in colonialism, imperialism and capitalism. Judith Stacey (1991) argues that there are two particular areas of contradiction for feminist ethnographers. First, fieldwork is always unequal and potentially treacherous, since everything in the lives and deaths of the researched is grist to the ethnographer's mill. Second, the researcher remains powerful as author of the research text, and this includes the power to expose research subjects to harm.

Researchers working in their own societies face power relationships and barriers to understanding that may be less apparent. But Michelle Fine and Lois Weis say that when ethnographers 'came home' from studying other cultures, and began to study their own societies, their informants could move next door and read the books that had been written about them (1996: 271). The possibility of the researched judging what the researcher has made of them considerably sharpens the problems of conceptualizing and representing 'others', and markedly problematizes relationships between researcher and the researched. Researchers, however, are often protected by producing texts for specialist academic consumption that are not intended to be available to non-specialists. The knowing feminist uses rhetorical devices in a given genre, as we are doing here (the textbook, the monograph, the journal article, the lecture, the seminar, the public meeting, the thesis, the essay), to convey a persuasive interpretation to a given audience.

The possibilities for sharing knowledge are limited when researcher and researched have no political interests in common. But Fine and Weis try to bring their rhetoric and politics out into the open, while also making visible their activity as privileged authors studying poor and working-class people in the US.

> [W]e are still a couple of White women, a well-paid Thelma and Louise with laptops, out to see the world through poor and working-class eyes [. . .]. We work with activists, policy makers, church leaders, women's groups and educators in these communities to try to figure our how best to collect data that will serve local struggles rather than merely to document them. [. . .] We write through our own race and class blinders, and we try to deconstruct them in our multiracial and multiethnic coalitions. (1996: 270–1)

They note, however, that while 'more than a few Whites see us as race traitors [. . .] a good number of people of color don't trust two white women academics to do them or their communities much good' (1996: 271).

The logic of acknowledging difference and seeking to avoid exploitation in the process of knowledge production may seem to limit ethical research practice to relationships between those who share as much as possible, and so are experts on each other. Linda Tuhiwa Smith (1999), from a Maori perspective in New Zealand, suggests that in the aftermath of imperial and colonial encounters, indigenous people can and should initiate their own research agendas within their own communities, making the knowledge their own. This could be seen as a version of standpoint or critical gaze. Her appeal to the reclaiming of Maori language, history, culture and values through indigenous research is thus also a political reframing of relationships between Maori and Pakeha (whites); not only a retelling of history from the inside, but also a challenge to existing political relations and so a claim to a Maori-centred story as a 'better story'. It is hard to see how this knowledge could be produced from outside Maori language, values, knowledge and experience.

However, the shifting complexity of identities, and the complex intersections of social divisions, make confining emancipatory research to insider knowledge difficult to achieve more generally in practice. Although, for example, Maori women can understand the culture and history they share with each other, they can also be differentiated by generation, locality, history, intermarriage with others, sexual orientation, education, class, experiences of other cultures, and so on. Linda Tuhiwa Smith works within a higher education system already removed from Maori culture, so Maori life is also being interpreted in terms that make sense to English-speaking audiences, and are persuasive in rewriting history.

The power of researchers to interpret their selection of data through their own ideas and values, and in terms of their chosen epistemology, remains dominant. A critical point in the politics of representing 'others' across difference is, then, the process of interpreting data.

The power of interpretation: data analysis

Producing knowledge through empirical research is not the same as acting as a conduit for the voices of others, or assuming that experience can speak for itself. Interpretation is a key process in the exercise of power. It marks a critical point of decision about the possibility or impossibility of connecting ideas, experience and realities, but also marks points of divergence, as feminists draw on different epistemological assumptions in making or refusing connections. The process of interpretation can be skilled, creative, reasoned and intuitive, but researchers cannot know for sure whether their connections and meanings can be justified, or what epistemological, ethical and political effects follow (Holland and Ramazanoğlu 1994).

Dorothy Smith comments that turning people's talk into academic texts risks 'reinscribing the moment of discovery of women's experiences as women talk with women, into the conceptual order that locates the reader's and writer's consciousness outside the experience of that talk' (1989: 35). The researcher cannot set aside her own language, life and understandings when she produces her interpretations (Smith 1989: 43). What is feminist in the process of interpretation is the theoretical framework, and the political and ethical concern with deconstructing power relations, and making the researcher accountable for the knowledge that is produced.

Some feminists have made particular efforts to take their knowledge back to the researched, to empower the researched through the research process, or to work on strategies for inclusion and alliance (Acker et al. 1983; Mies 1983). One strategy is for the researcher to negotiate interpretations of data with the researched where understandings conflict. This strategy, however, depends on a high degree of trust in the research relationship, and does not offer any consistent method for dealing with conflicting understandings among the researched, conflicting political interests or the ethics of informed consent.

Cathleen Armstead illustrates the difficulties of managing conflicting interpretations: 'I began my ethnographic research [of white, working-class women in the US] with a commitment to partial and multiple truths, sensitized to power relations and prepared for divided loyalties' (1995: 630). But dealing with divided loyalties meant that she took critical decisions in deciding how to represent these women. Where some expressed racism in ways that she did not share, she could have presented them as ignorant and bigoted. But she also understood them as constructing their own positions as clean, respectable, good mothers. In part, they did this by disparaging other women, including through racism. Armstead felt that her research should express women's understandings of their lives, but she also felt under academic pressure to present her findings in terms of existing theoretical categories that did not 'fit' these understandings (1995: 633).

Katherine Borland (1991) also illustrates the difficulties of managing disagreement in reporting on an 'interpretive conflict' with her grandmother, Beatrice Hanson, over their understandings of her grandmother's life. Borland (from her own feminist standpoint) tells Hanson's story as a struggle for female autonomy in a hostile male environment. Hanson furiously retorts that this is now Borland's story. 'You've read into this story what you wished to [. . .] the story is no longer MY story at all' (cited in Borland 1991: 70). Feminism was of no moment to Hanson, so she could not take a feminist standpoint in making sense of her life and her love for her father. Ten months later, Borland and Hanson worked on repairing their fractured relationship by negotiating a joint meaning for Hanson's story (Borland 1991: 74). This meant that the older woman accepted something of the feminist account of her life, but did so by moderating the meaning of feminism.

Rather than conflating the two accounts, Borland could have clarified and respected the differences between them by explaining why these stories of the same life differ. Merging conflicting accounts implies that they then represent one true reality. This position does not acknowledge that only partial, situated and contingent knowledges are possible, or that a shared theory, conscious-ness and normative framework are required in order to achieve a shared feminist standpoint. Borland and Hanson are differently situated in women's history, to which they bring different experiences and understandings. They each have different theories of women's interests, and so interpret the older woman's life differently. The decision as to whether one account is 'better' than the other is then contingent on criteria derived from theory and politics as well as from the (often contradictory) ways in which actualities are experi-enced and expressed. Acknowledging disagreement, inconsistencies and contradictions in interpretations of data helps to show the situatedness of the researcher's own position, and the specificity of her approach to connecting ideas, experience and reality.

In Holland et al. (1998) the researchers' interpretations of young people's accounts of their sexuality and sexual risk-taking were not explicitly shared by most of the young people, whose accounts were varied and often contra-dictory. The research team's conceptualization of the 'male-in-the-head' (the surveillance power of male-dominated, institutionalized heterosexuality) is rooted in interview talk (including hints and silences). But the team's con-clusions on heterosexuality were arrived at through the interaction of three levels of conceptualization: the terms and meanings offered by the young people and explicit in the data; the researchers' interpretations of these data in the light of their feminist theory and knowledge of their own experiences; and explanation of the differences between the understandings of researchers and researched (Holland et al. 1998: 222). This brings out the difference between young people's assumptions about 'normal' femininity and mas-culinity as complementary, and the researchers' interpretations of the largely hidden relations of institutionalized heterosexuality and dominant mas-culinity. It also explains contradictions and diversity in young people's accounts.

Feminist politics put pressure on researchers to consider how their own texts are produced, how power is exercised in the production process, and what gets constituted as extraneous, in the sense of being ruled outside the matter at hand (D.E. Smith 1998). Feminist researchers cannot determine in advance what inter-pretations can be made of their data, but they can reflect on how interpretation is made, what concepts, assumptions, and rules are drawn on, and why they use some categories rather than others (though this process of self-examination is not easy). There are critical differences (particularly between realist, empiricist and postmodern conceptions of reality) in how feminist researchers view the wider discursive, social, economic and political contexts of fieldwork encounters. There is also human variation in self-knowledge, empathy and imagination. Patricia Collins argues that 'who to trust, what to believe and why something is true are not benign academic issues. Instead these concerns tap the fundamental question of which versions of truth will prevail and shape thought and action' (1990: 202–3).

Language has powerful effects in producing meanings, so interpretation of data is like translation in constructing rather than just conveying meaning. Gayatri Spivak (1992) argues that feminist solidarity literally requires learning the other languages in which women express gendered existence. Bogusia Temple (1998) also links interpretation with translation in making the researcher responsible for what is produced, and what gets lost, between the researched and the researcher. Translation and interpretation of data are processes of knowledge production in which researchers are accountable for the understandings they produce. While there is a case that some issues cannot be translated between different modes of thought (Collins 1990: 232–3), there is also a case that hidden power relations should not be treated as only explicable in terms of local knowledges. It does not seem consistent with feminist politics to leave the powerful to enjoy knowledge of their powers, or to leave the subordinated to represent themselves only to themselves.

By treating interpretation as a political as well as an intellectual process, feminists can make sense of contested and unstable negotiations between the researcher and the researched. But people's lives are not open to just any interpretation. The researcher's conclusions need somehow to unite the contingency of knowledge of social life with a passion for telling a 'better story'. (This demands explicit criteria that can offer reasoned grounds for judging some conclusions to be stronger than others – an issue we return to in Chapter 7.) Given the impact of explicit and hidden power relations on social research, and the problems of making knowledge claims across difference, feminists have favoured processes of critical reflection, or reflexivity, to make these difficulties more manageable.

Reflexivity in the research process

Reflexivity as a principle of good feminist research practice is widely agreed. What reflexivity means, and how it can be achieved, is more difficult to pin down. Reflexivity generally means attempting to make explicit the power relations and the exercise of power in the research process. It covers varying attempts to unpack what knowledge is contingent upon, how the researcher is socially situated, and how the research agenda/process has been constituted. The distinctive feminist interrelation of politics and epistemology means that, despite differences in feminist approaches to knowledge production, the identification of power relations in the research process is generally seen as necessary.

Reflexivity is valued as critical reflection at a number of interrelated levels.

1 *Identification of the exercise of power, power relationships and their effects in the research process.*
2 *The particular theory of power that enables a particular conceptualization of power relations (hidden or otherwise) in this instance.*
3 *The ethical judgements that frame the research and mark the limits of shared values and political interests.* (This also requires reflection on any possible harm that could come from the research and how this should be avoided.)
4 *Accountability for the knowledge that is produced.* This includes reflections on what community of knowers (epistemic community) the researcher produces knowledge within, why researchers tell some stories rather than others, and how their knowledge is authorized.

The reflexive researcher needs effective practical strategies for achieving reflexivity with integrity at the four levels suggested here.

Feminism has perhaps been stronger on honourable intentions for examining power relations than on effective skills and strategies to enable fallible researchers to overcome limits of understanding, and the difficulties of seeing ourselves as others see us. Ann Phoenix (1994) comments on the difficulty of understanding which aspects of social location and identity actually impinge on any particular research relationship. Hidden power relations remain hidden if they are not imagined, but no rule of method can ensure the conceptual imagination and political insight that can make sense of hidden power. Exactly how accountability is arrived at, what trust can be built on, and how power should be theorized are disputed issues within feminism. These disputes mark points of divergence in understanding the complexities of intersecting power struggles in any form of social research, and also the problems of putting reflexivity into practice.

Feminist reflexivity is also an invitation to other voices to challenge the researcher's knowledge claims and conceptions of power (though academic feminists experience human difficulties in hearing criticism, and potential threats to academic careers in being openly criticized). But other voices may have limited means of challenge. Tikka Jan Wilson points out that Australian aboriginal women have been vocal critics of Australian feminism but, since they have limited access to public means of expression, their voices are not widely heard. Generally, interaction with feminism is a low priority on their 'very long list of pressing survival issues' (Wilson 1996: 20).

Any researcher's critical consciousness is constrained by the limits of their knowledge, culture and experience, and also by their personal skills, powers of empathy and political openness to silences and exclusions. Bola et al. (1998) argue that reflexivity cannot be an individual reflection, since researchers do not have this capacity as individuals. Reflexivity has to be both collective and contested because of the limits of individual visions and experiences. At least as an intention, reflexivity opens up possibilities for negotiation over what knowledge claims are made, for whom, why and within what frame of reference. Attempts to be reflexive are potentially productive despite human fallibility and the practical problems involved.

Conclusion

The problems of taking difference into account in social research are not directly soluble by methodological rules. Feminists cannot escape the complex interrelations of power that constitute them as knowing selves, and situate them in relations of difference. Taking account of difference in research practice is a sensitive, contested, personal and often painful process. There are often long and complicated histories behind women's differences that need skilled work in recovery, as well as political and emotional work in hearing them (Jones 1999). The skills and emotions involved should not be underestimated. Hallil Berktay, a Turkish historian working with Balkan historians to rethink their conflicting accounts of Ottoman history, describes their efforts as a 'kind of group therapy' (cited in Jones 2000). This is perhaps a useful concept for feminist researchers struggling with unmerited privileges, contradictory knowledges, incompatible frames of reference, conflicting value systems and hidden power relations.

The human agency of the researcher remains a critical level of moral action in interpreting and representing differences, even if our moral selves are themselves socially constituted. How researchers contribute to the negotiation of research relationships, and how they conceive power, difference and 'othering', affects the representations of actualities and experiences that they produce as knowledge, and their own accountability for this knowledge. The politics of feminism imply a general intention of sharing knowledge of what women actually do and do not have in common, and how their lives could be 'better', despite methodological and theoretical divergence between feminists. This gives feminist research the potential for using conflicting understandings productively and pragmatically in making alliances across differences.

Representations of difference affect what political coalitions are possible, since 'being a woman' is variously constituted in specific histories, localities, politics and cultures, and in particular relationships to patriarchal institutions, colonialism and capitalism (Mohanty 1988; Smith 1999; Tripp 2000). There is a difference between empowering individual research subjects and making any difference to entrenched, institutionalized power relations. Examining similarities and differences in women's knowledge and experiences, however, can provide some basis for generalization. It is from such (initially limited) generalizations that practical grounds for strategic alliances across differences can be considered, and common aims and interests conceived (Braidotti 1994: 105, 257; Lorde 1983: 100; Moraga 1983; Tripp 2000; Yuval-Davis 1997: 130),

Feminist research undoubtedly has radical potential for negotiating alliances across profound differences, for listening to experiences of 'othering', for addressing the effects of privilege, and identifying the situatedness and politics of any research process. The point of investigating gendered lives across difference is still to establish the best possible stories of diverse gendered social realities. Political transformation requires being able to judge between competing knowledge claims, and being able to locate the exercise of power in the production of knowledge. This makes it harder to reject the insistence by standpoint theorists that feminist knowledge is somehow grounded in women's experience. In Chapter 7 we take up the consequent difficulties of claiming connections between experience and reality.

Notes

1. Moira Gatens summarizes Simone de Beauvoir's claim that there is no necessary relation between femininity and woman:

> [W]oman today can escape the appellation of the absolute Other provided that she also escapes the female body and femininity and takes them as her (absolute) Other. The female body is other to her humanity, her subjectivity, in short, to her transcendence, which can be asserted only on condition that she escapes the grip of the female body. Man and woman may, at the level of consciousness, each be the other's other but the absolute Other remains essentially feminine. (1991: 59)

2. Thinking about how 'others' are constituted also draws on psychoanalytical theories of how we learn to be particular sorts of 'selves' distinct from 'others', and on reflections on how western thought subordinates its representations of what is 'other' (Kitzinger and Wilkinson 1996). Judith Butler cautions that inner psychic selves can be seen as a process of becoming in which a 'self' only exists in relation to its 'other', rather than as a stable state. She argues that neither heterosexual nor lesbian and gay identities are truly natural but are constituted in relation to each other: 'the disruption of the Other at the heart of the self is the very condition of that self's possibility' (1991: 27).

3. Reina Lewis criticizes Said's notion of Orientalism for treating the colonial subject as male, and questions how to take account of the diversity of what has been constituted as 'Oriental' (1996: 18).

4. Morwenna Griffiths (1995) usefully examines the complexity of how people come to be selves, and how the politics of identity can be connected to possibilities of liberation.

5. Ideas of postfeminism are responses to critical reflections on feminist achievements and failures, and to the diversification of feminism (especially the passing of a particular phase of feminist theory and politics from the 1960s to the 1980s) and the meanings given to these changes (for example, the shift from 'women's liberation' to 'girl power') (Coppock et al. 1995; Rosenfelt and Stacey 1987). Postfeminism tends to be contrasted with a version of unified, simplistic, western feminism with one political programme to be imposed on all women, and one history of 'waves', largely grounded in US history (Drake 1997; Garrison 2000; Orr 1997). Postfeminism can also be conceptualized as the effect of postmodern theories on thinking about gender. More generally it can imply that feminism is moving from prior simplicity into a positive new stage of multiplicity, especially from the 1990s (Brooks 1997). This stage celebrates women's diverse interests, as fragmented feminisms respond to multiplicity in women's lives and to the deconstruction of 'woman'. Feminist struggles remain, but feminist politics diversify. Postfeminism in this sense incorporates postmodern thought in deconstructing the foundations of feminist knowledge and politics (Barrett 2000) (with the consequences for methodology that have been considered in Chapter 5). Going beyond this position, to one which merges postfeminism with postmodern theory, leaves feminism without methodology, and without a notion of 'woman' (Hird 2000; Modleski 1991).

6. Rosi Braidotti (1994) suggests another version of agency in difference. She draws on Deleuze's notion of the nomadic subject as a means of deconstructing identity and so as a form of resistance. The nomadic subject is a political fiction that conceives the subject as simultaneously occurring in several social locations at once. What is nomadic is the critical consciousness that resists settling into socially coded modes of thought and behaviour. Felski (1997b) and Gedalof (1999) argue against this that it is easy for privileged westerners to refuse the constraints of particular boundaries of identity when the existence of their privileges remains unmarked. Braidotti's concept of the nomad does not

recognize that some historical and political specificities of actual relations between women in different social locations are much more constraining than others.

7. Feminists face particular problems of women employing women in exploitative relationships of domestic service (Andall 2000; Cock 1989; Gregson and Lowe 1994; Lorde 1983; Rollins 1985; Romero 1992; Sexwale 1994). Privileged women in developing countries with landless or subsistence farming populations are routinely dependent on the employment of personal servants, including men, producing complex dynamics of gender and class (Bujra 2000).

8. bell hooks has also noted a more subtle operation of exclusionary practices where the work of white feminists is accepted as 'theory' but the work of working-class women and women of colour is treated as 'experiential' (1989: 37), leading Deborah McDowell to question how the privileging of theory contributes to exclusion (1995: 106).

7

Knowledge, experience and reality

Justifying feminist connections

Introduction

One effect of postmodern thought on feminist research has been pressure to transform questions about what exists into multiple deconstructions of how people think about what exists. This leaves investigations of experience, embodiment and material reality, and the consequent problems of establishing criteria of validity, primarily as matters of language. These pressures have been productive but, since gender is more than language, a focus on language cannot explain all the relations of power, 'othering' and domination that structure particular gendered experiences (Friedman 1995: 38). Feminist social researchers are drawn back to some of the unresolved issues of modern thought. Questions about possible connections between knowledge and material realities, and about the validity of knowledge claims, creep back into knowledge production when the focus is on connecting knowledge and experience.

The passion in struggles over knowledge of difference comes from actual and personal experiences of difference. Feminists do not have any intellectual, moral or other authority to decide for others what their experience really is. However strongly it is felt, there is no guarantee that one woman's experience will be comprehensible to another, or that any one human being can ever fully understand themselves or others. Given these difficulties, it can seem reasonable to value personal experiences, but to write off experience as a critical connection between knowledge and reality, and so give up trying to ground feminist knowledge in women's experiences. In practice, however, feminist researchers have tended to be reluctant to take this step. The political expediency of having to choose between conflicting knowledges of gendered lives means that accounts of experience make a difference to what is known, and can change what counts as knowledge. Experiences, and how these feel, remain central to understanding similarities and diversity in gendered lives, and to investigation of inequalities, injustices and institutionalized power.

In this chapter we examine the case against taking experience as a source of knowledge and then consider whether feminists can make a counter case, using the example of knowledge of rape. Taking experience as a source of knowledge confronts feminist researchers with particular difficulties in connecting experience and material reality, and with problems of whether feminist knowledge requires criteria of validity or authorization within an epistemic community.

The case against taking experience as a source of knowledge

We take 'experience' in this context to be a loose, commonsense term referring to people's consciousness of their social existence.[1] Since the social realities and relations that people experience cannot be directly presented in research texts, researchers have to find ways of representing them or declaring them to be inaccessible. Representation of the social realities of the researched, and interpretations of experience, are ways of claiming (or disclaiming) particular connections between people's experiences, the theory, language and ideas that make sense of these experiences, and the realities that are experienced.

The methodological difficulties of founding feminist knowledge on women's experience are explored by standpoint feminists, but have been decisively attacked both by postmodern theorists and in older criticisms of empiricism and its limitations. Empiricists can suggest various connections between experience and reality through claims that evidence and experience can provide empirical adequacy by establishing testable connections with reality (Longino 1994; Nelson and Nelson 1994).[2] In defence of feminist empirical adequacy, Nelson and Nelson argue that empiricism should include critical examination of how knowledge and adequacy is constructed (1994: 489) (but these examinations too would have to be established as adequate).

Critics of empiricism generally sweep aside any argument that people can make connections between ideas and reality from their own experience, because this experience cannot be communicated independently of the ideas in which it is expressed. Experiences have to be expressed in some language (oral, written, body, sign) that is already part of a specific way of thinking in a particular culture, period and location. What is important for postmodern critics is not to connect experience with reality, but to deconstruct how people think about connections, and so focus on the power of language, or performativity, to constitute social realities.

> It is still common for those who express interest in the study of experience to confront an objection that runs something as follows: 'You cannot really study experience, because all experience is mediated by language – therefore one can only study language or discourse, i.e. representation.' (Csordas 1994: 11)

In representing others, feminists (like other social researchers) do have to conceptualize relationships, social locations and boundaries, to interpret meanings, and to make sense of experiences that they personally may not have had in the same way, or at all. These conceptualizations and meanings are shaped by the researcher's language, theory and ontology.

Feminists have been criticized for having simplistic beliefs in experience as a direct source of general knowledge of material social realities. Judith Grant (1993), for example, sees the core tenets of Anglo-American feminist theory as flawed, including the claim that feminist knowledge can be grounded in experience. She argues that since actual women have varied experiences, any claim that feminist knowledge is founded in experience requires an abstract, universal category of 'women' and results in a tautology: feminist theory is derived from raw experience that is only known through feminist theory (Grant 1993: 156). Feminists could accept that knowledge does not simply flow from experience, but Grant's accusation of tautology depends on a conceptual separation of theory and experience that is unrealistic in practice (as Dorothy Smith [1997: 393] argues against Susan Hekman – see Chapter 4). Feminist knowledge of gender is framed by theory, but if theory is not grounded in, and informed by, women's knowledge of their experiences, it is hard to see what is feminist about it.[3] Feminists have explored diverse ways of drawing on personal experience without losing wider connections to theory and material reality (Griffiths 1995; Stanley 1994).

Postmodern critics deal particularly severely with any attempt to treat experience as factual, since facts imply direct connections between knowledge and a foundation of material reality. Diana Fuss argues that facts themselves are socially constituted: 'experience is not the raw material knowledge seeks to understand, but rather knowledge is the active process that produces its own objects of investigation, including empirical facts' (1989: 118). Joan Scott (1992) criticizes historians' claims to factual knowledge in an argument that can also apply to any feminist case for treating experience as factual. She denies that an appeal to experience as 'uncontestable evidence' can stand up, because appealing to experience does not take into account the language through which people make sense of experience. Following Foucault, Scott takes experience to be a discursive construct. It is the history of the construct – the interpretations made of experience – that can be grasped, rather than the experience itself (Scott 1992: 37). Knowledge claims that are based on people's accounts of their experience are discursive and political constructs, and so simply identify what requires explanation. The tension between treating the same event as 'forced marriage' rather than problems created by 'undutiful daughters' (see Chapter 3) illustrates Scott's point. A change in political consciousness changes what is discovered as 'reality'.

A second criticism of experience as a source of knowledge is that any one person's experience will be limited, partial and socially located, and so cannot be taken as general knowledge of how social phenomena are organized as social relations. Feminists go beyond common sense and personal experience in order to claim knowledge of gender. The socially constituted knowing self is always partially grounded by the specificities of its existence. A person can experience an earthquake, for example, without any direct knowledge of its causes but, within their own culture and language, can make a particular sense of what has happened. Where one experiences a shift in the earth's tectonic plates, another lives through the wrath of God. While the unbeliever may find a theory of plate tectonics convincing, they may still look for meaning at the level of 'why me?' if they experience harm while others escape. If people generalize from their own experience (on which they are experts) or about people 'like themselves' (of whom they have insider knowledge), they will still only have a specific understanding of what happens to them, and this will affect how they connect their own experiences and social existence to those of others.

A third problem in making sense of experience is, as Descartes argued, that people can dream, hallucinate, be deluded and yet experience the evidence of their senses as real. Accounts such as those of alien abductions, ghosts, out-of-body experiences, premonitions, religious visions and other events that only some can sense make any clear boundary between actual and imagined events problematic. Different ways of thinking produce different boundaries and different meanings, and so different events. In contrast to Descartes's use of reason by the knowing subject to ensure certainty in his knowledge, postmodern thinkers embrace uncertainty. They dismiss experience as a source of general knowledge if the researcher assumes an extra-discursive, neutral vantage point from which a knowing subject can claim to know from experience what social/power relationships 'really' are. This offers the possibility of abandoning 'experience' to a relativist irresolution of multiple readings or progressive deconstructions.

If feminists accept the case that accounts of experience cannot be taken as reliable representations of a real world that is hidden behind them, this makes it problematic to claim women's experience as grounding feminist knowledge. Beverley Skeggs comments:

> I want to hold on to experience as a way of understanding how women occupy the category 'women', a category which is classed and raced and produced through power relations and through struggles across different sites in space and time. I do not, however, want to argue for experience as a foundation for knowledge, a way of revealing or locating true and authentic 'woman'. (1997: 27)

Feminists, however, need not make simplistic claims about authenticity or regard experience simply as evidence of reality. The argument against experience is less clear-cut, as Skeggs suggests, when accounts of experience are not regarded as factual. Gendered social relations and decentred subjects may be discursively constituted, but this does not mean that they do not exist. Embodiment, violence, institutionalized dominance, material resources, for example, produce experiences that are more than discourse or performativity.

Skeggs takes the Foucauldian position that it is not individuals who have experiences but subjects who are constituted through experience (1997: 27). 'This enables the shift to be made from experience as a foundation for knowledge to experience as productive of a knowing subject in which their identities are continually in production rather than being occupied as fixed' (Skeggs 1997: 28). While this may be a plausible argument, particular relationships between experience and knowledge cannot be assumed without investigation in specific situations. A feminist might ask how Skeggs knows that identities really are continually in production, or how particular experiences really produce particular knowing subjects. Skeggs' answers draw in part on her own experience, and on her empirical investigations in the light of her theory.

Making sense of experience, and of the diversity of experiences, has been a critical element in social and political transformation. Twentieth-century feminist claims that women in modern societies very generally experienced subordinated relationships to male power were founded in part on sharing accounts of experiences, and also on making new sense of them through new concepts (some experiences of 'marriage', for example, became experiences of 'domestic violence'). These interpretations had a powerful political impact when they resonated with women's sense of their own experiences. They also provoked political uproar and resistance when claims about gender subordination did not fit with women's experiences, or were culturally specific, or when they conflicted with dominant masculinist understandings. These strong emotional responses to feminist knowledge claims suggest that experiences of power relations can provide information on the realities of people's lives that is otherwise unavailable, and so that there is a case for grounding feminist knowledge in experience.

A case for taking experience as a source of knowledge

Outside debates on feminist philosophy and epistemology, the reasons for feminists insisting on retaining the possibility of connections between ideas, experience and material reality have probably been mainly pragmatic. Despite the problematic status of accounts of experience, they provide knowledge that otherwise does not exist. Although feminists take different approaches to the problems of interpreting experience, we argue that there is a strong case for taking people's accounts of their experiences as a necessary element of knowledge of gendered lives and actual power relations. While there are powerful criticisms of the methodological grounds of this case, the argument against ignoring experience as a source of knowledge is also powerful. Nelson and Nelson comment that 'the claim that theories which leave out entirely the experiences of those on the underside of society are likely to be suspect, or at least incomplete, is not outrageous. It smacks, in fact, of the obvious' (1994: 491). Despite the difficulties of making sense of accounts of experience in making knowledge claims about hidden power relations, and the problems of judging between knowledge claims, feminists have had to grasp the nettle of experience and face the consequences.

Ien Ang, for example, draws on her own experience to claim different knowledge of real, racialized power relations from that of white women:

> Time and again I have found myself in the uncomfortable position of realizing that I cannot bridge the gulf of difference separating me and my white counterparts, no matter how willingly they engage in the conversation (which is not, I should say, all that often when it comes to the personal politics of 'race'): there is always a residual personal truth, the irreducibly particular experiential knowledge of being the object of racialized othering, which I cannot share and the impact and repercussions of which they cannot ever fully understand. (1997: 59)

Ang's knowledge of these racialized differences is expressed in a particular conceptualization of experience, but her experience does not simply come from her theory of 'racialized othering', and her theory does not just come from reasoning. Theory and reason contribute to her interpretation of what she does and does not share with her white counterparts, and what the differences in their experiences mean, but Ang is also referring to actual conditions of existence: something that happens to her and not to her white counterparts, that affects the relationships between them and how these relationships are understood. The theory does not exist independently of the experience.

Although Joan Scott (1992) argues that experience can be only be accessed as a discursive construct and as a political construction, and so is not a reliable guide to what is real, she stops short at abandoning it altogether. There is a distinction between the claim that experience does not directly connect ideas and reality, and the claim that experience cannot tell us anything. She concludes:

> Experience is not a word we can do without. [. . .] It serves as a way of talking about what has happened, of establishing difference and similarity, of claiming knowledge that is 'unassailable'. [. . .] Experience is at once always already an interpretation *and* is in need of interpretation. What counts as experience is neither self-evident nor straightforward; it is always contested, always therefore political. (1992: 37)

Scott sees the historian's task as analysing how knowledge, including experiential knowledge, is produced, rather than treating experience as factual. Historians need not deny that experiencing subjects exist, but should focus on how these subjects are socially constituted (Scott 1992: 38).

Scott's critical questioning of how knowledge is produced from experience is a useful shift from the position of taking experience as simply connecting ideas and reality. But 'how' questions are not the only ones that can be asked. Feminists also need to establish 'what' experiences people have and 'why'. Questions about what an experience is like, and why it happens as it does, are not independent of how this experience is constituted in theory, politics, conceptions of injustice, and through the emotions of having, or not having, particular experiences. But these questions are not independent of something that happens. Accounts of experience are already interpreted in the ideas in which the people who have them express them, but these ideas do not come from nowhere. All experiences have social and cultural contexts (Skeggs 1995b).

Theories are not simply determined by experience, but there do not seem to be adequate grounds for claiming, in general, that experiences are wholly constituted by the theories and language that make sense of them. It is central to much feminist knowledge production that there is also something there to make sense of (although feminists are not agreed epistemologically or ontologically on how to deal with this issue [Stanley and Wise 1993: 132]). The case for grounding feminist knowledge, to some extent at least, in women's experiences seems to imply the necessity of making connections with extra-discursive realities – the hidden power relations that exist and happen outside language. These connections are difficult to justify, and we illustrate the problems and possibilities through the example of knowledge of rape.

Knowledge of rape: what can experience tell you?

Feminists have made the extent and meanings of rape a significant public and political issue. Accounts of rape illustrate both the necessity of grounding knowledge in experience, and the impossibility of treating experiential knowledge as simply true. The knowledge that comes from actual experience, emotion and embodied violation cannot make a clear and direct connection between: (1) feminist theory (or any other cultural conception) of rape; (2) people's experiences of raping/being raped; (3) an ultimate reality that is truly what rape is, independently of experience, language and theory. Feminists need to go beyond competing stories of experience if they are to produce valid knowledge of rape and its connections to sexuality and power relations.

To speak of one's own experience is not enough. Feminists have long claimed that the personal is political in order to alert the subordinated to common features of their subordination (for example, 'domestic violence') which may only be directly experienced as private and personal (for example, 'a bad marriage'). A wider debate on identity politics and expressions of pain raises problems about the complex connections between people's expressions of their feelings and afflictions, and more general knowledge of power relations. Bell (2000), Berlant (2000) and Probyn (2000) raise specific difficulties about connecting ideas, experiences and realities in considering how personal pain can inform collective political struggles to transform injustice. Experiences of rape are variable, and the meanings of rape are expressed in particular languages and ways of thinking. There are differences between legal, feminist, psychiatric and commonsense definitions of rape, and also cultural and historical variations in each of these. Rape is neither a single concept, nor a standard experience, so cannot directly connect a personal experience with a general power relation.

Feminists cannot, then, claim to know the sexual politics of rape by generalizing from personal experience, or within a single culture or period. However, Robert Scholes argues that there is a difference between having an experience and not having it, and especially between never having it, and having it again and again (1989: 99). Feminists take rape seriously because people have particular experiences. Sharing accounts of these experiences builds up not foundational facts, but knowledge of what the experiences conceptualized as 'rape' are like. Many similar accounts provide systematic information not only on the language in which experiences can be expressed, but also on what happens, how it feels, and how common the experience is. Feminists constitute the political significance of these experiences through the ways they are conceptualized in feminist theory. The theory and the experience are interrelated.

If the 'knowing self' that knows its own experiences is socially constituted, then, in producing an account of rape, a person becomes the author of a text – the story that they are telling. Rather than relating a 'fact' that simply connects their experience to some real structure, context or underlying relationship, the author cannot escape expressing their story in a particular language, style and set of assumptions, and addressing it to a particular audience. 'The author is not simply "subject" and the text "object"; the "author" produces him- or herself through the text' (Giddens 1979: 43–4). An account of rape can be told differently to the police, a counsellor, a partner, a child, your mother. In these accounts, authors produce themselves in terms that also exist outside the experience (as victim, as survivor, as terrified, as brave, as violated, as respectable, as innocent, as culpable). The author cannot fully control either the meanings in the text, or the effects that the text can have. 'These meanings are never "contained" in the text as such, but are enmeshed in the flux of social life in the same way as its initial production was' (Giddens 1979: 44).

Without experiential knowledge, however, there could be no general knowledge of what raping and being raped is. Rapists, lawyers, police, doctors, counsellors, activists, theorists, those who have been raped, and those who have not, can all produce knowledge of rape, what harm can be done, and what sense should be made of the event. This puts feminists in the position of having to decide how to judge between conflicting theories and accounts of rape, a problem that goes to the heart of feminist methodological struggles.

Susan Brownmiller explains why (in 1975) she wrote a book on rape as a political crime against women (rather than as an individual sexual act, or as a crime against male property). She recounts a dramatic transformation in her own understanding of well-hidden power relations when first hearing American women 'speak out' about their experiences of rape: 'what they came up with blew my mind' (Brownmiller 1986: 9). Much of the political impact of feminism in the twentieth century came from providing outlets for inexpressible personal experiences to be expressed. It was the mind-blowing impact of sharing silenced experiences and speaking out about areas of social life that previously had no public space that gave feminism in the 1960s and 1970s its sharp political edge (one that has become considerably blunted in subsequent academic attempts to be methodologically rigorous). Stevi Jackson comments that since Brownmiller made her very general claims about rape, '[f]eminists have become much more cautious about the dangers of sweeping cross-cultural and historical comparisons, much more reluctant to stray beyond the boundaries of our expertise, and habitually anxious about the criticisms other feminists might make of our work if we fail to carefully qualify every statement we make' (1997: 61). Brownmiller's lack of care in these respects brought widespread charges of essentialist and reductionist logic, and specific charges from African American women of collusion in racism, and of insensitivity to differences in women's experiences of rape (Davis 1982; hooks 1982; Jackson 1997).

Criticisms of Brownmiller indicate that any account of rape is already theorized, conceptualized and given meanings. Rape can also be silenced knowledge by being experienced as an extra-discursive reality that one may feel but have no language for knowing (Cain 1993). Access to counselling, exposure to feminist theory, or other forms of reflection can change the language in which an experience can be expressed, and so produce an experience of rape from an event that, at the time, had been experienced as something else (Holland et al. 1998). Speaking out, theorizing and political struggles develop together in making something out of people's experiences, but the events constituted as 'rape' also exist independently of their discursive constitution. Women's differing experiences are in part embodied, in part cultural, and in part shaped by structural divisions and differences in the material realities that enable and constrain people's lives.

The growing awareness, for example in the UK and the USA, of women as abusers, and of male rape by heterosexual men, has also had to be accommo-dated in feminist theories of rape. Until recently, very little practical or political support has been available to women abused by women, or to men who have been raped, and they have been left with the kinds of interpretations that were available to women prior to feminist interpretations (Kelly 1991). These inter-pretations, for example, make men who have been raped responsible for their rape, since somehow they must have 'asked for it' or consented to it. They con-stitute violation and assault as potentially pleasurable sexual experiences, and so position all men who have been raped as harbouring homosexual desires (McMullen 1990).

In contrast, feminists have constituted rape as an unethical exercise of male power, as a violation of the self, and as a particular, sexualized form of assault. Feminist theorists are not agreed on whether rape is primarily sexual, primarily political, primarily violent or some complex and variable interaction between these (Bell 1991). If knowledge of rape is grounded in the specificities of experi-ence, rather than general theory, however, different interactions of sexuality, power and violence can be expected in different situations. Feminist conceptions of, and political opposition to, rape come from situating experiential and emo-tional knowledge of what rape is like in the context of the judgement that rape is an immoral exercise of real, sexualized power that adversely affects people's lives. This judgement is clearly political and also potentially universalizing. Producing understandings of the many forms of rape, and judging what consti-tutes non-consensual assault and an unethical exercise of power, requires well-qualified and specific examinations of similarities and differences in expe-riences, of different social, cultural and political contexts, and the variable intersection of men's exercise of power with other power relations.

There are significant variations in experiences of what actually happens, as well as in understandings of rape. Sexualized power relations interact with other forms of power, particularly heterosexuality and racialized and classed relations. In the Indian subcontinent, for example, rape by the military, police or landlords has been used in specific nationalist and political struggles, and has needed to be conceptualized and resisted in these circumstances (Jahan 1995: 95; Kumar 1995: 68). Julia O'Connell Davidson (1998) analyses the diversity of con-texts and power relations within which adult and child prostitutes can experience or resist rape.

Christine Helliwell (2000) draws on Michel Foucault and Judith Butler to claim that rape has become both political and traumatic in a specific heterosex-ualization of desire in the West. She does not belittle the trauma and violence of rape, but argues that specific systems of male/female heterosexual opposition cannot be generalized to all societies. Helliwell takes her work in the Dayak community of Gerai, in Indonesian Borneo, as a case in point.

In this small community, rape and sexual assault did not occur and so were not experienced or conceptualized. Gerai women were puzzled by Helliwell's concept, since they could not see what harm a penis could do. In Gerai, per-sonhood derives not from gender, or the body, but from a sexual division of labour around rice production and human reproduction. Men are seen as stronger and braver than women, but also as nurturing, and not as sexually aggressive. Male and female genitals are differentiated only by being inside or outside the body. (Helliwell's gender remained in doubt because she clearly lacked elementary female rice skills, showed some male qualities and, as a westerner, could possibly have male genitals 'inside'.) Heterosexual intercourse in Gerai is thought to stem from mutual need, and is not accompanied by a heterosexual regulatory regime. In the absence of the theory and practice, there was no fear of rape or male sexual aggression (though there were fears of harm to rice and reproduction).

Experiences of rape in Gerai could presumably be changed, for example, by invading soldiers using rape as a political weapon. This would provide traumatic experiences comparable to those of many other parts of the world, but would not provide the same cultural meanings. If something happens in much of the world that does not apparently happen in Gerai, it is reasonable to insist that knowledge of rape should be informed by accounts of experience, without insisting either that accounts of rape simply tell the truth, or that theory/language/discourse can wholly constitute what experience of rape is. Feminists have to work out the grounds on which feminist theories of rape as political, sexualized violence and personal violation can be authoritative. They also need to attend to the possibility of other experiences in other contexts.

Rape cannot be known without being conceptualized, but similarities and differences in experience also need to be investigated at the level of accounts of experience. Robert Scholes distinguishes between *how* we know the world, and *what* there is to be known: '[R]eading a book is one thing, throwing it at someone is another. To be sure, the act of throwing can be read, but it is not itself only a reading. The world is a text, but it is not only a text' (1989: 91). Experiences of rape suggest that there is something to be known that is more than what gets constituted in theory and language. Feminists' focus on women's experience of rape and how accusations of rape are treated, rather than on men's experience of raping, has shaped feminist knowledge in particular ways. Rape is an area of encounters with reality that can illuminate hidden power relations, and so offer hope for change.

As feminists come under pressure to ground their knowledge in experience, they also come under pressure to reflect on the material realities of power. The knowing feminist cannot simply claim to know the truth of rape, but feminism's emancipatory impulse pulls researchers back into claiming connections between accounts of experience and material aspects of social existence.

The difficulties of connecting experience and material realities

If feminists want to make claims about people's experiential knowledge of material, social realities, they come up against the same argument – all that can be known is the language through which reality is discursively constituted. This makes 'reality' an effect of language, rather than a possible cause of experience. There is a clear epistemological split within feminism between those who believe that social relationships (such as patriarchal marriage) can exist without people being aware of them (Cain 1990), and those who criticize this realist epistemology on the grounds that the 'real world' is always socially constituted, and so cannot ever be 'discovered' (Haraway 1991: 198; Stanley and Wise 1993: 132).

Kate Soper (1993) argues, nevertheless, against severing the connections between experience and material structural inequalities when she questions Foucault's account of the 'Lapcourt incident'. Foucault uses this incident to give an example of 'the paedophile' being brought into discursive existence at a particular moment (Foucault 1984a: 31). Soper summarizes this incident as telling of

> a simple-minded farmhand from the village of Lapcourt [in France] who in 1867 was reported to the mayor for obtaining, as Foucault (1984a: 31) puts it, 'a few caresses from a little girl' [. . .]. The mayor reported the incident to the gendarmes, who led him before the judge, who indicted him (though he was eventually acquitted), and turned him over to a doctor, who contacted two other experts, who eventually wrote and published a report on the case. (1993: 42)

The point of Foucault's account is to show how all this discursive activity produces a new, deviant, sexual identity:

> So it was that our society – and it was doubtless the first in history to take such measures – assembled around these timeless gestures, these barely furtive pleasures between simple-minded adults and alert children, a whole machinery for speechifying, analyzing, and investigating. (Foucault 1984a: 32)

Soper suggests that connecting Foucault's account to some sense of what actually happened at Lapcourt can provide an alternative understanding. She accepts Foucault's analysis of the effects of discursive activity in bringing the 'paedophile' into existence, but she also considers the Lapcourt incident as a possible event of child abuse. Soper asks, does Foucault's interpretation have the effect of:

> exonerating, displacing and repressing the 'event' that it is really about: this 'alert' (terrified?) little girl, who runs to her parents to report her 'inconsequential bucolic pleasures' (her distress at being slavered over in a ditch by a full-grown, mentally-disturbed male?), thus summoning forth a 'collective intolerance' (alarm and sympathy?) over an episode remarkable only for its 'pettiness' (for the fact that something of this kind was for once accorded the attention it deserved?)? (1993: 42–3)

Soper considers whether Foucault's reading of this incident serves to shift attention from the reality of what happened at Lapcourt to the rhetoric of the discourse of sexuality that subsequently comes into being. She argues that child abuse neither precedes, nor gets constructed in, Foucault's own discourse.

Soper suggests that perhaps Foucault is right. Perhaps nothing very serious was going on at the edge of that field, and 'Foucault precisely targets, therefore, the degree to which "sexuality" is summoned into being out of a lot of discursive fuss about nothing' (Soper 1993: 43). But she also asks how Foucault knows that 'nothing' was going on. If he knows that there was nothing to justify the talk, then he appears to think that discourses of sexuality are about some extra-discursive reality. Why should anyone accept the 'truth' of his account of this reality? If child abuse is not simply trivial, its importance lies in the reality it constitutes, not just in the new set of beliefs, norms and values it brings into being.

Sue Wise (1999) comes to the same issue from a different perspective, by looking at the practical difficulties that feminist researchers face in specifying that discourses of child abuse are grounded in realities of experience. She reflects on her own experience in moving from being a social worker dealing with cases of child abuse, to being a sociologist looking at how 'child abuse' has been discursively constituted as a social problem. She argues that feminists should not be primarily concerned with establishing whether, for example, 'ritual child abuse' really exists or not. Since a connection between the concept and actual experiences can never be absolutely established, attempting this fruitless task can be emotionally draining.

Instead, Wise assumes that 'abuse' does exist, since she and others have experienced 'the daily, taken for granted and normalised existence of unspeakable acts of cruelty to children' (1999: 1.2). She urges feminist researchers not to become paralysed by the difficulties of justifying their connections between conceptions of child abuse and the realities that children suffer. She sees feminists as being caught in a similar situation to those at the extreme positions on Haraway's greasy pole (see Chapter 4), in which either they are criticized for failing to prove the 'facts' of abuse, or they accept 'abuse' as variably discursively constituted and so lose any way of connecting accounts of abuse with the everyday reality of experiences. Wise argues that feminists should put their resources into understanding what experience of 'abuse' means to people who experience it 'as terribly and terrifyingly real' (1999: 1.11), what consequences these meanings have, and how 'orthodox' notions of 'abuse' can be countered. Feminist research into child abuse can explore connections between ideas, experience and reality and investigate what political consequences follow from different connections.

Soper suggests that the same possibilities for seeking connections between ideas, experience and reality also apply to feminism. This means deciding whether the knowledge that feminism produces is actually about something. Otherwise, following Foucault, the significance of feminism only lies in producing new discourses through which it displaces previous 'truths' (Soper 1993: 44). Foucault's analysis is productive in showing the difference that new discourses can make, but Soper and Wise make strong arguments against severing child abuse, or feminism, from the material circumstances that give rise to them and the impact of these circumstances on human experience (Soper 1993: 45–6).[4]

Any claims that women's experiences are directly connected to underlying material realities can be contested. But people live in real bodies, in real social relationships, in a real world. These realities cannot be reduced to the language in which they are expressed, or discourses through which they are constituted (Alcoff 2000: 857–8). Establishing that discourses have real consequences entails specifying connections between particular ideas and particular realities. If discourses have real impacts on people's lives, then knowledge of these effects cannot be inferred simply from ideas or language. Real effects are variable and complex, and knowledge of them requires empirical investigation as well as interpretation of experience.

Lorraine Code argues that the epistemic-political challenge for women in grounding knowledge in experience is to devise strategies for claiming their competence and authority as knowers (1991: 218). Taking this view, however, links attempts to connect experience and materiality with the much maligned issue of specifying criteria of validity. In the rest of this chapter we look first at the question of validity, and then at the related issue of epistemic community.

Should feminists specify criteria of validity?

As long as feminists want to judge between competing knowledges, to evaluate well-founded knowledge claims against ill-founded ones, and to distinguish general knowledge from limited local truths, opinion or flights of fancy, they need practical ways of deconstructing the contingency and adequacy of their knowledge. If relativism is not an epistemological and political option, then, whether they state them openly or not, feminists (and their critics) must be using some criteria for judging between differing accounts of gendered lives (for example, between claims that rape is primarily a sexual encounter and so potentially enjoyable, and claims that rape is harmful and political). Criteria of validity need not generate crude claims to know the Truth. They are used in practice (although not necessarily explicitly) to justify judging between claims to connections (or disconnections) between ideas, experience and reality.

Feminists have become cautious about openly stating that they do use criteria of validity. The notion that valid knowledge is achievable has become widely criticized as a simplistic, foundational and indefensible claim to treat observable facts as direct evidence of the Truth. Defenders of standpoint feminism have insisted that feminist knowledge should not be conceived as truths that neutrally mirror reality. If validity in this sense is dismissed, however, feminists are still in the position of wanting to claim some accounts of gender as better than others. However partial, situated or contingent their knowledge, they want to judge between competing accounts of gendered lives.

Since there are no universal criteria of validity that can hold across time and cultures, feminists have no general grounds for deciding which knowledge claims are 'better'. Criteria of validity differ according to ontological and epistemological assumptions that shape particular knowledge claims and particular notions of science, research and curiosity. They also differ according to notions of reason, grounds for generalization, norms and values. The power of researchers to interpret their selection of data through their own ideas and values, and in terms of their chosen theory remains dominant, but can be challenged. Ultimately all truth claims are contingent on their conditions of production, but these conditions are variable and can be examined.

If it is possible to have a notion of validity (or contingent adequacy) without assuming a direct line to Truth, feminists can specify the criteria that are actually used in producing and evaluating particular knowledge claims. This need for explicit criteria of validity brings feminism back to modern concerns with evidence, empirical adequacy and reasoned argument that have become deconstructed, fragmented or marginalized in postmodern thought (Felski 2000; Phoenix 2000; Walby 2000).[5]

One approach to contingency is to abandon claims to general knowledge. Bogusia Temple (1997) considers how an author's text can be judged if it is not appropriate to judge it by some universal criteria of validity. She takes the example of a paper by Mykhalowskiy (1997), on his talks with his family around the kitchen table, in which he questions whether there is a correct way of reading academic texts across different understandings. Mykhalowskiy attempts to represent the multiple voices and differing views around the table as group writing with no final resolution of meaning: '[A]s the author he refuses to finish his work with the definitive conclusion traditionally expected from a researcher' (Temple 1997: 4.3). This refusal gets him out of the problem of claiming authority for his own voice, but feminist researchers have problems in abandoning their claims to authority.

Temple's solution is to abandon any general attempt to connect knowledge and experience to reality. She suggests that each researcher should declare their own hand, and each reader should compare what they read with their own views (Temple 1997: 5.3). This attempt at reflexivity is intended to avoid the problem of limited academic communities silencing the experience of others (especially through a 'booming voice of reason') by specifying what can constitute proper knowledge (Temple 1997: 5.1). This puts feminists in the contradictory position of not being able to state what criteria can reasonably be used in judging some stories to be better than others, but not accepting that all knowledge claims are of equal validity (Temple 1997: 2.4) The overlaps and contradictions between accounts still need explanation. Temple acknowledges that criteria for judging between accounts *are* used in practice, but leaves open the question of how to evaluate differing criteria of validity against each other when researchers make competing knowledge claims.

From a more empiricist position, Mary Hawkesworth makes the case that feminists must not only resist relativism, but also retain some notion of external reality, use reasoned argument, and work with some notion of truth (1989: 556): for example, the truth that some obstacles to women's participation in social, political and economic life are humanly created.

> In the absence of claims of universal validity, feminist accounts derive their justificatory force from their capacity to illuminate existing social relations, to demonstrate the deficiencies of alternative interpretations, to debunk opposing views. They must examine more and assume less about the world than the 'truths' that they oppose. (Hawkesworth 1989: 557)

This clarion call to the explicit validation of knowledge claims requires some sense of empirical adequacy in claiming connections between evidence, experience and theory. Hawkesworth criticizes the impact of postmodern relativism that slides too easily into treating accounts of what happens as political fictions: 'Rape, domestic violence, and sexual harassment [. . .] are not fictions or figurations that admit free play of signification. The victim's account of these experiences is not simply an arbitrary imposition of a purely fictive meaning on an otherwise meaningless reality' (1989: 555). The person who experiences power relations in a particular way can give a partial, situated account of the event that differs from the accounts of those who are differently situated.

Arguments against conceiving knowledge of gender as better stories (rather than as socially constituted, political fictions) rely on notions of rational argument as a means of discriminating between knowledge claims (Nelson 1990; Walby 2000). From this perspective, telling stories is not the same as making truth claims based on reasoned evidence, even though these truth claims and their evidence will be shaped by theory. Helen Longino says that much feminist (and anti-racist and other oppositional) effort has gone into discrediting existing knowledge claims on the grounds of their empirical inadequacy, but empirical adequacy alone does not establish validity since feminists have differing beliefs about what actually exists, and so can make different connections between ideas and reality (1994: 476–8).

The epistemological problems of how to justify criteria for deciding whether a disruptive story of difference is 'better' than a story of benign diversity are considerable, and are given urgency by the politics of difference. Feminists who want to draw on the insights of experience, and to consider what stories of experience are stories of, need to recognize the grounds of their own judgements as well as those of the tellers of stories and their various audiences. Rita Felski (2000) argues that telling stories can be reasonable, and also powerful, since stories can create new meanings or acts of redescription that can be performed in the public sphere. Stories can convey experiential truth and situate subjects in their specific histories. Ann Phoenix (2000) adds that these stories can also be transformative. (The redescriptions of 'forced marriages', 'whiteness as unmerited privilege' and 'rape as sexualized political violence' are cases in point.) New narratives of women's lives are intertwined with normative claims for justice.

Feminist analysis is in the contradictory position of invoking some explicit, common frame of reference for judging between knowledge claims, even though a universal framework of validity cannot be justified. Any common framework has to recognize the existence and political significance of conflicting frames of reference (Ang 1997: 59; Felski 2000; Phoenix 2000: 232; Walby 2000). Common frameworks for representing experience are thus produced, rather than discovered, and require agreements and alliances to be negotiated across differences.

There is no way of judging between competing stories of gendered lives that is not flawed, but abandoning reasoned grounds for judgement seems politically defeatist, conceals the criteria of validity that are being actually used, and actively reproduces the status quo. Feminists may not be able to lay down neutral or universal criteria for divining what is 'better' in all cultures and value systems, but they can urge (on both political and epistemological grounds) that all criteria of validity should not abandoned just because none can be universal. Rather than being inhibited by the inevitable contingency of truth claims, readers of feminist texts can identify how knowledge claims are framed in theory, how they are connected to experience, and also ask what makes some claims stronger, more general or more plausible than others. This means researchers specifying (at least as far as possible) what criteria are being used and why, and how local or general these criteria are.

Specifying criteria of validity can be a matter of reflexivity (see Chapter 6) in recognizing research practices, rather than of the prescription of general rules. Feminists should, for example, be able to support their knowledge claims by stating:

1   *what forms of reasoning this knowledge claim depends on;*
2   *whether this knowledge claim is confined to a local truth game or is more general;*
3   *how the knowing feminist who makes this knowledge claim is constituted;*
4   *whom this knowing feminist speaks for, why and with what authority;*
5   *what evidence or other grounds exist for the claims made;*
6   *how this evidence/grounding is constituted and assessed;*
7   *how counter-evidence/grounding is acknowledged and assessed;*
8   *what normative framework structures this process of knowledge production;*
9   *what connections/disconnections are claimed between ideas, experiences and realities;*
10   *whether and how these connections are conceived, denied or left unclear.*

While this may seem a formidable list, in practice criteria like these are (often unreflectively) employed in making routine decisions about what feminists and their critics do or do not believe. By making criteria explicit, and comparing them with those used by others, researchers and their readers can identify varying connections between ideas, experience and possible realities, and submit these connections to critical appraisal. Different feminist knowledge claims have had different degrees of success in being accepted. Much depends on what claims to validity and contingency are made and how these mesh with existing experiences and understandings.

Just as feminists are not isolated individuals as knowing subjects, so they are not individual producers of criteria of validity or theories of contingency. 'The construction of knowledge is an intersubjective process, dependent for its achievement on communal standards of legitimation and implicated in the power and institutional structures of communities and social orders' (Code 1991: 132). Feminists produce knowledge in relation to a category of 'knowers' (Nelson 1993), and this category has been conceptualized as a feminist epistemic community (or communities) in relation to, but distinct from, existing academic and scientific communities. The primary agent of the validation of feminist knowledge, in this view, is not, then, the individual researcher, but her epistemic community (Alcoff and Potter 1993: 9).

The idea of a feminist epistemic community

An epistemic community is a notion of a socially produced collectivity, with shared rules, that authorizes the right to speak as a particular kind of knowing subject. Such a community recognizes criteria for judging between (or being unable to judge between) knowledge claims. Nelson and Nelson comment: '[k]nowledge is, and will continue to be, generated by, endorsed by, and refined and modified by, groups and social processes' (1994: 495). In this view, the knowing feminist is distinguished from the knowing self who follows rules of method in a scientific community in which 'reasonable' academics question or accept communal assumptions, and act collectively, neutrally and rationally in deciding between knowledge claims (Assiter 1996; Code 1987). What is rejected here is both the notion of the knower as an independent individual, and the neutrality of rationality, from which apparently general criteria of validity can be derived.

(In order to have knowledge claims accepted as legitimate academic knowledge, and enhance their careers, feminists may still have to satisfy the demands of existing epistemic communities within established institutions and hierarchies, which demand that knowledge should be gender-neutral [Warnock 1996].)

Feminists exist as an imagined epistemic community in the sense that they do not need to meet together to exist as a collectivity and they are not simply a collection of women. It is open to investigation, however, as to what women or knowing feminists actually do have in common. A community of knowing feminists does not depend on feminists being the same, sharing every aspect of identity or living a common social existence. It does depend on a collectivity actually existing that is in some respect constituted as feminist. There is a difference between the varied communities and collectivities that people actually live in (from the most local to those of cyberspace) and epistemic communities organized around specific validating and authorizing practices for specific purposes.

Relatively little attention has been paid as yet to exactly what does, or could, constitute a feminist epistemic community (Assiter 1996). Every community implies an inside and an outside (with the outside playing a critical role in the constitution of the inside) and so potential struggles over where boundaries fall, who has the power to draw them, how permeable they are, how inclusion and exclusion operate, and whether there are multiple, separate or overlapping communities. A notion of a feminist epistemic community implies the negotiation of commonalities across differences.

Feminist epistemic communities may differ from existing academic epistemic communities not so much in their ability to authorize the adequacy of particular knowledge claims, but in their judgements of what constitute adequate and proper processes of knowledge production. This would cover the values incorporated into research practices, including openness to criticism, community standards in managing intellectual disputes and standards of intellectual authority (Longino 1990). These are issues that cannot be known prior to investigation, but at least feminist researchers can reflect on how their knowledge claims are actually established, how and why they can be challenged or defended, and what power relations are implicated in feminist authorizing practices. Alison Assiter argues that in the real world of epistemic communities, knowledge is both relative to particular communities and generally unequally shared within communities as well as between them (2000: 334). What is shared and why is also an empirical question.

Western feminism is always in danger of colonizing other people's experiences by incorporating them into western categories of thought, and judging them by western values. Maori women, in contrast, can tell a 'better story' of Maori/Pakeha histories, but are not politically and discursively positioned to have this colonizing power. Their epistemic empowerment constitutes a form of resistance to the colonizing power of western thought and practices (Smith 1999). It is open to investigation as to whether feminist knowledge can actually be shared or negotiated in common ways of authorizing and validating knowledge. It is an epistemological/political question as to whether they should. Feminist knowledge is more powerful when it can claim authority, but the exercise of authority brings powers of exclusion. There are dangers in claiming that knowledge authorized by an epistemic community does not need to be justified (Haack 1996: 285). Given the lack of any political centre, the nature and effectiveness of feminist authorizing practices remain unclear.

The conception of a feminist epistemic community also brings up the question of whether men, or others, can be feminist researchers. The critical question is not, for example, whether men, transsexuals, intersexuals or others can use feminist theory, be politically sympathetic to feminism's emancipatory impulse, or engage sensitively and reflexively with research subjects. The point is whether these researchers are in practice members of feminist epistemic communities, and if not, why not. Robert Scholes warns: 'I think no man should seek in any way to diminish the authority which the experience of women gives them in speaking about that experience' (1987: 217–18). This raises direct questions about the connections between feminist consciousness, differences in experiences of 'being a woman' (social, political, relational, embodied), and the nature and grounds of exclusionary epistemic practices.

Paul Connolly (1996) challenges Stanley and Wise's claim (1993: 31–2) that men cannot be feminists because they lack women's experience. (He also asks who can research across racialized power relations where experiences of racial and gender inequality are not shared.) He argues that men can be feminists by virtue of appropriate experience, ethics and politics, rather than being automatically excluded by a gendered identity. It is the nature of the experience, and the ethical and political consequences of the research, that should be at issue. Mark Liddle suggests that men can understand and share feminist perspectives and politics, and that opposition to men's involvement in feminism is most persuasive when it is defending feminism's hard-won territory from abuse by those men who lack appropriate politics and experiences (1996: 180).

Empirical investigation is needed of how specific processes of authorizing knowledge are constituted and operate. If researchers can identify actual epistemic communities within which feminist, or any other, knowledge is generated, the constitution, ideas of validity, and exclusionary practices of actual epistemic communities can be examined (Nelson 1993: 123). Attention to the grounds of particular forms of epistemic authority can help to clarify how particular knowing selves are constituted, how particular knowledge claims are authorized, and how particular challenges to authority are managed in specific conditions. The feminist researcher can then consider the politics, ethics, rationality and validity of authorizing practices, and make explicit the grounds on which judgements are made between knowledge claims.

Conclusion

Feminist researchers have to live with the contradictions that arise when feminism's humanist inheritance of universal norms, justice and emancipation is brought to bear on the diversity of women's differences, relationships and experiences. The distinctiveness of feminist methodologies lies in adopting a normative framework of respect between human beings within which some ideas, inequalities and modes of gendered social organization can be judged unjust, and some power relations and practices judged improper. These normative frameworks cannot be derived from universal norms (since these do not exist) and so can vary. Once chosen, they frame empirical explorations of what women do or do not share, and what gender/power relations do or do not exist. Without an agreed normative framework, feminists take ethical, epistemological and political risks in judging between differing stories of gendered existence. It is on moral, political and epistemological grounds that they deem these risks worth taking.

Feminist knowledge, however thoroughly reasoned, connected and grounded, will always be subject to change. Since struggles over the rationality and empirical adequacy of knowledge of gender are also struggles over the politics of theory and values, knowledge claims move on (for example, from 'women', 'battered wives', 'third world women'). Theories shift as concepts are qualified and refined, as new questions are asked, as more experiences are expressed and new evidence is addressed. Claims to clearer connections between ideas, experiences and realities will continue to be lodged, authorized and contested.

Although making sense of one's own and other people's experience remains a problem in any social investigation, feminists have been willing to tackle the tricky epistemological and ontological pitfalls of methodology. Taking account of the reality of women's experience still provides a powerful challenge to male-centred knowledge. Challenging male-centred knowledge brings feminist knowledge up against the complex interrelations of gender with other power relations. While different decisions on epistemology and ontology pull feminists in differing methodological directions, the political necessity of confronting actual power relations, and being able to justify what sense researchers make of them, pulls feminist researchers back to the problematic grounding of feminist knowledge in women's experience.

In Part III we look at where this leaves the feminist researcher faced with the practicalities of a small-scale project.

Notes

1. Notions of experience raise much wider issues about consciousness, agency, intention, cause and effect, that complicate claims that people can know their own experience, let alone that they can know the experience of others (Nelson 1990). Questions of the unconscious, the subconscious, the constitution of subjectivity, and so on, are beyond the scope of this chapter. Debates on these issues produce significant qualifications to generalizations about the nature of experience, self-knowledge, and any possible connection to 'reality' (Lazreg 1994).

2. We do not have space here to comment on the range of epistemological debates within modern thought on the status of experience as a source of knowledge. There are significant differences, for example, between empiricist, realist and relativist positions (Benton 1978; Outhwaite 1987; Tudor 1982).

3. If feminists do claim direct and simple connections between ideas, experience and reality, this is certainly a weak position. But, although this is a common accusation, it is not commonly defended as a methodological position (as standpoint theorists argue).

4. Maureen Cain (1986, 1990) suggests a perspective of 'humble realism' from which connections between knowledge, experience and reality can be theorized. She proposes

limited claims about real relationships that can endure for the time being, until challenged. Cain notes Roy Bhaskar's realist assertion of a disjunction between ontology and epistemology in asserting a difference between what is real and our ability to know what is real. Bhaskar (1979) argues for an ontology in which objects (for example, death, floods, relationships of class and gender) are taken to be real in the sense of being independent of people's knowledge of them, so these objects can directly affect people. But this need not entail claims that gender relations can be directly apprehended (Cain 1990).

5. Even though all truths may be contingent, every time a feminist flies, for example, she wants to be sure (barring acts of God, terror or human error) that the aircraft will go up, stay up, and come down, according to well-validated, predictable and reliable specifications.

PART III

MEETING CHALLENGES, MAKING CHOICES

8

Choices and decisions

Doing a feminist research project

Introduction

A feminist research project is where the methodological action starts. Reading or writing about debates on methodology is different from sticking your head above the parapet, taking up the challenge of putting your own reflections into practice, and committing yourself to a particular methodological strategy. It is hard to bring the wealth of argument on feminist methodology to bear on actual research practice, to make links between general abstractions, specific experiences and the practicalities of a small-scale study. Taking any methodological decision makes you vulnerable to criticisms from those taking other decisions. Since feminism offers no methodological means of reconciling differences in how people think about the nature of, and relations between, ideas, experience and reality, novice researchers cannot choose the reassurance of some uncontested middle ground. (If your research area seems uncontested, you should look more carefully.)

Despite the challenges facing researchers, however, embarking on your own project and making your own contribution to knowledge can be very positive.

> [. . .] I wouldn't swap my research experience for anything. It was brilliant, it made me engage in issues, taught me to think in different ways, stopped me being reliant on badly thought through theories and forced me to engage in political practicalities. It stopped me remaining in an ivory tower and it made me wary of seductive pretentious theory. I made excellent friends and had some great times. It was a rich and rewarding, if also traumatic and painful, experience. (Skeggs 1995b: 203)

This is a personal comment on a particular experience of feminist ethnography, but suggests the roller-coaster possibilities of a research project.

Planning any social research project requires decisions on what to study, what information to produce, and how to go about making sense of it. Abstractions of theory, ontology and epistemology have to be translated into a practical research question with appropriate research techniques and practices. Feminist researchers should be reflexive about the exercise of power in the research process (though power can be conceived positively as well as negatively). Reflexivity (see Chapter 6) also means making clear the ethics of your research practice and your moral and epistemic accountability. The knowledge claims that result have to be both persuasive and justifiable. Unleashing demands for this range of decisions on an unsuspecting novice can produce an advanced state of academic insecurity. This chapter is intended to offer some support in managing the decisions required by a small-scale feminist social research project.

Faced with the impossibility of reconciling irreconcilable methodological and political positions, it is appealing to abandon abstractions in favour of just getting on with the job. It can be tempting to identify with researchers who proceed imaginatively in haphazard, contradictory or eclectic ways, bypassing the task of acknowledging any explicit ontological and epistemological position. But if feminist knowledge claims are to be well-founded, well-justified and useful for social transformation, they must be able to stand up to criticism. Researchers should be clear about how their claims can be challenged and defended (not only in academic debate, but also at the level of everyday knowledge and personal practices).

Perhaps your decision will be not to attempt a feminist project, on the grounds, for example, that gender analysis cannot be sufficiently disentangled from other ideas, representations or relationships, that your own experiences are inappropriate, or that you situate yourself as politically indifferent or opposed to feminism. What does it mean to you to refuse the possibility of feminist knowledge? These are personal, theoretical and political, rather than primarily methodological, decisions.

What makes social research feminist?

We argued in Chapter 1 that there is no universal definition of what is or is not feminist, so any attribution of 'feminist' (or 'not-feminist', or 'not-feminist-enough') rests on claims rather than facts. Planning any feminist project raises problems about the politics of constituting boundaries, and how these powers (according to how they are conceived) are relevant to knowledge production. In our view, the point of doing feminist social research is not to score points for political correctness, or to attain methodological purity, but to give insights into gendered social existence that would otherwise not exist. Feminist approaches to research can be identified largely by their theories of gender and power, their normative frameworks, and their notions of transformation and accountability, even though these are not uniform. Methodologically, there is likely to be overlap with the concerns and visions of other approaches to social investigation.

It is not the investigation of gender, or gendered social lives, as such that makes a research project feminist. There have been investigations of 'child sexual abuse', for example, that have claimed abuse as an aberration, or as produced by pathological men, seductive children, defective mothers, or as an effect of specific discourses. Feminist approaches are distinguished by conceptualizing taken-for-granted male power in the family/household as a critical issue in making sense of experiences of abuse. What appears to make some projects feminist (despite political, theoretical and epistemological variations) is dependence on a normative framework that interrelates 'injustice', a politics for 'women' (however these categories are understood), ethical practices that eschew the 'unjust' exercise of power, and theory that conceptualizes gendered power within this normative framework. Since this identification of 'feminist' depends on socially constituted, and so variable, norms, concepts and experiences, it is never an open and shut case.

Research projects can be thought of as feminist if they are framed by feminist theory, and aim to produce knowledge that will be useful for effective transformation of gendered injustice and subordination. But this does not mean that feminists have to study women, or only study gender, or treat women as innocent of abuses of power. First, the politics of gender makes investigation of men's, intersexuals' and other gendered lives relevant. During the 1960s and 1970s in the West, feminist researchers tended to feel that previous attention had been focused almost exclusively on men's lives as central and normal, and on women's lives as dependent, marginal or deviant. They took on the task of grounding their new knowledge in women's voices and experiences. These efforts have been enormously productive, but they are not incompatible with looking more generally at gendered lives, power relations, hierarchies and institutionalized dominance.

Second, the numerous interrelations of gender with, for example, racialized power, heterosexism, the effects of capitalism or disability, complicate any study that is focused exclusively on gender. Gender relations are difficult to separate in practice from other power relations. Working out whether gender is a primary focus for a project, a contributory factor or an area of contradiction may become a shifting area of decision during the course of a study. Since researchers approach their projects from varying social locations, with diverse experiences, varying access to power and different expertise on social life, they can have strong feelings about what is or is not appropriate in focusing a particular study. Targeting gender can have the effect of excluding, silencing or marginalizing significant divisions between women, and empowering the researcher to privilege gender over other differences.

Third, envisaging a feminist research strategy does not mean that feminist knowledge is necessarily favourable to women. Feminists have had to come to terms with the discomforts of producing knowledge of how women exercise power, promote injustice, collude in their own subordination, or benefit from the subordination of 'others'.

We are not proposing that all work on gender should be feminist, nor that feminist work should focus exclusively on gender or fit any standard normative framework. Although feminism implies that projects should be reflexively conceived and justified, the critical categories of 'women' and 'justice' remain caught in the contradictions between the humanist universalism of feminist emancipatory politics and the specificities and divisions of difference. No project is ever feminist in some politically pure and incontrovertible state, and new ways of imagining gender are always possible. Rather than struggling to fit into a particular category, your efforts would be better spent in making your aims, assumptions, politics and ethics clear and justifiable.

The research process

No social researcher starts from scratch in a state of social, intellectual or political isolation. All researchers, however inexperienced, carry intellectual, emotional and political baggage with them. Planning a small-scale project requires critical and imaginative reflection on what you are free to do with this luggage. What must be packed for the journey, and what can be added or thrown out? What can or cannot fit comfortably with what else? What makes your knees buckle? What new packages could ease the journey?

This chapter is not a guide on exactly how to pack your bags for an ideal feminist project. There are too many productive possibilities, and no advantage in prescription. Instead we sketch a simplified process of social research in which an intrepid researcher has to make all the key decisions. Even novice researchers can feel empowered to take decisions, take stock of what they already know and believe, and take into account that different decisions have different consequences. Since all approaches to research are contested, what is approved as good research practice in any field is subject to change, but we suggest that in managing your own knowledge production it can be helpful to follow the convention of envisaging your research process in terms of a series of interrelated decisions.

The institutional context of research

Your project may be located within an academic, state, charitable, non-governmental or other institution that has control over how you do research. This context will structure expectations and possibilities for your project. In some institutions it may be difficult even to suggest using feminist methodology if dominant assumptions about method and epistemic community (see Chapter 7) are critical of feminist knowledge. Academic colleagues may take a postmodern stance that is critical of empirical research, or a positivist stance that is critical of feminist politics, or, less commonly, be feminist scholars who can ease your passage into research. Your decisions about your research can be framed both by the realities of institutional demands and, where appropriate and possible, by resistance to them.

Research funded by scholarships or grants is carried out within many and complex restraints that can limit the pursuit of feminist principles. Funding for academic research is generally highly competitive. Editors of journals and books, and peer reviewers of funded research, can also regulate what counts as knowledge and demand particular ways of presenting your findings. Young researchers may be constrained by their location in a hierarchical research team. A female researcher, early in her career, for example, might be able to gain sensitive information from vulnerable women through her empathy and understanding, but then be required to pass these data on to others who do not share her feminist sensibilities (Kay 1990). Feminist researchers may need considerable ingenuity to work around institutional and funding constraints.

In the rest of this chapter we consider the kinds of decisions a feminist researcher faces in carrying out a small-scale social research project. Throughout the process of research, researchers have responsibility for the practical and ethical implications of their decisions, and feminist research implies some stance on the possibilities of social transformation.

Situating your research question

It can be challenging to have to come up with a well-focused research question, particularly under pressure to conform to a specific model of research practice within a limited time and for assessment. A useful way of meeting this challenge is to ask yourself what you would like to find out that you do not know now; what puzzles you that you would like to explain. (It can be useful to get a friend to act as interrogator, and to eliminate what you are certain that you do not want to investigate.) Your project will have to be tailored to meet limitations of scale, timing and resources. Novice researchers often choose too broad a question for their resources, and take too long to fix on a final version. The same technique of questioning can help from the start to break a broad research question into smaller, more manageable questions. From these narrower concerns, your objectives and aims can be targeted.

Clarifying your research question clarifies what you care about and can be an emotional process. It also makes it necessary to reflect on how you are constituted as a knowing subject (for example, how you have become a socially constituted 'feminist', a 'student', an 'academic researcher', how you juggle and value multiple aspects of identity). Your research question starts you off on a social process of exploration, including exploration of the research process and your place in it. From the start, your project will incorporate your own values (whether explicitly or implicitly), your theory (your assumptions about gender and power), your ontology (what you believe to be the nature of the aspects of gender/power that you have chosen to study) and your epistemology (what will count as authoritative knowledge of gender).

Conceptualizing your starting point

Having to make and justify decisions about theory, ontology and epistemology does not mean inventing a position from nothing, or having to defend general abstractions. These decisions are more manageable if you see them as conceptualizing your starting point by making explicit what you already believe about gender and power, clarifying how you already think about authoritative knowledge, and considering whether you want to make any changes in order to tell the best possible story about what you want to know. Your existing beliefs and knowledge will provide what seems obvious to you in starting your research.

We have emphasized the centrality in debates on methodology of struggles over how to conceptualize connections (or lack of connections) between a social world that actually exists, experiences of social life, and the ideas through which people imagine, produce or make sense of their realities. Any feminist research project starts in practice from some position in these debates (even if this is not explicit in the research question or obvious to the researcher). Whether you think it through or not, your research will entail assumptions about what your knowledge claims are based on, whether any particular connections are unknowable or irrelevant, and the place of power in knowledge production. Making these assumptions explicit will ensure that your beliefs have some logical consistency. We have, for example, seen students embrace postmodern theory without having worked out that their own pre-existing assumptions still incorporate the common sense of modern scientific method, giving them strong but unquestioned beliefs in the superiority of 'objective knowledge' on the grounds that this mirrors 'reality'. Their explicit postmodern intentions are incompatible with their implicit epistemology, leaving them unable to justify their knowledge claims. While eclectism might seem imaginative and unconstrained, it is only consistent with some form of relativism, and so is incompatible with emancipatory politics.

Theory

Your choice of theory will powerfully shape your research question. In the dualisms of the common sense of western thought, theory is a set of interrelated ideas – how people imagine things to be – as opposed to the factual nature of how reality actually is. In planning a new project, it is more useful to think of choosing a theory as deciding between different ways of conceptualizing and explaining aspects of social life and their interconnections (for example, gendered identities, relationships, representations, sexuality, division of labour).

There are a number of ways, for example, in which inequalities between women and men could be theorized. (1) Differences could be conceptualized in terms of men's greater aggression, bodily strength and need to control reproduction through control of women's bodies. (Resistance to innate male power could lie in valuing women's feminine specificity.) (2) Subordination could be conceived as resulting from men's institutionalized, patriarchal power, and control of the sexual division of labour. (Resistance to repressive male power could lie in challenging areas of institutional power, such as marriage or law.) (3)

Differences could be seen as repeatedly socially constituted in everyday practices that produce gendered inequalities, including women's practices – for example, in socializing girls and boys differently. (Resistance could lie in identifying subordinating ideas and changing practices.) (4) Inequalities could be constituted through effects of discourses of gendered difference. (Resistance could lie in the positive power of producing counter discourses.) These are oversimplified examples, but serve to show that different theories of gender lead researchers to pursue different questions, with different implications for emancipation. Your choice of theory will be closely related to your ontological assumptions.

Ontology

As with your research question, a potentially helpful way of identifying your ontological position is to ask yourself questions, and to note when you say, 'No, that is not the way I see it.' You can make your ontological assumptions clear by asking how you already think about the nature of the aspects of gender that you want to study. Jennifer Mason comments:

> Ontology can seem like a difficult concept precisely because the nature and essence of social things seem so fundamental and obvious that it can be hard to see what there is to conceptualize. [. . .] [I]t is only once it is recognized that alternative ontological perspectives might tell different stories that a researcher can begin to see their own ontological view of the social world as a position which should be established and understood, rather than as an obvious and universal truth which can be taken for granted. (1996: 11)

Mason offers an extensive list of what can count as essential aspects of social reality from different (and often conflicting) ontological positions, including: people, social actors; understandings, interpretations, motivations, ideas; attitudes, beliefs, views; stories, narratives, biographies; texts, discourses; interactions, situations, social relations; institutions, structures; order, chaos; one objective reality, multiple realities (1996: 11–12).

The knowledge of gendered social life that you produce will depend not only on what you believe to be the nature of gender, the nature of power, the nature of social relationships, and so on, but also on how you see potential connections between these beliefs and what is to be discovered. Differences in beliefs about the nature of gender have different theoretical and political implications, and suggest different strategies for knowledge production and social transformation. These cannot logically be strung together in any combination.

Epistemology

Different decisions about epistemology have different implications for relationships between knowledge and power. Situating your research question in relation to epistemology means deciding what can constitute authoritative knowledge of gender, and whether you expect your knowledge to be believable. This is hardly an individual decision. Different epistemologies propose different rules for establishing what counts as authoritative knowledge. A researcher who, say, claims general knowledge of a crisis of masculinity in a given location and period, based entirely on their personal opinion, is likely to learn the hard way that authorizing knowledge is not simply a matter of asserting a claim to truth. Although an individual can adopt any epistemological position, authorizing knowledge is a collective process within a particular cultural context (as the notions of discourse and of epistemic community indicate). Both communities and discourses can result in unequal access to processes of authorization. Feminists have had to fight (not always successfully) for feminist knowledge to be treated as authoritative knowledge, and some epistemological positions are more open to the authorization of feminist knowledge than others.

If you are uncertain of your epistemological position, you could start by asking whether you believe that you can produce objective knowledge. If so, you face a barrage of criticism (see Chapter 3). If not, this will help you to clarify the grounds on which you can challenge the binary thinking that deems objective knowledge superior to subjective knowledge, and to consider what you think your knowledge will be contingent on.

A simple example of an epistemological question is whether you believe that reality exists independently of people's beliefs about it. That is, whether, through reason and theory, knowledge can be produced of a level of social reality that exists whether or not people are aware of it. This belief would allow you to claim knowledge of patriarchy, heterosexism or racialized gender relations as real, but not necessarily conceptualized in everyday life. If you say no to this question, you are rejecting a realist epistemology.

An alternative question is whether social reality can be accessed through observation, experiment or the evidence of the senses (for example, evidence of oppressive social relationships or predictable patterns of behaviour). Knowledge could then be produced, for example, from attitudes and beliefs, investigated from a psychological perspective, using the rules of positivist methodology and generating statistical data as evidence of what exists. Alternatively the understandings, interpretations and ideas that people actually use could be studied from an interpretivist perspective, employing a qualitative approach to produce evidence of people's meanings. If you say no to this kind of approach to knowledge production, you are rejecting an empiricist epistemology.

You could also ask whether there are multiple realities which are knowable only through representations of culture, or deconstructions of language and discourse, with no single truth or accessible reality, or whether realities are only what people believe them to be. If you say no to these questions, you are rejecting a relativist epistemology and a postmodern perspective.

Levels of analysis

The investigation of gendered lives, meanings, representations, power or relationships can be conceptualized in terms of a number of interrelated analytical 'levels'. Considerable disagreements between claims to knowledge can arise from analyses being made at one level rather than another, or at more than one level. Because interrelations between gender and power can be both complex and sensitive, it can be useful to clarify which, or how many, levels of existence and their interconnections you are trying to explore in your project. There are various ways of differentiating between analytical levels, but we take as an example the difference between choosing to analyse gender and power at the level of language and at the level of institutionalized social relations.

Social investigation at the level of language could include analysis of ideas, beliefs, norms, discourses, the reproduction of culture, and their effects. This is a significant level of gendered existence and the exercise of power. Feminists have argued, for example, that patriarchal ideas of the nature of masculinity and femininity are powerful social constructions that can be challenged (as can ideologies of race or class). Ideas can determine what people take to be real, and how reality is understood. Postmodern thought has been particularly influential in showing how gender is brought into being in particular discourses and representations. Gendered identities, subjects and subjectivities are continuously produced, accepted, resisted, modified, fragmented. At this level there can be agency, in the sense that people can accept, resist or counter constructions of gendered identities, and be empowered or disempowered by them.

Language is a critical element in connecting knowledge and experience if it is through language that identities, subjectivities and experiences are made, given meaning and remade. But, in studying gender and power, language is not all there is to know. Patti Lather argues, following Foucault, that language is particularly powerful in producing categories (such as the classification of genders), but that since reality is heterogeneous, she does not want to 'collapse the real into language' (1991: 124). There is a critical difference between focusing on gender and power as effectively constituted by language, and seeing gender as partly constituted by language.

Gender and power can also be investigated in terms of social structures, relationships, institutions, states and resources. At this level, researchers can locate gendered experiences within more general conceptions of material conditions of existence and their histories. Those who focus on language do not generally deny the existence of persistent networks and hierarchies of relationships (hidden or otherwise) and their associated everyday practices. Differences lie in how this level of social existence is conceived and, critically, how connections between social structures and ideas are envisaged. Analysis at this level does not mean ignoring language and its effects, but it does mean making connections between ideas, institutions and hierarchies. For example, people's struggles to counter experiences of sexualized, racialized or other forms of subordination with new and positive identities, cultures, histories and values can illuminate entrenched relations of domination, unequal access to resources and constraints on agency and change.

The question of how bodies are relevant to social analysis of gender illustrates possible analytical distinctions between these levels. While analyses of language, discourse and representations can show how bodies are made meaningful, and how these meanings can vary and change, bodies also have a material and social existence that is not entirely produced by language. Having another human being growing in your own body, having another human being force themselves or objects into your bodily orifices, having disability, disease, age or accident constrain bodily activity, choosing to 'improve', beautify or reshape the body, are all events that can be produced in discourses and carry different meanings in different languages and value systems. But they are also constituted as experiences and grounded, to varying extents, in inescapable embodiment, as specific aspects of the material conditions of life. Feminist concerns with unjust power relations require analysis of the interconnections between language, relationships and the material grounding of power.

Since you can investigate gender as simultaneously discursive, institutionalized, relational, experiential and material, you need to decide what difference it will make to your project to choose one level rather than another, or more than one. Differences in levels of analysis will affect the practicalities of your project. Thinking about the possibilities of investigating gender at interrelated, but analytically different, levels also brings you up against the interaction of gender with other dimensions of social existence in practice.

Once you have focused your questions, sorted out your beliefs about knowledge and reality, and decided on the level or levels of your gender analysis, you can design your research project and select techniques of data production.

Face to face with the research: data production

The term 'data production' implies that information gathered by the researcher is produced in a social process of giving meaning to the social world. This is distinct from 'data collection', which, at its simplest, can imply that 'facts' are lying about waiting for the researcher to spot them. There is some tension here between theories of social construction that imply that some human agent or social force (for example, the knowing subject, a discourse, patriarchy) is producing the data, and those versions of postmodern thought that see the researcher's knowledge as produced through repeated practices of imagining and constituting 'data'. Whether you think in terms of data collection, data production or postmodern reiteration will depend on how you think about possible relations between what is observable, ideas of what is observable and some notion of underlying realities. Most feminist social research probably falls into the category of data production, but there is considerable variation in approaches (McRobbie 1997; Maynard and Purvis 1994; Skeggs 1995a).

Choosing one or more techniques for producing knowledge of gender is a critical point in your research. Your decisions will depend on what sort of data you think appropriate to the kind of knowledge claim you want to make, and what you think data are (facts, social constructs, ideas). Many practical and possibly pragmatic decisions have to be made, but there is nothing inherently feminist about research design – the integration of your process of investigation and techniques of data production with your theory, ontology and epistemology. Different specialisms in social research tend to favour particular techniques, but there is generally a wide range of sources and techniques, at least potentially, available to any researcher.

Some feminist researchers, particularly during the 1970s and 1980s, developed face-to-face, qualitative and interactive methods as the most appropriate way to produce data on the realities of women's lives. This approach was specifically taken in opposition to a particular positivist methodological position that assumed quantitative data could best represent reality, and was also intended to counter the absence of knowledge of women's lives. It encouraged researchers to give voice to personal, experiential and emotional aspects of existence (which dependence on 'scientific method' had ignored, or marginalized as 'subjective knowledge') and to deconstruct power relations in research. Feminist social research has thus often been equated with a woman-to-woman, sensitive style of qualitative interview, observation or life history, or one that involves research participants in the production of knowledge. These approaches to data production are valued for respecting the understandings and experiences of research subjects, and making explicit the politics of knowing and the possibilities of empowerment (Acker et al. 1983; Mies 1983; Morris 1993). But in planning your project you need not take for granted that this is how feminist data production is always, or must be, carried out (Maynard 1994; Pilcher and Coffey 1996; Reinharz 1992).

While small-scale, qualitative/interactive approaches have been powerful and productive, feminists have offered spirited defences of what can be learned using quantitative methods, and have proposed that feminists should avail themselves of whatever techniques are useful for investigating their research questions (Jayaratne and Stewart 1991; Kelly et al. 1995; Stanley 1995). Feminists can familiarize themselves with quantitative methods, computer-aided data analysis and the resources of the Internet, and also investigate whether these are used to enhance male power over women. As well as promoting sensitive, qualitative methods, feminists also use: large-scale social survey; statistical analysis; methods combining quantitative and qualitative techniques; ethnographic and participatory methods; explorations of discourses, texts or representations; methods of providing informants with the means to represent their own lives (diaries, cameras, tape- or video-recorders). If, for example, quantitative data or visual images are appropriate for your research question, these can be approached with varying epistemological assumptions.[1] Quantitative data do not require a positivist methodology or empiricist epistemology, and these approaches do not depend on quantitative data.

If you are to be reflexive about your research design, you need to reflect on the implications of choosing one technique over another. Quantitative methods offer limited access to accounts of experiences, nuances of meaning, the nature of social relationships, and their shifts and contradictions. Qualititative methods offer limited means of generalization. Different methods can be appropriate for different levels of analysis. You will need to decide on the analytical levels and their interrelationships that are relevant to your research question.

If you want direct contact with research subjects, it may be useful to reflect on your own experiences and to clarify your taken-for-granted assumptions where these could be relevant. This can be useful for reflections on difference, 'othering', the constitution of subjects and objects of the research, inclusion and exclusion of subjects, and how this may affect your approach to, and relationships with, research participants.[2] You need to allow for complexity in establishing what you may or may not have in common with those you study.

Decisions about techniques of data production will be helped by breaking down the abstractions of your general theory into key concepts that can be specified in relation to your data. General concepts such as 'gender' or 'power relations' could be specified in particular sites, for example in terms of: how young people experience 'coming out' as gay or lesbian at school; how women experience ill health; how childcare is organized in an area of high male unemployment; how African-Caribbean boys come to be disproportionately excluded from school; what women of different ages think about feminism; how women's family labour in agriculture is valued; how particular representations of ideal bodies are racialized and sexualized.

Operationalizing your key concepts for specific locations and levels of analysis will enable you to target what data you want to produce, and so help to specify what research subjects or sources of data will be most appropriate, and how far your resources will stretch. Practical questions (such as which situations to observe, how many people to interview and how to select them, whether your selection should represent a wider population, which texts or images are appropriate, how focus groups should be constituted, how an ethnography should start, whether autobiography is appropriate) cannot be answered in general, or from a specifically feminist stance. These are not, however, merely matters of personal creativity or free choice, since they are also technical issues with specific consequences for your knowledge claims. They are best chosen in a critical relationship to textbooks on methods, in relation to your chosen epistemology and, if relevant, to the demands of your system of assessment (Fine 1992; Hall 1997a; Holland et al. 1995; Maynard and Purvis 1994; Pilcher and Coffey 1996; Reinharz 1992; Rose 2001; Wilkinson 1996).

Face to face with the researched: putting reflexivity into practice

Focusing your research question, selecting your method and operationalizing your concepts will frame your decisions about how to situate yourself in relation to those whom you research. It is possible to investigate inanimate objects – things, texts, images, representations. The exercise of power is not necessarily absent in relations between the researcher and their treatment of these objects, but the situation is more complex when the researcher enters into a social relationship with research subjects. A reflexive approach demands awareness of, and appropriate responses to, relationships between researcher and researched.

Where your prospective sources are people, your relationships with them, and what they understand you to be doing, are ethical issues, and raise questions about the exercise of power in the production of data. Given your own understanding of how power can operate in the research process, its possible impact on both researcher and researched, you have to decide how to put good intentions into practice. You will need to decide both how to conceptualize power and what to do about power relations in your own research, including situations where the people you are studying can exercise power over you.

Gatekeepers

To come face to face with the researched you must first have access to them. This may involve gatekeepers (for example, school heads, committees that run institutions, employers, community leaders, local officials) who must be persuaded of the value of your research, the ethics of your research practice and the standing of any organization that backs you. Decisions about who is likely to grant access to feminist projects have to be realistic, and some gatekeepers are so slow to grant assent that your research time may run out. If you are upfront about the politics and intentions of a feminist project, feminism's negative reputation can mean your project being greeted with suspicion, or access being denied. Much will depend on how you present yourself and to whom. Ruth Frankenberg, for example, in seeking access to 'white women' for her anti-racist, feminist project on white women's relationship to racism in California, was refused access by organizations whose gatekeepers thought it racist to target white women and not others, or who thought gender had nothing to do with race (1993: 33). The potential value of your project to the researched will need to be taken into account in your presentation of yourself and your aims. Obviously it is not just feminist researchers who face these decisions, but the political and ethical stance of feminism makes for sensitive choices. At all stages in the research you have to decide on ethics and accountability, to consider whom your work is for, and its political and practical implications. Practical considerations about how to get access to the people you have selected are entwined with ethical issues about informed consent, and possible harm to research subjects or others.

Access, ethics and informed consent

Even the most committed feminist researcher is in the game of research out of self-interest. (Although committed feminist research may not offer an ideal route to academic advancement.) You will need to work out your ethical position in relation to the researched, your accountability for the research, how you should present yourself, what the researched are to be asked to consent to, and what information it is proper to give them to this end.

Your account of your aims and methods, and the way you present yourself in terms of multiple possible aspects of identity and social location, will be critical in negotiating the engagement of your participants, and in how they respond to you. In presenting yourself and your project you will be seeking informed consent. This is a particularly difficult issue in any social research, since researchers often do not want to inform the researched or their gatekeepers too fully because of the possible impact on data production. If you state, for example, that you are interested in homophobia, or in researching men in positions of power in order to ascertain ways in which they control women, or that you want to investigate power play between women, you are likely to inhibit what participants will discuss.

Even if you conscientiously offer information, you cannot be sure of what people think they are consenting to. The researched are not necessarily aware of the nature of research activity in general, let alone the specific instance you represent. What may be a burning issue for you may be far from their experience or interests. Your concepts, values, concerns and ethical stance may not mesh with theirs. Being curious or generous enough to participate in your research could mean just taking the implications on trust. It is questionable how far social research can ever be adequately ethically justified, and whether the value of the knowledge claims that result should ever be taken to outweigh a lack of fully informed consent. Inadequate informed consent can be countered by accountability for what is made of the research. A feminist might not be too troubled by slipping a radical project past the powerful in order to investigate abuses of power, but would still bear responsibility for negotiating consent that is as fully informed as possible with those to whom harm could result (Kelly 1988: 9).[3]

One possibility is to investigate your own social location, where your identities are already known and accepted, and the value of your project is clear to the participants, as in Gillian Dunne's (1997) investigation of local lesbian lifestyles. If Dunne had come in as an outsider with the explicit intention of investigating domestic violence in lesbian relationships, her reception and responsibilities would presumably have been different.

If your project demands spending long periods of time with research subjects, people can become accustomed to your presence, drop their guard, and perhaps reveal more than they might wish. For the researcher the entire experience is data, but ethics and accountability to the researched demand that you are alert to the interests of your participants, and accountable for producing knowledge that could harm them (Stacey 1991). The pressure on researchers to gain accounts of meanings, experiences and understandings from respondents can lead to subtle, or not so subtle, manipulation of potential areas of shared experience, and possible exploitation of the participant's trust in the researcher (Cotterill 1992). Where research subjects feel shared sympathy with, and trust in, the researcher, they can be particularly vulnerable. Janet Finch has famously noted that she has 'emerged from interviews with the feeling that my interviewees need to know how to protect themselves from people like me' (1984: 80).

Social location and relationships

Reflexivity, in the sense of making explicit the play of power relations in your research process, and in identifying your relationship to the researched, is particularly important given the interrelation of politics, ethics and epistemology in feminist research. It is also particularly tricky because of the difficulty of knowing in advance exactly what effects different aspects of social locations and identities will have in practice, and what expectations, understandings and relationships will develop during your project. Taking reflexivity personally means reflecting critically on the consequences of your presence in the research process.

A precise match of researcher and researched to eliminate any effects of difference is impossible. The researcher and researched may agree or differ on a range of factors that impinge on the possibilities of interaction. Where the researcher sees similarity or shared identity (for example, gender, sexual orientation), the researched might see difference (for example, age, racialized status, education, access to resources). They may then defer to the researcher, or feel relatively powerless, or refuse co-operation, or offer careful resistance. Similarities or differences that appear obvious to the researched may not occur to the researcher in the same way. Even given apparent similarities, different interpretations of the research relationships are still possible.

Decisions on how to control the complex interactions of research relationships through best ethical practice cannot be fully taken in advance. If you expect to be in a position of power, you can decide to attempt to subvert your own exercise of power by undertaking research as a collaborative interactional process, with reciprocal inputs from researcher and researched, and agreed conclusions on interpretation of the data (Acker et al. 1983; Graham 1984). In the many situations where this approach is not appropriate or practicable, you will retain moral responsibility for the power you can exercise, and how you try to make this power explicit in your account of your research. You will need to identify the fragmented and multiple intersecting identities/subjectivities of both researcher and researched, and also the persistent, institutionalized privileges and inequalities that impinge on research relationships. Key questions to ask yourself both initially and with hindsight are: what relationships you have with the researched; what effects your presence and knowledge could have on your research subjects or sources; to whom you are accountable for the knowledge you produce.

Face to face with the data: analysis and conclusions

Once you have produced your data (for example, observations, tape-recordings, notes, diaries, questionnaires, deconstructions), you will have to communicate to others what these mean. Interpretation does not merely enter at this stage since interpretation and analysis will have permeated the research process. While interpretation may feel a demanding but wholly open process, any approach to interpretation is already constrained. Your conclusions will be framed: (1) by your general approach to your investigation (your theory, ontology and epistemology) and so by how you conceive gender and any connections between your ideas, your findings and possible social realities; (2) by your own location in your process of data production and your interest in your research question; (3) by the politics of your process of interpretation and the ethics of your research practice.

Making your data speak, even when you are drawing on the exact words of the researched, is a creative process of imagining gendered social existence. However closely you aim to represent and respect your research subjects, human life is so complex and multifaceted that researchers constantly have to make decisions on selecting, refining and organizing their perceptions to avoid drowning in data. Novice researchers can be daunted by the sheer quantity of complex material that even a short period of research can produce (Coffey and Atkinson 1996: 1–2). The conventions of social research, like those of everyday life, however, do not require that every nuance of communication, verbal and non-verbal, is captured for every research subject, or that every millimetre of an image is deconstructed. Even if interactions, emotions and body language are tape-recorded or videoed, analysing them is still a process of selection and organization on which your prior assumptions, meanings, politics and expectations are brought to bear. Data analysis is a process of envisaging patterns, making sense, giving shape and bringing your quantities of material under control.

The everyday world is already extensively organized and categorized in order to make the complexity of everyday life manageable, and research subjects will draw on the categories and meanings familiar to them, even if these are unfamiliar to you, diverse and contradictory. Your notions of what to look for will come in part from what you learn from your data, in part from interaction with your initial decisions about your project and its framework of ideas. You can get initial guidance on how to look at your data by working out what questions you are asking of them. The results of this interaction between your interpretative creativity, the constraining framework of your prior beliefs, and what appears new to you in your data constitute your conclusions.

If you cannot neutrally unpack your data to discover direct evidence of an unproblematic reality, then your findings are open to multiple readings, and so can be interpreted in different ways, with different strategies for representation, selection and interpretation, and so different consequences (Reay 1996). This is as true of modern as of postmodern thought. Researchers with different theories of power will interpret the same observations of social life differently. Just as data are not lying around waiting to be collected, so meanings are not lying in your data waiting to be found. Data do not speak for themselves. You have to do the work of deciding what you take your data to mean, whether they constitute 'evidence', and so whether your data are just ideas, or whether you want to claim that they can suggest connections with something else (for example, power relations, gendered inequalities, the power of ideas).

Patti Lather, for example, takes a short journal entry written by a women's studies student on her developing understanding of sexism in television commercials, and gives two possible interpretations (1991: 135–41). Lather's (less than sympathetic) reading through modern notions of ideology and hegemony takes the journal as indicating the operation of structural forces of domination and subordination through advertising. Her (more sympathetic) postmodern, deconstructive analysis of the same data, focuses on how the process of learning shapes the student's experience of thinking differently, and the possibilities of grasping complexity and contradictions in commercials. This reading leads Lather to reflect on how the emancipatory intentions of the women's studies course itself can produce conformity in ideas, and so in politics. She attempts to subvert this power by analysing the political work that each of these interpretations is doing (1991: 151) (though this analysis too could be analysed differently).

Since there is no general feminist methodological strategy on interpretation, you will need to decide how to put reflexivity into practice. Any words you use to convey meaning already carry meanings. It is always possible that your research subjects, or other researchers analysing your data, could come to different conclusions. It is in walking away with the data and making your own interpretation of them that your power as a researcher is most acute (Smith (1989: 35–6).

Anne Opie also considers how to avoid feminists' potential for the 'textual appropriation of the researched' (1992: 53) and to facilitate empowerment. She found in interviews with family carers of elderly, confused relatives that carers constituted their caring as family labour exploited by the state healthcare system, and as destructive of personal relationships. But she also caught brief and ambiguous expressions of love, and heard 'hesitation, contradictoriness and recursiveness of the spoken voice' (Opie 1992: 55). Since the language of the researcher tends to dominate interpretation, Opie had the problem of conveying the instability of the 'otherness' of the researched in her own text. She suggests treating interview accounts as contingent and incomplete, but also identifying: how the data are conceptualized; how a range of positionings of the researched can be represented; how interpretative control can be shared with the researched. Sharing control of interpretations can open up what is going on in an interview, and how the researched are connecting ideas and experiences, but it also brings out disagreements over interpretation both between different research subjects, and between the researcher and researched (see Chapter 6).

Feminist researchers face 'the conundrum of how not to undercut, discredit or write-off women's consciousnesses' (Stanley 1984: 201) when these differ from their own. At best you can be as aware as possible that interpretation is your exercise of power, that your decisions have consequences, and that you are accountable for your conclusions. Simple decisions over how to categorize, what to include and what to exclude also carry theoretical, political and ethical impli-cations. You can check your analysis for silences and absences, and consider who does not appear to be present in the research project. Van Maanen (1988) identi-fies a silent hierarchy in ethnographies determining which sort of details get mentioned, and which do not.

Making your process of reading/interpreting your data as explicit as possible will include taking a position on how you justify your knowledge claims. This includes taking a position on who is speaking, what authority you are claiming, and how much certainty you feel you can claim: for example, whether others (the researched, feminists, other social researchers, an epistemic community) should believe what you say, whether you have a notion of validity (see Chapter 7), empirical adequacy or contingency, and whether your findings can be generalized.

There is no point at which the possibility of competing interpretations and analyses stops, but there will be pressures on you to come to a point of decision, both from the conventions of the research process, and from the demands of feminist politics. This is the point at which you have to make a stand on whether or not you want to claim that you can tell a better story about gendered social existence than existing knowledge claims, rather than just proposing one among other possibilities.

Face to face with a blank sheet: writing up

The research process ends in some form of writing up your conclusions, or pre-senting them to an audience. This is, in part, a continuation of the general process of analysis, but it is also a matter of persuading your audience that you have a compelling case. Persuasion means constructing a text or presentation in a particular genre, with a particular take on reasoned argument, and with a particular rhetoric and ethics. Feminists have experimented with different styles of communication and persuasion, but they are still under pressure to make their social research believable or otherwise convincing. In filling the blank pages of your presentation, report, essay, thesis, article, book or other account, you have to make decisions about your audience and your genre.

The audience

Your intended audience, or audiences, will affect what you can say and how you say it. The same research could produce bullet points for a campaign strategy, a thesis for a PhD committee, a press release, radio or TV interview, an academic article, essay or conference paper, a leaflet for research participants, a presentation to a local community. Your choices are likely to be severely restricted by your resources, institutional constraints and your initial decisions on the nature of your project. You should be able to exercise some choice, though, over whom the research is for, to whom you are accountable, and what sort of audiences can be targeted.

Meeting your audience (whether in person or in print, by negotiation, invitation or in competition with others) is the point at which you make yourself vulnerable by offering your knowledge claims up to be challenged. Making this commitment can be not only politically and intellectually challenging, but also emotionally demanding. It can be a baptism of fire to present feminist conclusions to an audience that shares none of your assumptions; it can encourage complacency only to target audiences where all your assumptions are shared. The possibility of challenge encourages any researcher to defend their position as best they can and, as fallible humans, it is easier to concentrate on defence and persuasion rather than take on uncomfortable challenges to entrenched positions or areas of contradiction, confusion or ignorance.

Genre and rhetoric

Just as there is nothing neutral in your production of knowledge, so there is no way of presenting your findings that is independent of a particular style (for example, a brief report, an academic article, a newspaper article, a journal entry). Even student essays have specific requirements of form and style that have to be learned in each institutional context. (This book conforms to a particular textbook style of formal academic argument.) The genre in which you present your findings may be dictated by your institution or other conventions, and choices of genre are generally limited. As young researchers, we were required to express ourselves in an impersonal style intended to convey the objectivity and validity of our conclusions. Today, some students are still reluctant to use 'I' in their own work, having been taught that this is an inferior style, or conveys subjectivity. But conventions of any genre can be disrupted and radical critiques of method generally allow for authors to make their presence felt throughout the research process. (Feminists may bring in the personal, express emotions, ground abstractions or use poetry). But the point of presenting your findings is to be persuasive, and disruption of conventions may or may not serve your purpose.

You can be as reflexive as possible about your techniques for making your account persuasive, and how you aim to make your knowledge claims authoritative. The rhetorical devices available to you will tend to constitute your text in particular ways that make your story seem the only one possible (Giddens 1979; D.E. Smith 1998; Van Maanen 1988). Reflexivity can then take the form of critical reflection on your own presence in your text, admission of problems and awareness that a process of persuasion is underway (just as we are attempting to persuade you here of the necessity and mechanisms of reflexivity in feminist work).

Conclusion

Decision-making in feminist social research means overcoming considerable challenges, so achieving a feminist project is a considerable accomplishment. Knowledge of gender relations is still disputed, but has been transformed by the enormous range of feminist work, particularly over the last thirty years of the twentieth century. Knowledge of gender relations has been changed not only through developments in theory, but also through successful struggles to establish resources for empirical research, and spaces and support for feminist thought and practice. Your project may have limited objectives, and specific items of feminist knowledge rarely rise to the challenge of unravelling the complex interconnections of gendered social life and wider causes of subordination, exploitation and injustice. But the point of producing feminist knowledge is both to understand the realities of gendered lives, and to be able to transform them. Even a small-scale study has the potential to change the possibilities of people's lives. The liberatory potential of feminist knowledge is rarely straightforward, however, because of the contradictions and complexities of gendered social existence.

The links between your conclusions, competing notions of justice and practical strategies of transformation may be circuitous. Kelly et al. (1994) caution against simplistic expectations that feminist research will necessarily be empowering. In practice, gender is intermeshed with other aspects of social life, and academic researchers may have little to offer. '[P]articipating in a research project is unlikely, in the vast majority of cases to change women's lives. We cannot, for example, provide access to alternative housing options, childcare places, or a reasonable income' (Kelly et al. 1994: 37). Even knowledge that is eventually useful may have little to offer directly to specific research participants.

Research may help to clarify how transformation of gendered inequalities could make a difference, but the politics of defining who should transform what, for whom, how and why is a wider issue. Ideas can be politically effective without being well-grounded in experience, as patriarchal, racist, homophobic, disablist and other notions of natural inferiority have shown. It is possible that your results could become incorporated into policy in unanticipated ways that could themselves contribute to further subordination. Over time, and in interaction with challenges to it, however, feminist research can make a difference.

Notes

1. If, for example, statistics on working mothers are taken simply as facts that mirror some absolute reality of work and motherness, a very specific relationship between reality and ideas is assumed. But if these 'facts' are assumed to be socially constituted, they cannot reflect reality – they actively create the 'reality' of a category of 'working mother'. The statistics measure socially constituted categories of 'working mother' in political and epistemological struggles to establish particular 'facts' as authoritative in particular ways, for particular purposes. Statistics on 'working mothers' may not recognize a category of 'working fathers' (as opposed to workers/working men). The category of 'working mother' can then be conceived, at least in part, as an effect of discourses of gendered parent/worker that allocate moral and practical responsibility for childcare to mothers rather than fathers. Since the statistics help produce a category of 'working mother', they contribute to the existence of what they document. But it is still possible to document this category. In practice, much feminist knowledge of the extent of, and variations in, inequalities comes in statistical form.

2. Whilst undertaking, respectively, an ethnographic investigation of gender relations in schools and a study of young people's values (Gordon et al. 2000; Holland et al. 2000), the research teams used memory work (Crawford et al. 1992; Haug 1987) to examine their own experiences at the age of the young people they were investigating. This helped to make sense of the researchers' hidden assumptions that were relevant to the experiences of the young people who were being studied. It also suggested connections between the researchers' meanings and understandings, similar and different meanings produced by the young people, and the discourses, meanings and relationships that constituted the broader social context of these studies.

3. Universities and other academic organizations have been made aware of the need for an ethical approach towards social research subjects, if only from the need to cover themselves should a researcher cause participants to object to their activities. Like medical research organizations, university ethics committees scrutinize planned research projects. Professional organizations (such as the British and American Sociological Associations) have guidelines on ethical practices to which researchers can refer, and these also exist in other areas of social research. (For an example see the British Sociological Association website.)

9

Conclusion

Debates on feminist methodology are struggles over different possibilities for knowing what gendered lives are like, different conceptions of relationships between knowledge and power, and different strategies for transformation. Knowledge of gender, however methodologically problematic, has flourished, but the validity and authority of feminist knowledge are always contested, and the problems of judging between different knowledge claims remain. Feminists have been effective in tackling hidden power relations and their interconnections, in bringing out the diversity of gendered identities, relationships and conditions, and in promoting social change. They have not resolved the contradictions of methodology, but they have risen in productive ways to the challenges of scientific method, postmodern thought and differences between women.

Scientific method has been a powerful influence on feminist methodology, but this shifted during the twentieth century as ways of understanding science itself changed. Scientific and technical knowledge now underlie every aspect of human existence from the cutting edges of military, industrial and medical technology, to the impact in remote rural areas of satellite television, school textbooks, pesticides or seed quality. Understandings of science have been affected by social research on how scientists think and behave, and by shifts in scientific thought from assumptions that rules of method can discover an orderly, predictable universe to explorations of the possibilities of chaos and uncertainty. Rather than social research becoming more rigorously 'scientific', science can be seen to be more like social research in that 'discoveries' depend on imagining and theorizing possible connections between knowledge, experiment and realities. Rationality has been reconsidered, and it is now perhaps more widely recognized that technology is not neutral, that certainty is unattainable, and that politics, resources and the personal enter into the production of scientific knowledge.

Feminists retain three elements in particular of scientific method: (1) the possibility of being able to differentiate between better-grounded and worse-grounded stories of gendered social existence; (2) a general commitment to reasoned argument (despite the problematic history of rationality); (3) the need to justify knowledge claims. These are points of debate rather than of unity, but they have not been abandoned. Feminist hopes for challenging unjust power relations entail curiosity about the nature of the social world, and a desire to explain similarities in gendered social existence as well as differences.

The challenge to feminist knowledge from postmodern thought is perhaps not as acute as it was during the 1980s and 1990s. Feminist interactions with postmodern thinking vary in different academic cultures but have brought positive reappraisals of feminist knowledge as well as critical deconstructions. Postmodern thought has encouraged additional caution in making general knowledge claims. It has shattered claims to the general validity of feminist knowledge, and has promoted awareness of social research as a particular kind of thinking with its own history, norms and power relations. Postmodern sensitivity to the multiplicity and flux of 'truths', and work on the deconstruction of difference, subjectivities and knowledge production, have brought new attention to the power of language. Postmodern thinkers have made it particularly difficult for feminists to claim that any one story is better than another. Patti Lather sees the impact of postmodernism as making feminists 'wrestle with postmodern questioning of the lust for authoritative accounts' (1988: 577).

This criticism of connections between feminist knowledge and 'better stories' is accompanied by postmodern criticism of feminist hopes for emancipation. Seyla Benhabib (1992) asks what vision of feminist politics is then left. 'Postmodernism can teach us the theoretical and political traps of why utopias and foundational thinking can go wrong, but it should not lead to a retreat from utopia altogether' (Benhabib 1992: 230). Her point is not that feminists have the answer, but that women have much to lose. She argues that as the world becomes more intricately global, feminists should beware of being deflected by postmodernism into only focusing on fragmentation and the local (1992: 241).

An unfortunate side-effect of postmodern thought on feminism can be the condoning of a powerful, hierarchical intellectual culture. While these effects are variable, and can be resisted, it seems that the difficulties and abstractions of much postmodern thought have coincided with a period of competitive career pressures in higher education so that only certain kinds of feminist thought are deemed worthy of respect, funding or promotion. Much academic education in social research can entail scholars learning to pour scorn on those who connect ideas, experience and reality differently from themselves. Feminists cut their political teeth on overturning patriarchal truths and disparaging those who upheld them. In their turn they have had to dodge terms such as 'empiricist', 'essentialist', 'foundationalist' (see Glossary), as these became fashionable weapons for trashing traces of modern thinking – often without having to specify in any detail what is at issue. (Pity the unsuspecting empiricist caught in a circle of contemptuous postmodern thinkers – and vice versa.)

A vivid example of scholarly cut and thrust appears in a less than sisterly attack on Mary Hawkesworth by Joan Scott, although both authors express explicit feminist and emancipatory intentions, and concern about inequality and injustice. Hawkesworth (1997a) reviews four recent works on gender in order to interrogate gender as an analytical category. She defends the power of theoretical analysis to improve understandings of actual social and political problems and so to clear the ground for effective political alliances (Hawkesworth 1997b: 708). Scott crossly dismisses Hawkesworth's analysis as misrepresenting, distorting and contorting 'some of the most original feminist scholarship that we [sic] have' (1997: 697). She picks on Hawkesworth as exemplifying a wider tendency to patrol the boundaries of feminist inquiry in the name of emancipation in a futile attempt to purge feminism of its contradictions (1997: 698). (Although Scott herself proposes strictures on what feminists, and the editors of Signs, should and should not do.) Scott sees contradiction in feminism as inherent and insoluble, and postmodern thinking as liberating since it can crash through the restrictive boundaries of modern thought and allow feminists freedom to do more effective political work.

Scott argues that Hawkesworth imposes her own logic on the authors she reviews in her efforts to judge whether their work is empirically adequate and how it can serve the liberation of women. Scott's postmodern sensibilities are outraged by this whiff of empiricism. We are concerned here not with the details of Hawkesworth's critique, but with the passion it aroused. Passion is located in the difference between believing that the apparent 'realities' of gender can be an *effect* of how gender is thought about, and the belief that some underlying 'reality' can *produce* gender (1997: 700). Scott expresses admiration of 'impurity, nonconformity and unruliness' (Scott 1997: 702) in promoting breakthroughs in feminist knowledge. But she does not tolerate Hawkesworth's strategy for connecting ideas, experiences and realities in producing knowledge of gender. Where Scott believes that ideas of gender produce gendered realities, Hawkesworth targets emancipatory projects at the level of social institutions, relations and interrelated differences, and so allows for the possibility that some underlying reality actually produces experiences of gender (1997a: 680). Scott's anger expresses strategic disagreement on which approach is effective in understanding gender, and so in tackling injustices. Hawkesworth could productively question how Scott knows that connections have been wrongly made, or that unruliness, for example, works. Answers, presumably, would need investigations of specific connections, leading to qualified conclusions, and allowance for variations.

Scott and Hawkesworth illustrate acute differences in envisaging possible connections between ideas, experience and reality. Material reality or embodiment cannot be even a contributory factor in producing gendered social relationships if materiality itself is a product of how gender is thought or repeatedly performed. Politically the key for both authors is their evaluation of how knowledge of gender can be effective in contributing to progressive social transformation. Scott's anger and Hawkesworth's (1997b) pained defence do not just express a difference of opinion. They convey theoretical, epistemological and political disagreement about the realities of gender, how knowledge of them can be produced, how the knowing feminist is constituted, whom she speaks for, and what use her knowledge can be.

Disagreements over possibilities for producing knowledge of gender are not just scholarly disputes over authorizing particular ways of knowing. They have practical and political consequences for conceiving what exists, what can be changed, and what strategic alliances are possible. Efforts in the 1970s and 1980s to provide sisterly support in feminist debate, space for speaking and listening, and for the nurturing of tentative ideas seem largely to have collapsed as more feminist scholars become academically skilled and climb the career ladder successfully in hierarchical, highly competitive and pressured academies. The subversive power of feminism becomes considerably muted as it is incorporated into existing institutions and justified within dominant modes of thought. Women's studies centres, sections or departments can make a difference, but often have to struggle against marginalization within their institutions.

While the challenges of scientific method and postmodern thought have changed over time, the challenge of difference is a permanent feature of feminist social research. A strong streak of idealism runs through the impulse to research gender from a feminist perspective. In the wake of idealism trails feminism's radical humanism. The necessity of deconstructing feminist universalism (and so 'woman' as the object of feminist knowledge) is widely accepted, but any commitment to notions of emancipation, transformation, progress or improvement faces feminists with a contradiction that cannot be resolved. How can there be an emancipatory project for 'women' that has no common goal? Feminism is only distinctive in terms of its emancipatory impulse, which entails some universal ideal of justice. This universality is incompatible with the diversity of gendered lives and the diversity of relationships between women. Feminists have responded to contradiction by continuing to diversify, both at the level of theory and in interaction with varied local practices. They continue to address the considerable tensions between their ideas of women and the social divisions between women, through their conceptions of what women have (or could have) in common, what their rights should be, and how gender engages with other social divisions. The problems continue of claiming connections between knowledge and reality across the diversity of women's experiences and relationships.

Our reflections on feminist methodology are not intended to test the purity of any particular version of feminism. They are intended to clarify what can be productive in feminist reflections on methodology, to point to the significance of political, theoretical and epistemological decisions in feminist research, and to explain why feminist approaches to methodology have diversified. Feminists tend to be relatively pessimistic in their analyses of the present, but ambitiously optimistic about future possibilities. The potential for alliances between women both allows new visions of possible human relations and demands effective analyses of present realities.

While it is difficult to generalize, feminist methodology has been developing during a period of increasing globalization and localized warfare, accompanied by the spread of a dominant, macho culture, and degradation of the environment. Feminism remains inherently contradictory because gender is only part of people's lives. In order to transform unjust gender relations, more than gender must change. Maureen McNeil (2000) comments that while feminists have produced powerful analyses of what is happening (for example, in the work of Haraway [1997], Martin [1998] and Plant [1997] on technoscience), they have had virtually no impact on the direction of significant areas of life. 'Feminists have looked at and conjured "the male gaze of science", modest (and immodest) witnessing of science, both amazed and critical gazing at technologies and spectacles, cyborgs, the citadels of technoscience studies, and yearned for diffractions, but there is little indication that technoscience has been transformed' (McNeil 2000: 231).

Women's situations are very varied, but they have increasingly burst into male-dominated areas of public life, diversified their positions outside the home, and transformed their expectations. There is, though, much ambivalence in these shifts, and often little effective change in gender relations, or in the interrelations of gender with production systems and other sites of powerful inequalities. In places where gender relations had been relatively balanced, conquest, modernization, education and globalization can promote new forms of male dominance. While a minority of women can compete successfully, the majority can still be subordinated in public life and at work. Few women have access to centres of influence and action, and those who do achieve powerful positions may feel little political sympathy with women-in-general. There are also counter-pressures towards putting women's resources into motherhood, local issues, emotional and service work and domestic economy.

There have, however, been considerable changes in women's lives wherever male power has been made visible and rendered unjust. Many women in the twenty-first century have a lot to lose. But while women are increasingly able to access aggression, competition, mastery, and to fend for themselves, there is little evidence of dominant men moving internationally into femininity, dependence, emotional labour, co-operation or nurturing. Alternative masculinities tend to be localized and limited. What is most damaging about aggressive forms of dominant masculinity has been illuminated, but remains dominant. Feminist political action has probably been most effective in periodic grass-roots campaigns, in networks organized around specific issues, and in local activities and movements.

For many women around the world, caught up in struggles to survive, raise children, cope with poverty, natural disasters, corrupt regimes or varieties of social exclusion, resources for thinking about thinking are irrelevant luxuries. The interrelations of gender with other power relations leave the inequities and injustices of everyday life barely changed for the most disadvantaged. But for those who have the resources to do so, thinking about how and why feminists can justify their claims to knowledge has significant political and ethical implications. The inseparability of epistemology, ethics and politics encourages feminists to imagine how human relationships could be different, and how a better social world could work. Despite feminists' human limitations, there are still numerous connections through which women can work pragmatically on their differences and can pursue justice, exercise choice and make alliances. If feminists can make effective challenges to dominant understandings of reality, and offer well-grounded strategies for telling better stories of gender, at least for the time being, struggles over methodology will be worthwhile, even though struggles between competing knowledge claims will continue.

Glossary

Accountability Feminists claim that people are responsible, and so accountable, for the knowledge they produce and its effects. *Feminism* implies a moral responsibility for feminist knowledge and a general ethic of accountability to a community of women.

Agency The assumption that people can act rationally and by choice to achieve particular goals. This is opposed to actions and ideas being determined by social position, genes, the subconscious, impersonal historical forces or other factors. If people have power to make choices and act on them, they can be held morally responsible for their actions.

Cartesian dualisms In particular, René Descartes's claim that the reasoning mind is separate from and superior to unreasoning matter. Also used more generally to characterize dualistic or binary thinking in western culture that attributes mastery to mind over body, reason over passion, culture over nature, male over female, civilized over primitive, objectivity over subjectivity.

Difference The notion of difference is used to contest any assumption that 'women' share a common embodied state or are similarly subordinated. Differences of political interest are identified between women and men (and others), and also between women. Difference indicates contradictions in how people are actually situated in relation to each other and how divisions between people are regulated and experienced.

Emancipation The emancipation or liberation of women presumes a universal category of women who are subject to some common form of patriarchal oppression from which individual women can be liberated. This liberal assumption of universal humanity and universal rights transcends actual inequalities, contradictions and *difference*, and so overlooks the actual specificities of women's diverse situations, relations and interests. It takes emancipation to be the outcome of decision-making by rational individuals. A more radical notion of emancipation requires massive social transformation of interlinked forms of oppression. Strategies for achieving emancipation incorporate a range of cognitive, moral and political judgements on what constitutes the injustice, subordination or oppression from which freedom is sought, and diverse visions of what freedom could be like, and what potential for alliances between women exists.

Empiricism An empiricist *epistemology* assumes that knowledge of reality derives from what can be established through the senses and experience, rather than from innate ideas or reasoning. Empiricists rely on their observations and experiments to make connections between human experience, external reality and ideas about what really exists.

The Enlightenment A period of European science, philosophy, politics and society, particularly during the seventeenth and eighteenth centuries. It was during this period that *scientific method* developed its modern forms, that reason became particularly valued, and that science and reason became imbued with notions of progress.

Epistemic community The idea of a socially produced collectivity, with shared rules, that authorizes the right to speak as a particular kind of *knowing self*.

Epistemology A theory of knowledge that specifies how researchers can know what they know. Different epistemologies (for example, *empiricism, realism*) offer different rules on what constitutes knowledge, and what criteria establish knowledge of social or natural reality as legitimate, adequate or valid.

Essentialism Essentialists claim particular connections between knowledge, reality and experience as due to inherent qualities. Essences are taken to be natural (for example, an innate female nature, or innate racial characteristics). These essences are taken as explaining social characteristics, identities or relationships (for example, men's access to reason, feminine powers of intuition, racial or ethnic inequalities).

Feminism An unstable intellectual, political and practical activity grounded in some sense of women having common political interests across their social divisions, and so having some potential interest in acting together to transform unjust gender relations. Various theories of male dominance that take relations between women and men to be political and are entwined with political activity on behalf of women. There is no unified feminist theory of power or political movement, and so there are a range of political strategies for transforming the specific representations, power relations and practices that are taken as subordinating women.

Feminist methodology Feminist *methodology* is distinctive to the extent that it is shaped by feminist theory, politics and ethics and grounded in women's experience. Feminists draw on different epistemologies, but take politics and *epistemology* to be inseparable.

Feminist standpoint An area of debate on how to produce the best current understanding of the relationship of feminist knowledge to women's experiences and the realities of *gender*. Knowledge can (potentially) be produced from a feminist standpoint wherever women live in unequal gendered social relationships, and can develop a feminist political consciousness. It covers various ways of exploring (as opposed to assuming) the specificities of how women experience life differently from men, or intersexuals, or others, where they live in specific social relationships to the exercise of male power.

Foundationalism Rules of method for establishing a foundation of scientific knowledge that is built on more or less certain connections between knowledge and reality. Reality is taken to exist independently of the *knowing self*, and current knowledge can be revised as further knowledge of reality is progressively accumulated. Any *knowing self* using the same rules should be able to produce the same knowledge.

Gender A contested term that has been analysed from differing perspectives and with differing assumptions. It covers conceptions of sexuality and reproduction; sexual difference, embodiment, the social constitution of male, female, intersexual, other; masculinity and femininity; ideas, discourses, practices, subjectivities and social relationships.

Humanism The version of humanism referred to in this book is an attitude in western thought that has influenced feminist approaches to social investigation. The human subject ('man') is an autonomous individual with *agency* who can take himself as his own object, since he is the reasoning 'I' who can discover the 'truth'. His rationality is universally valid in a universal humanity. (In order to deny this common humanity to those inferior to the *knowing self*, humanity's 'other' can be defined as not fully, or not yet, human.) Since the human subject can use reason progressively to discover the truth about the world, he has the potential to be emancipated, and the power and the right to study, and speak for, humanity.

Knowing feminist There is no agreed version of the theorist who produces feminist knowledge. Conceptions of the knowing feminist vary from humanist notions of an authentic, feminine *knowing self*, who knows as a woman, to deconstructions of multiple historically and culturally specific feminist subjects, identities and selves. The idea of a knowing feminist entails some claim to the production of authoritative knowledge of *gender* and female experience. Debates focus on how knowing feminists are socially constituted and for whom they speak.

Knowing self The subject of *humanism* is the individual, rational self with a fixed identity who produces authoritative knowledge. This autonomous knowing self is challenged in feminist and *postmodern thought* by asking how particular versions of knowing selves are socially constituted, and how they are historically situated as particular kinds of subjects, in particular power relations.

Methodology Methodology in social research entails: a social and political process of knowledge production; assumptions about the nature and meanings of ideas, experience and social reality, and how/whether these may be connected; critical reflection on what authority can be claimed for the knowledge that results; *accountability* (or denial of accountability) for the political and ethical implications of knowledge production. Each methodology links a particular *ontology* and a particular *epistemology* in providing rules that specify how to produce knowledge of social reality.

Ontology A way of specifying the nature or essence of something. Different ontologies offer different beliefs about social existence, and different distinctions between categories of existence (for example, rocks, primates, people).

Positivism There are a number of positivist approaches to *methodology*, which are all versions of *empiricism*, and argue that scientific knowledge can specify true connections between ideas and reality. Feminists have targeted in particular a *foundationalist* version of the application of scientific methods to the investigation of social life that claims that reality is accessible only through the correct production of facts and the control of subjectivity.

Postmodern thought This term is a loose characterization of aspects of postmodern and poststructural theory. Postmodern thought questions how knowledge claims become constituted and established. It deconstructs unified conceptions of 'women' or '*feminism*' and undercuts the notion of feminist knowledge as grounded in the experience of women. It abandons the idea that direct connections between experience, knowledge and reality can be achieved through rational, *scientific method* or from a *feminist standpoint*. It offers freedom from humanist conceptions of self, *agency*, power and *emancipation*.

Rationalism The discovery of rational truths about the nature of the world from innate ideas and reasoning rather than from empirical experience.

Realism Realist epistemologies assume that although reality is not fully available to the senses it can still be grasped. Theory is required in order to imagine what is hidden from the senses and cannot be directly observed. Reality may or may not be imagined correctly.

Relativism From a relativist position there are no general rules or criteria of validity that can establish a direct relationship between knowledge claims, experience and actual social reality. Valid knowledge of an external social world is neither directly nor indirectly accessible so there are no general grounds for judging between competing claims to truth. There are, therefore, multiple truths or different 'readings' of reality.

Scientific method Modern scientific method is a variety of approaches to the pursuit of truth, in the sense that scientists aim to specify connections between ideas (scientific theories), experience (what the scientist's observations and experiments can establish) and reality (what actually exists independently of human thought).

Validity Validity in social research is a way of establishing what counts as true. Valid knowledge implies that a connection can be established between knowledge and social reality (as opposed to producing variable readings, deconstructions or representations of inaccessible realities).

References

Acker, Joan, Barry, Kate and Essevold, Joke (1983) 'Objectivity and truth: problems in doing feminist research', *Women's Studies International Forum*, 6 (4): 423–35.

Adam, Barbara (1996) 'Time for feminist approaches to technology, "nature" and work', in J. Pilcher and A. Coffey (eds), *Gender and Qualitative Research*. Aldershot: Avebury.

Afshar, Haleh and Maynard, Mary (2000) 'Gender and ethnicity at the millennium: from margin to centre', *Ethnic and Racial Studies*, 23 (5): 805–19.

Ahmed, Sara (2000) *Strange Encounters: Embodied Others in Post-Coloniality*. London: Routledge.

Ahmed, Sara, Kilby, Jane, Lury, Celia, McNeil, Maureen, Pearce, Lynn and Skeggs, Beverley (eds) (2000) *Transformations: Thinking Through Feminism*. London: Routledge.

Alcoff, Linda (2000) 'Review essay: philosophy matters: a review of recent work in feminist philosophy', *Signs*, 25 (3): 841–82.

Alcoff, Linda and Potter, Elizabeth (1993) 'Introduction', in L. Alcoff and E. Potter (eds) *Feminist Epistemologies*. London: Routledge.

Amis, Kingsley (1997) *The King's English: a Guide to Modern Usage*. London: HarperCollins.

Andall, Jacqueline (2000) *The Politics of Gender and Domestic Service: Black Women in Contemporary Italy*. Aldershot: Ashgate.

Ang, Ien (1996) 'The curse of the smile: ambivalence and the "Asian" woman in Australian multiculturalism', *Feminist Review*, 52: 36–49.

Ang, Ien (1997) 'Comment on Felski's "The doxa of difference": the uses of incommensurability', *Signs*, 23 (1): 57–63.

Arditti, Rita (1982) 'Feminism and science', in E. Whitelegg (ed.), *The Changing Experience of Women*. Oxford: Martin Robertson.

Armstead, Cathleen (1995) 'Writing contradictions: feminist research and feminist writing', *Women's Studies International Forum*, 18 (5/6): 627–36.

Arpad, Susan S. (1986) 'Burnout', *Women's Studies International Forum*, 9 (2): 207–13.

Assiter, Alison (1996) *Enlightened Women: Modernist Feminism in a Postmodern Age*. London: Routledge.

Assiter, Alison (2000) 'Feminist epistemology and value', *Feminist Theory*, 1 (3): 329–46.

Atherton, Margaret (1993) 'Cartesian reason and gendered reason', in L.B. Anthony and C. Witt (eds), *A Mind of One's Own: Feminist Essays on Reason and Objectivity*. Oxford: Westview Press.

Attar, Dena (1987) 'The controversial feminist', in G. Chester and S. Nielsen (eds), *In Other Words: Writing as a Feminist*. London: Hutchinson.

Bacon, Francis (1995) 'The new science' [1620], in I. Kramnick (ed.), *The Portable Enlightenment Reader*. London: Penguin.

Baier, Annette C. (1993) 'Hume: the reflective woman's epistemologist?', in L.B. Antony and C. Witt (eds), *A Mind of One's Own: Feminist Essays on Reason and Objectivity*. Oxford: Westview Press.

Barrett, Michèle (1987) 'The concept of difference', *Feminist Review*, 26: 29–41.

Barrett, Michèle (2000) 'Post-feminism', in G. Browning, A. Halcli and F. Webster (eds), *Understanding Contemporary Society: Theories of the Present*. London: Sage.

Barrett, Michèle and Phillips, Anne (1992) *Destabilizing Theory: Contemporary Feminist Debates*. Cambridge: Polity Press.

Bartky, Sandra Lee (1990) *Femininity and Domination: Studies in the Phenomenology of Oppression*. London: Routledge.

Basu, Amrita (ed.) (1995) *The Challenge of Local Feminisms: Women's Movements in Global Perspective*. Oxford: Westview Press.

Bauman, Zygmunt (1988) 'Is there a postmodern sociology?', *Theory, Culture and Society*, 5 (2): 217–37.

Bauman, Zygmunt (1990) *Modernity and the Holocaust*. Cambridge: Polity Press.

Bazilli, Susan, (1991) 'Feminist conferencing', Agenda, 9: 44–52.

BBC News (1999) 'UK politics. Forced marriage – your views', <http://news.bbc.co.uk/hi/english/uk_politics/newsid_412000/412768.stm>.

BBC News (2000) 'Taskforce to fight forced marriages', <http://news6.thdo.bbc.co.uk/hi/english/uk/newsid%5F664000/664509.stm>.

Beal, Frances M. (1970) 'Double jeopardy: to be black and female', in R. Morgan (ed.), *Sisterhood is Powerful: an Anthology of Writings from the Women's Liberation Movement*. New York: Vintage Books.

Beauvoir, Simone de (1953) *The Second Sex*. New York: Knopf.

Begum, Nasa (1992) 'Disabled women and the feminist agenda', *Feminist Review*, 40: 70–84.

Bell, Diane and Klein, Renate (eds) (1996) *Radically Speaking: Feminism Reclaimed*. London: Zed Books.

Bell, Vikki (1991) 'Feminism, Foucault and the desexualisation of rape', *International Journal of the Sociology of Law*, 19: 83–100.

Bell, Vikki (2000) 'Owned suffering: thinking the feminist political imagination with Simone de Beauvoir and Richard Wright', in S. Ahmed, J. Kilby, C. Lury, M. McNeil, L. Pearce and B. Skeggs (eds), *Transformations: Thinking Through Feminism*. London: Routledge.

Benhabib, Seyla (1992) *Situating the Self: Gender, Community and Postmodernism in Contemporary Ethics*. Cambridge: Polity Press.

Benjamin, Jessica (1986) 'A desire of one's own: psychoanalytic feminism and intersubjective space', in T. de Lauretis (ed.), *Feminist Studies: Critical Studies*. Bloomington: Indiana University Press.

Benton, Ted (1978) *Philosophical Foundations of the Three Sociologies*. London: Routledge and Kegan Paul.

Berlant, Lauren (2000) 'The subject of true feeling: pain, privacy and politics', in S. Ahmed, J. Kilby, C. Lury, M. McNeil, L. Pearce and B. Skeggs (eds), *Transformations: Thinking Through Feminism*. London: Routledge.

Best, Steven and Kellner, Douglas (1991) *Postmodern Theory: Critical Interrogations*. London: Macmillan.

Bhabha, Homi (1995) 'Signs taken for wonders', in B. Ashcroft, G. Griffiths and H. Tiffin (eds), *The Post-Colonial Studies Reader*. London: Routledge.

Bhabha, Homi (1996) 'Culture's in-between', in S. Hall and P. du Gay (eds), *Questions of Cultural Identity*. London: Sage.

Bhaskar, Roy (1979) *The Possibility of Naturalism*. Brighton: Harvester.

Bhavnani, Kum-Kum and Haraway, Donna (1994) 'Shifting the subject: a conversation between Kum-Kum Bhavnani and Donna Haraway, 12 April 1993, Santa Cruz, California', in K.-K. Bhavnani and A. Phoenix (eds), *Shifting Identities, Shifting Racisms*. London: Sage.

Bhopal, Kalwant (1997) *Gender, 'Race' and Patriarchy: a Study of South Asian Women*. Aldershot: Ashgate.

Birke, Linda (1986) *Women, Feminism and Biology: the Feminist Challenge*. Brighton: Wheatsheaf Books.

Bland, Lucy (1995) *Banishing the Beast: English Feminism and Sexual Morality 1885–1914*. London: Penguin.

Bleier, Ruth (1984) *Science and Gender: a Critique of Biology and Its Theories of Women*. Oxford: Pergamon.

Bleier, Ruth (ed.) (1986) *Feminist Approaches to Science*. Oxford: Pergamon.

Bola, Manjit, Drew, Clair, Gill, Rosalind, Harding, Stella, King, Estelle and Seu, Bruna (1998) 'Representing ourselves: representing others: a response', *Feminism and Psychology*, 8 (1): 105–10.

Bordo, Susan (1990) 'Feminism, postmodernism, and gender-scepticism', in L.J. Nicholson (ed.), *Feminism/Postmodernism*. London: Routledge.

Bordo, Susan (1993) *Unbearable Weight: Feminism, Western Culture and the Body*. London: University of California Press.

Bordo, Susan (ed.) (1999) *Feminist Interpretations of Descartes: Re-reading the Canon*. University Park: Pennsylvania State University Press.

Borland, Katherine (1991) '"That's not what I said": interpretive conflict in oral narrative research', in S.B. Gluck and D. Patai (eds), *Women's Words: The Feminist Practice of Oral History*. London: Routledge.

Brah, Avtar (1992) 'Difference, diversity and differentiation', in J. Donald and A. Rattansi (eds) *Race, Culture and Difference*. London: Sage.

Braidotti, Rosi (1991) *Patterns of Dissonance: A Study of Women in Contemporary Philosophy*. Cambridge: Polity Press.

Braidotti, Rosi (1994) *Nomadic Subjects: Embodiment and Sexual Difference in Contemporary Feminist Theory*. New York: Columbia University Press.

Brennan, Teresa (ed.) (1989) *Between Feminism and Psychoanalysis*. London: Routledge.

British Sociological Association 'Statement of ethical practice', <http://www.britsoc.org.uk/about/ethic.htm>.

Brooks, Ann (1997) *Postfeminisms: Feminism, Cultural Theory and Cultural Forms*. London: Routledge.

Brownmiller, Susan (1986) *Against Our Will: Men, Women and Rape*. Harmondsworth: Penguin.

Bryan, Beverley, Dadzie, Stella and Scafe, Suzanne (1997) 'The heart of the race: Black women's lives in Britain', in H.S. Mirza (ed.), *Black British Feminism*. London: Routledge.

Buchanan, Ian and Colebrook, Claire (eds) (1999) *Deleuze and Feminist Theory*. Edinburgh: Edinburgh University Press.

Bujra, Janet (2000) *Masculinity and the Feminization of Domestic Service in Tanzania*. Edinburgh: Edinburgh University Press for the IAI.

Butler, Judith (1990) *Gender Trouble: Feminism and the Subversion Of Identity*. London: Routledge.

Butler, Judith (1991) 'Imitation and gender insubordination', in D. Fuss (ed.), *Inside/Outside: Lesbian Theories, Gay Theories*. London: Routledge.

Butler, Judith (1992) 'Contingent foundations: feminism and the question of "postmodernism"', in J. Butler and J.W. Scott (eds), *Feminists Theorize the Political*. London: Routledge.

Butler, Judith (1993) *Bodies That Matter: On the Discursive Limits of 'sex'*. London: Routledge.

Butler, Judith (1995) 'For a careful reading', in S. Benhabib, J. Butler, D. Cornell and N. Fraser, *Feminist Contentions: a Philosophical Exchange*. London: Routledge.

Cain, Maureen (1986) 'Realism, feminism, methodology and law', *International Journal of the Sociology of Law*, 14: 255–67.

Cain, Maureen (1990) 'Realist philosophy and standpoint epistemologies OR feminist criminology as a successor science', in L. Gelsthorpe (ed.), *Feminist Perspectives in Criminology*. Milton Keynes: Open University Press.

Cain, Maureen (1993) 'Foucault, feminism and feeling: what Foucault can and cannot contribute to feminist epistemology', in C. Ramazanoğlu (ed.), *Up Against Foucault: Explorations of Some Tensions Between Foucault and Feminism*. London: Routledge.

Caplan, Pat (ed.) (1987) *The Cultural Construction of Sexuality*. London: Tavistock.

Carby, Hazel (1982) 'White woman listen! Black feminism and the boundaries of sisterhood', in Birmingham University Centre for Contemporary Cultural Studies (ed.), *The Empire Strikes Back: Race and Racism in 70s Britain*. London: Hutchinson.

Chalmers, A.F. (1982) *What Is This Thing Called Science?* 2nd edn. Milton Keynes: Open University Press.

Clegg, Sue (1975) 'Feminist methodology: fact or fiction', *Quality and Quantity*, 19:83–97.

Clifford, James (1986) 'Introduction: partial truths', in J. Clifford and G.E. Marcus (eds), *Writing Culture: the Poetics and Politics of Ethnography*. London: University of California Press.

Cock, Jacklyn (1989) *Maids and Madams: Domestic Workers Under Apartheid*. London: Women's Press.

Code, Lorraine (1987) *Epistemic Responsibility*. Hanover, NH: University Press of New England.

Code, Lorraine (1991) *What Can She Know? Feminist Theory and the Construction of Knowledge*. London: Cornell University Press.

Coffey, Amanda and Atkinson, Paul (1996) *Making Sense of Qualitative Data*. London: Sage.

Collins, Patrica Hill (1990) *Black Feminist Thought: Knowledge, Consciousness and the Politics of Empowerment*. London: HarperCollins.

Collins, Patricia Hill (1997) 'Comment on Hekman's "Truth and method: feminist standpoint theory revisited": Where's the power?', *Signs*, 22 (21): 375–81.

Comer, Lee (1974) 'Medical mystifications', in S. Allen, L. Saunders and J. Wallis (eds), *Conditions of Illusion: Papers from the Women's Movement*. Leeds: Feminist Books.

Connolly, Paul (1996) 'Doing what comes naturally? Standpoint epistemology, critical social research and the politics of identity', in S.E. Lyon and J. Busfield (eds), *Methodological Imaginations*. Basingstoke: Macmillan.

Cook, Judith A. and Fonow, Mary Margaret (1990) 'Knowledge and women's interests: issues of epistemology and methodology in feminist sociological research', in J.M. Nielson (ed.), *Feminist Research Methods: Exemplary Readings in the Social Sciences*. Boulder, CO: Westview Press.

Coppock, Vicki, Hayden, Deena and Richter, Ingrid (1995) *The Illusions of Post-Feminism*. London: Taylor and Francis.

Cotterill, Pamela (1992) 'Interviewing women: issues of friendship, vulnerability and power', *Women's Studies International Forum*, 15 (5/6): 593–606.

Crawford, June, Kippax, Susan, Onyx, Jenny, Gault, Una and Benton, Pam (1992) *Emotion and Gender: Constructing Meaning from Memory*. London: Sage.

Crossley, Gay L. and Joyce, Elizabeth (eds) (1996) 'Postfeminist forum', <http://www.altx.com/ebr/ebr3/forum/forum.htm>.

Csordas, Thomas J. (1994) 'Introduction', in T.J. Csordas (ed.), *Embodiment and Experience: the Existential Ground of Culture and Self*. Cambridge: Cambridge University Press.

Curley, E.M. (1978) *Descartes against the Skeptics*. Oxford: Blackwell.

Daly, Mary (1977) *Beyond God the Father: Toward a Philosophy of Women's Liberation*. Boston: Beacon Press.

Daly, Mary (1978) *Gyn/Ecology: the Metaethics of Radical Feminism*. Boston: Beacon Press.

Damon, Gene (1970) 'The least of these: the minority whose screams haven't yet been heard', in R. Morgan (ed.), *Sisterhood is Powerful: an Anthology of Writings from the Women's Liberation Movement*. New York: Vintage Books.

Davis, Angela (1982) *Women, Race and Class*. London: Women's Press.

Deleuze, Gilles and Guattari, Félix (1983) *Anti-Oedipus*. Minneapolis: University of Minnesota Press.

Deleuze, Gilles and Guattari, Félix (1987) *A Thousand Plateaus*. Minneapolis: University of Minnesota Press.

Derrida, Jacques (1970) 'Structure, sign and play in the discourse of the human sciences', in R. Macksey and E. Donato (eds), *The Structuralist Controversy*. Baltimore: Johns Hopkins University Press.

Derrida, Jacques (1987) 'Women in the beehive: a seminar with Jacques Derrida', in A. Jardine and P. Smith (eds), *Men in Feminism*. London: Methuen.

Descartes, René (1995) 'I think therefore I am' [1637], in I. Kramnick (ed.), *The Portable Enlightenment Reader*. London: Penguin.

Dinny (1981) 'Feeling sick with doctors', in Feminist Anthology Collective (ed.), *No Turning Back: Writings from the Women's Liberation Movement 1975–80*. London: Women's Press.

Di Stefano, Christine (1990) 'Dilemmas of difference: feminism, modernity and post-modernism', in L.J. Nicholson (ed.), *Feminism/Postmodernism*. London: Routledge.

Drake, Jennifer (1997) 'Review essay: third wave feminisms', *Feminist Studies*, 23 (1): 97–108.

du Bois, Barbara (1983) 'Passionate scholarship: notes on values, knowing and method in feminist social science', in G. Bowles and R.D. Klein (eds), *Theories of Women's Studies*. London: Routledge and Kegan Paul.

Dunne, Gillian A. (1997) *Lesbian Lifestyles: Women's Work and the Politics of Sexuality*. Basingstoke: Macmillan.

Dworkin, Andrea (1988) 'Dangerous and deadly', *Trouble and Strife*, 14: 42–5.

Edwards, Rosalind (1996) 'White woman researcher: black women subjects', in S. Wilkinson and C. Kitzinger (eds), *Representing the Other: a Feminism and Psychology Reader*. London: Sage.

Elam, Diane (1994) *Feminism and Deconstruction: Ms. en Abyme*. London: Routledge.

Eze, Emmanuel Chukwudi (ed.) (1997) *Race and the Enlightenment: A Reader*. Oxford: Blackwell.

Feder, Ellen K., Rawlinson, Mary C. and Dakin, Emily (eds) (1997) *Derrida and Feminism*. London: Routledge.

Fee, Elizabeth (1983) 'Women's nature and scientific objectivity', in M. Lowe and R. Hubbard (eds), *Woman's Nature: Rationalizations of Inequality*. Oxford: Pergamon.

Fee, Elizabeth (1986) 'Critiques of modern science: the relationship of feminism to other radical epistemologies', in R. Bleier (ed.), *Feminist Approaches to Science*. Oxford: Pergamon.

Felski, Rita (1997a) 'The doxa of difference', *Signs*, 23 (1): 1–22.

Felski, Rita (1997b) 'Reply to Braidotti, Cornell and Ang', *Signs*, 23 (1): 64–70.

Felski, Rita (2000) 'Being reasonable: telling stories', *Feminist Theory*, 1 (2): 225–9.

Feminism and Philosophy, <http://www.cddc.vt.edu/feminism/phi.html>.

Feminism on Trial, <http://feminismontrial.webprovider.com/index.htm>.

Feminist Anthology Collective (ed.) (1981) *No Turning Back: Writings from the Women's Liberation Movement 1975–80*. London: Women's Press.

Finch, Janet (1984) '"It's great to have someone to talk to": the ethics and politics of inter-viewing women', in C. Bell and H. Roberts (eds), *Social Researching: Politics, Problems, Practice*. London: Routledge and Kegan Paul.

Fine, Michelle (1992) *Disruptive Voices: the Possibilities of Feminist Research*. Ann Arbor: University of Michigan Press.

Fine, Michelle and Weis, Lois (1996) 'Writing the "wrongs" of fieldwork: confronting our own research/writing dilemmas in urban ethnographies', *Qualitative Inquiry*, 2 (3): 251–74.

Firestone, Shulamith (1970) *The Dialectic of Sex: the Case for Feminist Revolution*. New York: William Morrow.

Flax, Jane (1987) 'Postmodernism and gender relations in feminist theory', *Signs*, 12 (4): 621–43.

Flax, Jane (1990) *Thinking Fragments: Psychoanalysis, Feminism and Postmodernism in the Contemporary West*. Berkeley: University of California Press.

Flax, Jane (1992) 'The end of innocence', in J. Butler and J.W. Scott (eds), *Feminists Theorize the Political*. London: Routledge.

Foucault, Michel (1973) *The Order of Things: an Archaeology of the Human Sciences*. New York: Vintage Books.

Foucault, Michel (1980a) 'Truth and power', in C. Gordon (ed.), *Power/Knowledge: Selected Interviews and Other Writings 1972–77 by Michel Foucault*. Hemel Hempstead: Harvester Wheatsheaf.

Foucault. Michel (1980b) 'The confession of the flesh', in C. Gordon (ed.), *Power/Knowledge: Selected Interviews and Other Writings 1972–77 by Michel Foucault*. Hemel Hempstead: Harvester Wheatsheaf.

Foucault, Michel (1984a) *The History of Sexuality Vol. I*. London: Penguin.

Foucault, Michel (1984b) 'What is Enlightenment?', in P. Rabinow (ed.), *The Foucault Reader*. Harmondsworth: Penguin.

Foucault, Michel (1988a) 'Power and sex', in L.D. Kritzman (ed.), *Michel Foucault: Politics, Philosophy, Culture*. London: Routledge.

Foucault, Michel (1988b) 'The concern for truth', in L.D. Kritzman (ed.), *Michel Foucault: Politics, Philosophy, Culture*. London: Routledge.

Foucault, Michel (1991a) *Discipline and Punish: the Birth of the Prison*. London: Penguin.

Foucault, Michel (1991b) 'Politics and the study of discourse', in G. Burchell, C. Gordon and P. Miller (eds), *The Foucault Effect: Studies in Governmentality*. Hemel Hempstead: Harvester Wheatsheaf.

Frankenberg, Ruth (1993) *White Women, Race Matters: the Social Construction of Whiteness*. London: Routledge.

Fraser, Nancy (1989) *Unruly Practices: Power, Discourse and Gender in Contemporary Social Theory*. Cambridge: Polity Press.

Friedman, Susan Stanford (1995) 'Beyond white and other: relationality and narratives of race in feminist discourse', *Signs*, 21 (1): 1–49.

Fuss, Diana (1989) *Essentially Speaking: Feminism, Nature and Difference*. London: Routledge.

Garrison, Ednie Kaeh (2000) 'U.S. feminism grrrl style! Youth (sub)cultures and the technologics of the third wave', *Feminist Studies*, 26 (1): 141–70.

Gatens, Moira (1991) *Feminism and Philosophy: Perspectives on Difference and Equality*. Cambridge: Polity Press.

Gedalof, Irene (1999) *Against Purity: Rethinking Identity with Indian and Western Feminism*. London: Routledge.

Gelsthorpe, Loraine (1992) 'Response to Martyn Hammersley's paper "On feminist methodology"', *Sociology*, 26 (2): 213–18.

Giddens, Anthony (1979) *Central Problems in Social Theory: Action, Structure and Contradiction in Social Analysis*. London: Macmillan.

Gill, Rosalind (1997) 'Colluding in the backlash? Feminism and the construction of "orthodoxy"', *Soundings*, 5: 1–15.

Gilroy, Paul (1993) *The Black Atlantic: Modernity and Double Consciousness*. London: Verso.

Glucksman, Miriam A. (1998) '"What a difference a day makes": a theoretical historical explanation of temporality and gender', *Sociology*, 32 (2): 239–58.

Gordon, Tuula, Lahelma, Elina and Holland, Janet (2000) *Making Spaces: Citizenship and Difference in Schools*. London: Macmillan.

Graham, Hilary (1984) 'Surveying through stories', in C. Bell and H. Roberts (eds), *Social Researching: Politics, Problems, Practice*. London: Routledge and Kegan Paul.

Grant, Judith (1993) *Fundamental Feminism: Contesting the Core Concepts of Feminist Theory*. London: Routledge.

Gregson, Nicky and Lowe, Michelle (1994) *Servicing the Middle Classes*. London: Routledge.

Griffin, Gabriele (ed.) (1994) *Difference in View: Women and Modernism*. London: Taylor and Francis.

Griffiths, Morwenna (1995) *Feminisms and the Self: the Web of Identity*. London: Routledge.

Griffiths, Morwenna and Whitford, Margaret (1988) 'Introduction', in M. Griffiths and M. Whitford (eds), *Feminist Perspectives in Philosophy*. Brighton: Wheatsheaf.

Grimshaw, Jean (1986) *Feminist Philosophers: Women's Perspectives on Philosophical Traditions*. Brighton: Wheatsheaf.

Grimshaw, Jean (1993) 'Practices of freedom', in C. Ramazanoğlu (ed.), *Up Against Foucault: Explorations of Some Tensions Between Foucault and Feminism*. London: Routledge.

Grosz, Elizabeth (1990) 'Contemporary theories of power and subjectivity', in S. Gunew (ed.), *Feminist Knowledge: Critique and Construct*. London: Routledge.

Grosz, Elizabeth (1994) *Volatile Bodies: Toward a Corporeal Feminism*. Bloomington: Indiana University Press.

Haack, Susan (1996) 'Susan Haack (1945–)', in M. Warnock (ed.), *Women Philosophers*. London: J.M. Dent.

Hall, Stuart (1990) 'Cultural identity and diaspora', in J. Rutherford (ed.), *Identity, Community, Culture and Difference*. London: Lawrence and Wishart.

Hall, Stuart (1992) 'New ethnicities', in J. Donald and A. Rattansi (eds), *Race, Culture and Difference*. London: Sage.

Hall, Stuart (ed.) (1997a) *Representation: Cultural Representation and Signifying Practices*. (Culture, Media and Identities Series Vol. 2). London: Sage.

Hall, Stuart (1997b) 'The spectacle of the other', in S. Hall (ed.), *Representation: Cultural Representation and Signifying Practices* (Culture, Media and Identities Series Vol. 2). London: Sage.

Hammersley, Martyn (1992) 'On feminist methodology', *Sociology*, 26 (2):187–206.

Hammersley, Martyn (1994) 'On feminist methodology: a response', *Sociology*, 28 (1): 293–300.

Hammersley, Martyn and Gomm, Roger (1997) 'Bias in social research', *Sociological Research Online*, 2 (1) <http://www.socresonline.org.uk/socresonline/2/1.html>.

Hampshire, Stuart (1999) *Justice is Conflict*. Princeton: Princeton University Press.

Haraway, Donna (1989) *Primate Visions: Gender, Race and Nature in the World of Modern Science*. London: Routledge.

Haraway, Donna J. (1991) *Simians, Cyborgs and Women: the Reinvention of Nature*. London: Free Association Books.

Haraway, Donna J. (1997) *Modest_Witness@Second_Millenium.Female/Man_Meets_ OncoMouse: Feminism and Technoscience*. London: Routledge.

Harding, Sandra (1986) *The Science Question in Feminism*. Milton Keynes: Open University Press.

Harding, Sandra (1987a) 'Introduction: is there a feminist method?', in S. Harding (ed.), *Feminism and Methodology: Social Science Issues*. Milton Keynes: Open University Press.

Harding, Sandra (1987b) 'Epistemological questions', in S. Harding (ed.), *Feminism and Methodology: Social Science Issues*. Milton Keynes: Open University Press.

Harding, Sandra (1991) *Whose Science? Whose Knowledge? Thinking from Women's Lives.* Milton Keynes: Open University Press.

Harding, Sandra (1993) 'Rethinking standpoint epistemologies: what is "strong objectivity"?' in L. Alcoff and E. Potter (eds), *Feminist Epistemologies.* London: Routledge.

Harding, Sandra (1997) 'Comment on Hekman's "Truth and method: feminist standpoint theory revisited": Whose standpoint needs the regimes of truth and reality?', *Signs,* 22 (2): 382–91.

Hartsock, Nancy C.M. (1983a) *Money, Sex and Power.* London: Longman.

Hartsock, Nancy C.M. (1983b) 'The feminist standpoint: developing the ground for a specifically feminist historical materialism', in S. Harding and M.B. Hintikka (eds), *Discovering Reality: Feminist Perspectives on Epistemology, Metaphysics, Methodology and Philosophy of Science.* London: Reidel.

Hartsock, Nancy C.M. (1990) 'Foucault on power: a theory for women', in L.J. Nicholson (ed.), *Feminism/Postmodernism.* London: Routledge.

Hartsock, Nancy C.M. (1997) 'Comment on Hekman's "Truth and method: feminist standpoint theory revisited": Truth or justice?', *Signs,* 22 (21): 367–74.

Hartsock, Nancy C.M. (1998) *The Feminist Standpoint Revisited and Other Essays.* Oxford: Westview Press.

Haug, Frigga (1987) *Female Sexualization: a Collective Work of Memory.* London: Verso.

Hawkesworth, Mary (1989) 'Knowers, knowing, known: feminist theory and claims of truth', *Signs,* 14 (3): 533–57.

Hawkesworth, Mary (1997a) 'Confounding gender', *Signs,* 22 (3): 649–85.

Hawkesworth, Mary (1997b) 'Reply to McKenna and Kessler, Smith, Scott and Connell', *Signs,* 22 (3): 707–13.

Hekman, Susan J. (1992) *Gender and Knowledge: Elements of a Postmodern Feminism.* Cambridge: Polity Press.

Hekman, Susan J. (1995) *Moral Voices, Moral Selves: Carol Gilligan and Feminist Moral Theory.* Cambridge: Polity Press.

Hekman, Susan J. (ed.) (1996) *Feminist Interpretations of Michel Foucault.* University Park: Pennsylvania State University Press.

Hekman, Susan J. (1997a) 'Truth and method: feminist standpoint theory revisited', *Signs,* 22 (21): 341–65.

Hekman, Susan J. (1997b) 'Reply to Hartsock, Collins, Harding and Smith', *Signs,* 22 (21): 399–402.

Helliwell, Christine (2000) '"It's only a penis": rape, feminism and difference', *Signs,* 25 (3): 789–816.

Hird, Myra (2000) 'Gender's nature: intersexuality, transsexualism and the "sex"/"gender" binary', *Feminist Theory,* 1 (3): 347–64.

Hochschild, Arlie (1985) *The Managed Heart: Commercialization of Human Feeling.* Berkeley: University of California Press.

Holland, Janet and Ramazanoğlu, Caroline (1994) 'Coming to conclusions: power and interpretation in researching young women's sexuality', in M. Maynard and J. Purvis (eds), *Researching Women's Lives from a Feminist Perspective.* London: Taylor and Francis.

Holland, Janet, Blair, Maud and Sheldon, Sue (eds) (1995) *Debates and Issues in Feminist Research and Pedagogy.* Clevedon: Multilingual Matters Ltd.

Holland, Janet, Ramazanoğlu, Caroline, Sharpe, Sue and Thomson, Rachel (1998) *The Male in the Head: Young People, Heterosexuality and Power.* London: Tufnell Press.

Holland, Janet, Thomson, Rachel, Henderson, Sheila, McGrellis, Sheena and Sharpe, Sue (2000) 'Catching on, wising up and learning from your mistakes: young people's accounts of moral development', *The International Journal of Children's Rights,* 8: 271–94.

Holland, Nancy J. (ed.) (1997) *Feminist Interpretations of Jacques Derrida.* University Park: Pennsylvania State University Press.

Holland-Muter, Susan (1994) 'Opening Pandora's box: reflections on whiteness in the South African women's movement', *Agenda*, 25: 55–62.

hooks, bell (1982) *Ain't I a Woman: Black Women and Feminism*. Boston: South End Press.

hooks, bell (1989) *Talking Back: Thinking Feminist, Thinking Black*. London: Sheba Press.

hooks, bell (1991) *Yearning: Race, Gender and Cultural Politics*. London: Turnaround.

hooks, bell (1992) *Black Looks: Race and Representation*. London: Turnaround.

hooks, bell (1994) *Teaching to Transgress: Education as the Practice of Freedom*. London: Routledge.

Humphries, Beth (1997) 'From critical thought to emancipatory action: contradictory research goals', *Sociological Research Online*, 2 (1) <http://www.socresonline.org.uk/socresonline/2/1/3.html>.

Hussain, Freda (ed.) (1984) *Muslim Women*. London: Croom Helm.

Jackson, Stevi (1995) 'Gender and heterosexuality: a materialist feminist analysis', in M. Maynard and J. Purvis (eds), *(Hetero)sexual Politics*. London: Taylor and Francis.

Jackson, Stevi (1997) 'Against our will', *Trouble and Strife*, 35: 61–7.

Jackson, Stevi and Scott, Sue (eds) (1996) *Feminism and Sexuality: A Reader*. Edinburgh: Edinburgh University Press.

Jaggar, Alison M. (1983) *Feminist Politics and Human Nature*. Brighton: Harvester Press.

Jahan, Roushan (1995) 'Men in seclusion, women in public: Rokeya's dream and women's struggles in Bangladesh', in A. Basu (ed.), *The Challenge of Local Feminisms: Women's Movements in Global Perspective*. Oxford: Westview Press.

James, Stanlie M. and Busia, Abena P.A. (eds) (1993) *Theorizing Black Feminisms: the Visionary Pragmatism of Black Women*. London: Routledge.

Jayaratne, Toby Epstein and Stewart, Abigail J. (1991) 'Quantitative and qualitative methods in the social sciences: feminist issues and practical strategies', in M.M. Fonow and J.A. Cook (eds), *Beyond Methodology: Feminist Scholarship as Lived Research*. Bloomington: Indiana University Press.

Johnson, Pauline (1994) *Feminism as Radical Humanism*. London: Allen and Unwin.

Jones, Cecily (1999) 'A darker shade of white? Gender, social class and the reproduction of white identity in Barbadian plantation society', in H. Brown, M. Gilkes and A. Kaloski-Naylor (eds), *White? Women: Critical Perspective on Race and Gender*. University of York, Women's Studies Centre: Raw Nerve Books.

Jones, Dorian (2000) 'Eyewitness', *The Times Higher Education Supplement*, 15 December: 12.

Joseph, Gloria and Lewis, Jill (1981) *Common Differences: Conflicts in Black and White Feminist Perspectives*. Garden City, NY: Anchor Books.

Kant, Immanuel (1995a) 'What is Enlightenment?' [1784], in I. Kramnick (ed.), *The Portable Enlightenment Reader*. London: Penguin.

Kant, Immanuel (1995b) 'Observations on the feeling of the beautiful and sublime' [1764], in I. Kramnick (ed.), *The Portable Enlightenment Reader*. London: Penguin.

Kay, Helen (1990) 'Research note: constructing the epistemological gap: gender divisions in sociological research', *Sociological Review*, 38 (2): 344–51.

Keller, Evelyn Fox (1985) *Reflections on Gender and Science*. New Haven, CT: Yale University Press.

Keller, Evelyn Fox (1992) *Secrets of Life, Secrets of Death: Essays on Language, Gender and Science*. London: Routledge.

Keller, Evelyn Fox and Longino, Helen E. (eds) (1996) *Feminism and Science*. Oxford: Oxford University Press.

Kelly, Liz (1988) *Surviving Sexual Violence*. Cambridge Polity Press.

Kelly, Liz (1991) 'Unspeakable acts: women who abuse', *Trouble and Strife*, 21: 13–20.

Kelly, Liz, Burton, Sheila and Regan, Linda (1994) 'Researching women's lives or studying women's oppression', in M. Maynard and J. Purvis (eds), *Researching Women's Lives from a Feminist Perspective*. London: Taylor and Francis.

Kelly, Liz, Regan, Linda and Burton, Sheila (1995) 'Defending the indefensible? Quantitative methods and feminist research', in J. Holland, M. Blair and S. Sheldon (eds), *Debates and Issues in Feminist Research and Pedagogy*. Clevedon: Multilingual Matters Ltd.

Kenny, Anthony (1997) 'Descartes to Kant', in A. Kenny (ed.), *The Oxford Illustrated History of Western Philosophy*. Oxford: Oxford University Press.

Kitzinger, Celia and Wilkinson, Sue (1996) 'Theorizing representing the other', in S. Wilkinson and C. Kitzinger (eds), *Representing the Other: a Feminism and Psychology Reader*. London: Sage.

Kuhn, Thomas S. (1970) *The Structure of Scientific Revolutions*. 2nd edn. London: University of Chicago Press.

Kumar, Radha (1989) 'Contemporary Indian feminism', *Feminist Review*. 33: 20–9.

Kumar, Radha (1995) 'From Chipko to Sati: the contemporary Indian women's movement', in A. Basu (ed.), *The Challenge of Local Feminisms: Women's Movements in Global Perspective*. Oxford: Westview Press.

Lanser, Susan S. (1997) 'Review essay: writing women into romanticism', *Feminist Studies*, 23 (1): 167–90.

Lather, Patti (1988) 'Feminist perspectives on empowering research methodologies', *Women's Studies International Forum*, 11 (6): 569–81.

Lather, Patti (1991) *Getting Smart: Feminist Research and Pedagogy With/in the Postmodern*. London: Routledge.

Latour, Bruno (1993) *We Have Never Been Modern*. Hemel Hempstead: Harvester Wheatsheaf.

Lazreg, Marnia (1994) 'Women's experience and feminist epistemology: a critical neo-rationalist approach', in K. Lennon and M. Whitford (eds), *Knowing the Difference: Feminist Perspectives in Epistemology*. London: Routledge.

Lewis, Reina (1996) *Gendering Orientalism: Race, Femininity and Representation*. London: Routledge.

Lewis, Brenda and Ramazanoğlu, Caroline (1999) 'Not guilty, not proud, just white: women's accounts of their whiteness', in H. Brown, M. Gilkes and A. Kaloski-Naylor (eds), *White? Women: Critical Perspectives on Race and Gender*. University of York, Women's Studies Centre: Raw Nerve Books.

Liddle, Mark (1996) 'Gender, power and epistemology: can men know feminist truths?', in S.E. Lyon and J. Busfield (eds), *Methodological Imaginations*. Basingstoke: Macmillan.

Lloyd, Genevieve (1984) *The Man of Reason: Male and Female in Western Philosophy*. Minneapolis: University of Minnesota Press.

Longino, Helen E. (1990) *Science as Social Knowledge*. Princeton: Princeton University Press.

Longino, Helen E. (1994) 'In search of feminist epistemology', *The Monist*, 77 (4): 472–85.

Longino, Helen E. and Hammonds, Evelynn (1990) 'Conflicts and tensions in the feminist study of gender and science', in M. Hirsch and E.F. Keller (eds), *Conflicts in Feminism*. London: Routledge.

Lorde, Audre (1983) 'The master's tools will never dismantle the master's house', in C. Moraga and G. Anzaldúa (eds), *This Bridge Called My Back: Writings by Radical Women of Color*. 2nd edn. New York: Kitchen Table Press.

Lovibond, Serena (1989) 'Feminism and postmodernism', *New Left Review*, 178: 5–28.

Luff, Donna (1999) 'Dialogue across the divides: "moments of rapport" and power in feminist research with anti-feminist women', *Sociology*, 33 (4): 687–703.

Lukács, Georg (1971) *History and Class Consciousness*. Boston: Beacon Press.

Lury, Celia (1995) 'The rights and wrongs of culture: issues of theory and methodology', in B. Skeggs (ed.), *Feminist Cultural Theory: Process and Production*. Manchester: Manchester University Press.

Lyotard, Jean-François (1984) *The Postmodern Condition: a Report on Knowledge*. Manchester: Manchester University Press.

Lyotard, Jean-François (1993) *Political Writings*. London: UCL Press.

McDowell, Deborah (1995) 'Transferences: black feminist discourse: the "practice" of theory', in D. Elam and R. Weigman (eds), *Feminism Beside Itself*. London: Routledge.

McKee, Lorna and O'Brien, Margaret (1983) 'Interviewing men: taking gender seriously', in E. Gamarnikow, D. Morgan, J. Purvis and D. Taylorson (eds), *The Public and the Private*. London: Heinemann.

McMahon, Martha (1996) 'Significant absences', *Qualitative Inquiry*, 2 (3): 320–37.

McMullen, Richie J. (1990) *Male Rape: Breaking the Silence on the Last Taboo*. London: Gay Men's Press.

McNay, Lois (1992) *Foucault and Feminism*. Cambridge: Polity Press.

McNeil, Maureen (2000) 'Techno-triumphalism, techno-tourism, American dreams and feminism' in S. Ahmed, J. Kilby, C. Lury, M. McNeil, L. Pearce and B. Skeggs (eds), *Transformations: Thinking Through Feminism*. London: Routledge.

McRobbie, Angela (ed.) (1997) *Back to Reality? Social Experience and Cultural Studies*. Manchester: Manchester University Press.

Magee, Brian (1987) 'Descartes: dialogue with Bernard Williams', in B. Magee *The Great Philosophers: an Introduction to Western Philosophy*. London: BBC Books.

Martin, Biddy and Mohanty, Chandra Talpade (1986) 'Feminist politics: what's home got to do with it?', in T. de Lauretis (ed.), *Feminist Studies/Critical Studies*. Bloomington: Indiana University Press

Martin, Emily (1989) *The Woman in the Body: a Cultural Analysis of Reproduction*. Milton Keynes: Open University Press.

Martin, Emily (1998) 'Anthropology and the cultural study of science', *Science, Technology and Human Values*, 23 (1): 24–44.

Martin, Rux (1988) 'Truth, power, self: an interview with Michel Foucault', in L.H. Martin, H. Gutman and P.H. Hutton (eds), *Technologies of the Self: a Seminar with Michel Foucault*. London: Tavistock Press.

Marx, Karl (1971) *A Contribution to the Critique of Political Economy* (with '1857 Introduction'). London: Lawrence and Wishart.

Marx, Karl (1976) *Capital, Vol. I*. Harmondsworth: Penguin.

Mason, Jennifer (1996) *Qualitative Researching*. London: Sage.

Maynard, Mary (1993) 'Feminism and the possibilities of a postmodern research practice', *British Journal of the Sociology of Education*, 14 (3): 327–31.

Maynard, Mary (1994) 'Methods, practice and epistemology: the debate about feminist research', in M. Maynard and J. Purvis (eds), *Researching Women's Lives from a Feminist Perspective*. London: Taylor and Francis.

Maynard, Mary (1995) 'Beyond the big three: the development of feminist theory into the 1990s', *Women's History Review*, 4 (2): 259–82.

Maynard, Mary and Purvis, June (eds) (1994) *Researching Women's Lives from a Feminist Perspective*. London: Taylor and Francis.

Mernissi, Fatima (1995) *The Harem Within: Tales of a Moroccan Girlhood*. London: Bantam Books.

Mies, Maria (1983) 'Towards a methodology for feminist research', in G. Bowles and R.D. Klein (eds), *Theories of Women's Studies*. London: Routledge and Kegan Paul.

Millett, Kate (1970) *Sexual Politics*. Garden City, NY: Doubleday.

Mirza, Heidi Safia (ed.) (1997a) *Black British Feminism: a Reader*. London: Routledge.

Mirza, Heidi Safia (1997b) 'Introduction', in H.S. Mirza (ed.), *Black British Feminism: a Reader*. London: Routledge.

Modleski, Tania (1991) *Feminism Without Women: Culture and Criticism in a 'Postfeminist' Age*. London: Routledge.

Mohammed, Patricia (1998) 'Towards indigenous feminist theorizing in the Caribbean', *Feminist Review*, 59: 6–33.

Mohanty, Chandra Talpade (1988) 'Under western eyes: feminist scholarship and colonial discourses', *Feminist Review*, 30: 61–88.

Moore, Henrietta (2000) 'Difference and recognition: postmillennial identities and social justice', *Signs*, 25 (4): 1129–32.

Moraga, Cherríe (1983) 'Refugees of a world on fire: foreword to the second edition', in C. Moraga and C. Anzaldúa (eds), *This Bridge Called My Back: Writings by Radical Women of Color*. 2nd edn. New York: Kitchen Table Press.

Moraga, Cherríe and Anzaldúa, Gloria (eds) (1983) *This Bridge Called My Back: Writings by Radical Women of Color*. 2nd edn. New York: Kitchen Table Press.

Morawski, S. (1996) *The Troubles with Postmodernism*. London: Routledge.

Morgan, Robin (1970) 'Introduction: the women's revolution', in R. Morgan (ed.), (1970) *Sisterhood is Powerful: an Anthology of Writings from the Women's Liberation Movement*. New York: Vintage Books.

Morgan, Robin (1978) *Going Too Far: The Personal Chronicle of a Feminist*. New York: Vintage Books.

Morris, Jenny (1993) 'Feminism and disability', *Feminist Review*, 43: 57–70.

Mouzelis, Nicos (1995) *Sociological Theory: What Went Wrong?* London: Routledge.

Murdolo, Adele (1996) 'Warmth and unity with all women? Historicizing racism in the Australian women's movement', *Feminist Review*, 52: 69–86.

Mykhalowskiy, Eric (1997) 'Reconsidering "table talk": critical thoughts on the relationship between sociology, autobiography, and self-indulgence', in R. Hertz (ed.), *Reflexivity and Voice*. London: Sage.

Nash, Kate (1994) 'Feminist production of knowledge: is deconstruction a practice for women?', *Feminist Review*, 47: 65–77.

Nelson, Jack and Nelson, Lynn Hankinson (1994) 'No rush to judgment', *The Monist*, 77 (4): 486–508.

Nelson, Lynn Hankinson (1990) *Who Knows? From Quine to a Feminist Empiricism*. Philadelphia: Temple University Press.

Nelson, Lynn Hankinson (1993) 'Epistemological communities', in L. Alcoff and E. Potter (eds), *Feminist Epistemologies*. London: Routledge.

Nicholson, Linda J. (ed.) (1990) *Feminism/Postmodernism*. London: Routledge.

Norris, Christopher (1987) *Derrida*. London: Fontana.

Norris, Christopher (2000) 'Post-modernism: a guide for the perplexed', in G. Browning, A. Halcli and F. Webster (eds), *Understanding Contemporary Society: Theories of the Present*. London: Sage.

O'Connell Davidson, Julia (1998) *Prostitution, Power and Freedom*. Ann Arbor: University of Michigan Press.

Opie, Anne (1992) 'Qualitative research, appropriation of the "other" and empowerment', *Feminist Review*, 40: 52–6.

Orr, Catherine M. (1997) 'Charting the currents of the third wave', <www.taasa.org/library/feminism/feminism_charting.htm>.

Outhwaite, William (1987) *New Philosophies of Social Science: Realism, Hermeneutics and Critical Theory*. Basingstoke: Macmillan.

Parry, Benita (1995) 'Problems in current theories of colonial discourse', in B. Ashcroft, G. Griffiths and H. Tiffin (eds), *The Post-Colonial Studies Reader*. London: Routledge.

Patai, Daphne (1991) 'U.S. academics and third world women: is ethical research possible?', in S.B. Gluck and D. Patai (eds), *Women's Words: The Feminist Practice of Oral History*. London: Routledge.

Pethu, Serote (1992) 'Issues of race and power expressed during gender conferences in South Africa', *Agenda*, 14: 22–4.

Phoenix, Ann (1994) 'Practising feminist research: the intersection of gender and "race" in the research process', in M. Maynard and J. Purvis (eds), *Researching Women's Lives From a Feminist Perspective*. London: Taylor and Francis.

Phoenix, Ann (2000) 'Aspiring to the politics of alliance: response to Sylvia Walby's "Beyond the politics of location: the power of argument in a global era"', *Feminist Theory*, 1 (2): 230–5.

Pilcher, Jane and Coffey, Amanda (eds) (1996) *Gender and Qualitative Research*. Aldershot: Avebury.

Plant, Sadie (1997) *Zeros and Ones: Digital Women and the New Technology*. London: Fourth Estate.

Probyn, Elspeth (2000) 'Shaming theory, thinking disconnections: feminism and reconciliation', in S. Ahmed. J. Kilby, C. Lury, M. McNeil, L. Pearce and B. Skeggs (eds), *Transformations: Thinking Through Feminism*. London: Routledge.

Ramazanoğlu, Caroline (1992a) 'What can you do with a man? Feminism and the critical appraisal of masculinity', *Women's Studies International Forum*, 15 (3): 339–50.

Ramazanoğlu, Caroline (1992b) 'On feminist methodology: male reason versus female empowerment', *Sociology*, 26 (2): 207–12.

Ramazanoğlu, Caroline (ed.) (1993) *Up Against Foucault: Explorations of Some Tensions Between Foucault and Feminism*. London: Routledge.

Ramazanoğlu, Caroline (1995) 'Back to basics: heterosexuality, biology and why men stay on top', in M. Maynard and J. Purvis (eds), *(Hetero)sexual politics*. London: Tayor and Francis.

Ramazanoğlu, Caroline (1998) 'Saying goodbye to emancipation? Where Lyotard leaves feminism and where feminists leave Lyotard', in C. Rojek and B. Turner (eds), *The Politics of Jean-François Lyotard*. London: Routledge.

Ransom, Janet (1993) 'Feminism, difference and discourse: the limits of discursive analysis for feminism', in C. Ramazanoğlu (ed.), *Up Against Foucault: Explorations of Some Tensions Between Foucault and Feminism*. London: Routledge.

Reay, Diane (1996) 'Insider perspectives or stealing the words out of women's mouths: interpretation in the research process', *Feminist Review*, 53: 57–73.

Reinharz, Shulamit (with the assistance of Lynn Davidman) (1992) *Feminist Methods in Social Research*. New York: Oxford University Press.

rhodes, dusty and McNeill, Sandra (1985) 'Introduction', in d. rhodes and S. McNeill (eds), *Women Against Violence Against Women*. London: Onlywomen Press.

Richardson, Diane (1996) '"Misguided, dangerous and wrong": on the maligning of radical feminism', in D. Bell and R. Klein (eds), *Radically Speaking: Feminism Reclaimed*, London: Zed Books.

Riley, Denise, (1988) *'Am I That Name'? Feminism and the Category of 'Women' in History*. London, Macmillan.

Rollins, Judith (1985) *Between Women: Domestics and Their Employers*. Philadelphia: Temple University Press.

Romero, Mary (1992) *Maid in the USA*. London: Routledge.

Ros (1984) 'Race riots: what was I doing there? What about my own racism?', in H. Kanter, S. Lefanu, S. Shah and C. Spedding (eds), *Sweeping Statements: Writings from the Women's Liberation Movement 1981–83*. London: Women's Press.

Rose, Gillian (2001) *Visual Methodologies: an Introduction to the Interpretation of Visual Materials*. London: Sage.

Rose, Hilary (1984) 'Hand, brain and heart: towards a feminist epistemology for the natural sciences', *Socialism in the World*, 8 (43): 70–90.

Rose, Jacqueline (1983) 'Femininity and its discontents', *Feminist Review*, 14: 5–21.

Rosenfelt, Deborah and Stacey, Judith (1987) 'Review essay: second thoughts on the second wave', *Feminist Review*, 27: 77–95.

Rossi, Alice S. (1973) *The Feminist Papers: From Adams to Beauvoir*, London: Bantam Books

Rousseau, Jean-Jacques (1995a) 'A critique of progress' [1751], in I. Kramnick (ed.), *The Portable Enlightenment Reader*. London: Penguin.

Rousseau, Jean-Jacques (1995b) 'Duties of women' [1762], in I. Kramnick (ed.), *The Portable Enlightenment Reader*. London: Penguin.

Ruddick, Sara (1980) 'Maternal thinking', *Feminist Studies*, 6 (2): 342–67.

Russell, Bertrand (1996) *A History of Western Philosophy*. 2nd edn. London: Routledge.

Said, Edward (1978) *Orientalism*. London: Routledge and Kegan Paul.

Sanday, Peggy Reeves (1981) *Female Power and Male Dominance: On the Origins of Inequality*. Cambridge: Cambridge University Press.

Sarup, Maden (1993) *An Introductory Guide to Postmodernism and Poststructuralism*. 2nd edn. Hemel Hempstead: Harvester Wheatsheaf.

Sawhney, Sabina (1995) 'Authenticity is such a drag!', in D. Elam and R. Weigman (eds), *Feminism Beside Itself*. London: Routledge.

Sawicki, Jana (1991) *Disciplining Foucault: Feminism, Power and the Body*. London: Routledge.

Scarry, Elaine (1994) *Resisting Representation*. Oxford: Oxford. Oxford University Press.

Scholes, Robert (1987) 'Reading like a man', in A. Jardine and P. Smith (eds), *Men in Feminism*. London: Methuen.

Scholes, Robert (1989) *Protocols of Reading*. London: Yale University Press.

Schott, Robin May (ed.) (1997) *Feminist Interpretations of Immanuel Kant: Re-reading the Canon*. University Park: Pennsylvania State University Press.

Scott, Joan W. (1990) 'Deconstructing equality-versus-difference: or, the uses of post-structuralist theory for feminism', in M. Hirsch and E.F. Keller (eds), *Conflicts in Feminism*. London: Routledge.

Scott, Joan W. (1992) '"Experience"', in J. Butler and J.W. Scott (eds), *Feminists Theorize the Political*. London: Routledge.

Scott, Joan W. (1997) 'Comment on Hawkesworth's "Confounding gender"', *Signs*, 22 (3): 697–702.

Seidler, Victor J. (1986) *Kant, Respect and Injustice: the Limits of Liberal Moral Theory*. London: Routledge

Seidler, Victor J. (1994) *Unreasonable Men: Masculinity and Social Theory*. London: Routledge.

Seidler, Victor J. (2000) *Shadows of the Shoah: Jewish Identity and Belonging*. Oxford: Berg.

Seller, Anne (1994) 'Should the feminist philosopher stay at home?', in K. Lennon and M. Whitford (eds), *Knowing the Difference: Feminist Perspectives in Epistemology*. London: Routledge.

Sexwale, Bunie M. Matlanyane (1994) 'Experiences of South African domestic workers', in H. Afshar and M. Maynard (eds), *The Dynamics of Race and Gender: Some Feminist Interventions*. London: Taylor and Francis.

Shah, Shaila (1984) 'Angry opinion', in H. Kanter, S. Lefanu, S. Shah and C. Spedding (eds), *Sweeping Statements: Writings from the Women's Liberation Movement 1981–83*. London: Women's Press.

Sharpe, Sue (1994) *Fathers and Daughters*. London: Routledge.

Shildrick, Margrit (1997) *Leaky Bodies and Boundaries: Feminism, Postmodernism and (Bio)ethics*. London: Routledge.

Skeggs, Beverley (ed.) (1995a) *Feminist Cultural Theory: Process and Production*. Manchester: Manchester University Press.

Skeggs, Beverley (1995b) 'Theorising, ethics and representation in feminist ethnography', in B. Skeggs (ed.), *Feminist Cultural Theory: Process and Production*. Manchester: Manchester University Press.

Skeggs, Beverley (1997) *Formations of Class and Gender: Becoming Respectable*. London: Sage.

Smart, Carol (1992) 'Disruptive bodies and unruly sex: the regulation of reproduction and sexuality in the nineteenth century', in C. Smart (ed.), *Regulating Womanhood: Historical Essays on Marriage, Motherhood and Sexuality*. London: Routledge.

Smart, Carol (1996) 'Desperately seeking post-heterosexual woman', in J. Holland and L. Adkins (eds), *Sex, Sensibility and the Gendered Body*. London: Macmillan.

Smith, Dorothy E. (1974) 'Women's perspective as a radical critique of sociology', *Sociological Inquiry*, 44 (1): 7–13.

Smith, Dorothy E. (1988) *The Everyday World as Problematic: a Feminist Sociology*. Milton Keynes: Open University Press.

Smith, Dorothy E. (1989) 'Sociological theory: methods of writing patriarchy', in R. Wallace (ed.), *Feminism and Sociological Theory*. London: Sage.

Smith, Dorothy E. (1997) 'Comment on Hekman's "Truth and method: feminist standpoint theory revisited"', *Signs*, 22 (21): 392–7.

Smith, Dorothy E. (1998) *Writing the Social: Critique, Theory and Investigations*. Toronto: University of Toronto Press.

Smith, Linda Tuhiwai (1998) 'Connecting pieces: finding the indigenous presence in the history of women's education', in S. Middleton and K. Weiler (eds), *Telling Women's Lives: Narrative Inquiries in the History of Women's Education*. Milton Keynes: Open University Press.

Smith, Linda Tuhiwai (1999) *Decolonizing Methodologies: Research and Indigenous Peoples*. London: Zed Books.

Soper, Kate (1990) *Troubled Pleasures: Writings on Gender, Politics and Hedonism*. London: Verso.

Soper, Kate (1993) 'Productive contradictions', in C. Ramazanoğlu (ed.), *Up Against Foucault: Explorations of Some Tensions Between Foucault and Feminism*. London: Routledge.

Spelman, Elizabeth V. (1990) *Inessential Women: Problems of Exclusion in Feminist Thought*. London: Women's Press.

Spivak, Gayatri Chakravorty (1987) *In Other Worlds: Essays in Cultural Politics*. London: Methuen.

Spivak, Gayatri Chakravorty (1988) 'Can the subaltern speak?', in C. Nelson and L. Grossberg (eds), *Marxism and the Interpretation of Culture*. Basingstoke: Macmillan.

Spivak, Gayatri Chakravorty (1992) 'The politics of translation', in M. Barrett and A. Phillips (eds), *Destabilizing Theory: Contemporary Feminist Debates*. Cambridge: Polity Press.

Stacey, Judith (1991) 'Can there be a feminist ethnography?', in S.B. Gluck and D. Patai (eds), *Women's Words: The Feminist Practice of Oral History*. London: Routledge.

Stanford Encyclopaedia of Philosophy <http://plato.stanford.edu/>.

Stanley, Liz (1984) 'How the social science research process discriminates against women', in S. Acker and D. Warren Piper (eds), *Is Higher Education Fair to Women?* London: Nelson.

Stanley, Liz (1992) *Is There a Lesbian Epistemology?* Manchester: Feminist Praxis, Dept of Sociology, University of Manchester.

Stanley, Liz (1994) 'The knowing because experiencing subject: narratives, lives and autobiography', in M. Lennon and M. Whitford (eds), *Knowing the Difference: Feminist Perspectives in Epistemology*. London: Routledge.

Stanley, Liz (ed.) (1995) *Sex Surveyed 1949–1994: From Mass-Observation's 'Little Kinsey' to the National Survey and the Hite Reports*. London: Taylor and Francis.

Stanley, Liz (ed.) (1997) *Knowing Feminisms: On Academic Borders, Territories and Tribes*. London: Sage.

Stanley, Liz and Wise, Sue (1990) 'Method, methodology and epistemology in feminist research processes', in L. Stanley (ed.), *Feminist Praxis: Research, Theory and Epistemology in Feminist Sociology*. London: Routledge.

Stanley, Liz and Wise, Sue (1993) *Breaking Out Again: Feminist Ontology and Epistemology*. London: Routledge.

Stoler, Ann L. (1995) *Race and the Education of Desire: Foucault's History of Sexuality and the Colonial Order of Things*. London: Duke University Press.

Sum, Ngai-Ling (2000) 'From politics of identity to politics of complexity: a possible research agenda for feminist politics/movements across time and space', in S. Ahmed, J. Kilby, C. Lury, M. McNeil, L. Pearce and B. Skeggs (eds), *Transformations: Thinking Through Feminism*. London: Routledge.

Temple, Bogusia (1997) '"Collegial accountability" and bias: the solution or the problem?', *Sociological Research Online*, 2 (4) <http://www.socresonline.org.uk/socresonline/2/4/8.html>.

Temple, Bogusia (1998) 'Watch your tongue: issues in translation and cross-cultural research', *Sociology*, 31 (3): 607–18.

Thompson, Elizabeth (1992) 'Mad women in the tropics', *Agenda*, 15: 60–3.

Tripp, Aili Mari (2000) 'Rethinking difference: comparative perspectives from Africa', *Signs*, 25 (3): 649–76.

Tudor, Andrew (1982) *Beyond Empiricism: Philosophy of Science in Sociology*. London: Routledge and Kegan Paul.

Van Maanen, John (1988) *Tales of the Field: On Writing Ethnography*. Chicago: University of Chicago Press.

Walby, Sylvia (2000) 'Beyond the politics of location: the power of argument in a global era', *Feminist Theory*, 1 (2): 189–206.

Walkerdine, Valerie (1997) *Daddy's Girl: Young Girls and Popular Culture*. London: Macmillan.

Ward, Lucy (2000) 'Help brides forced to wed study urges: practice should be treated like "rape and child abuse"', *The Guardian*, 6 June.

Warnock, Mary (ed.) (1996) *Women Philosophers*. London: J.M. Dent.

Waugh, Patricia (1992) 'Modernism, postmodernism, feminism: gender and autonomy theory', in P. Waugh (ed.), *Postmodernism: a Reader*. London: Edward Arnold.

Weedon, Chris (1997) *Feminist Practice and Poststructuralist Theory*. 2nd edn. Oxford: Blackwell.

Wilkinson, Sue (ed.) (1996) *Feminist Social Psychologies: International Perspectives*. Buckingham: Open University Press.

Wilkinson, Sue and Kitzinger, Celia (eds) (1993) *Heterosexuality: a Feminism and Psychology Reader*. London: Sage

Wilkinson, Sue and Kitzinger, Celia (eds) (1996) *Representing the Other: a Feminism and Psychology Reader*. London: Sage.

Williams, Malcolm and May, Tim (1996) *Introduction to the Philosophy of Social Research*. London: UCL Press.

Wilson, Tikka Jan (1996) 'Feminism and institutionalized racism', *Feminist Review*, 52: 1–26.

Wise, Sue (1999) 'Reading Sara Scott's "Here be dragons"', Sociological Research Online, 4 (1), <http://www.socresonline.org.uk/socresonline/4/1/wise.html>.

Witt, Charlotte (1996) 'How feminism is re-writing the philosophical canon', <http:www.uh.edu/~cfreelan/SWIP/Witt.html>.

Wolf, Diane L. (1996) 'Situating feminist dilemmas in fieldwork', in D.L. Wolf (ed.), *Feminist Dilemmas in Fieldwork*. Oxford: Westview Press.

Women and Science Group (1981) 'Women and science', in Feminist Anthology Collective (ed.), *No Turning Back: Writings from the Women's Liberation Movement 1975–80*. London: Women's Press.

Woolgar, Steve (1988) *Science: the Very Idea*. London: Tavistock.

Young, Iris, M. (1985) 'Humanism, gynocentrism and feminist politics', *Women's Studies International Forum*, 8 (3): 173–83.

Young, Robert (1990) *White Mythologies*. London: Routledge.

Yuval-Davis, Nira (1997) *Gender and Nation*. London: Sage.

Zinn, Maxine Baca and Dill, Bonnie Thornton (1996) 'Theorizing difference from mul-
tiracial feminism', *Feminist Studies*, 22 (2): 321–32.

Index